WHEN THE TAPES CAME ON, THE LAST WRAPS CAME OFF

First there were the extraordinary "Camillagate tapes," shockingly recording the intimate conversations between Prince Charles and Camilla Parker Bowles, and leaving no doubt about the love and the lust they shared for each other.

Then came the even more startling "Squidgy tapes" that recorded the late night telephone calls between Princess Diana and James Gilbey. The stunningly sexual parts were first censored, and then exploded into headlines.

With these tapes, the curtain of silence around "the love story of the century" began to unravel. Now with this frank close-up of the mockery of a marriage and shattering separation of Prince Charles and Princess Diana, the naked truth emerges in all its passion and pain, deception and desperation, with cruel consequences for the people involved and profoundly dangerous implications for the once sacred British throne.

The whole world watched the wedding. Now the whole world can learn what really happened— then, since, and now.

DIANA vs. CHARLES: ROYAL BLOOD FEUD

JAMES WHITAKER

DIANA *vs.* CHARLES

ROYAL

Blood Feud

A SIGNET BOOK

SIGNET
Published by the Penguin Group
Penguin Books USA Inc., 375 Hudson Street,
New York, New York 10014, U.S.A.
Penguin Books Ltd, 27 Wrights Lane,
London W8 5TZ, England
Penguin Books Australia Ltd, Ringwood,
Victoria, Australia
Penguin Books Canada Ltd, 10 Alcorn Avenue,
Toronto, Ontario, Canada M4V 3B2
Penguin Books (N.Z.) Ltd, 182–190 Wairau Road,
Auckland 10, New Zealand

Penguin Books Ltd, Registered Offices:
Harmondsworth, Middlesex, England

Published by Signet, an imprint of Dutton Signet,
a division of Penguin Books USA Inc.
Previously published in a Dutton Editon.

First Signet Printing, December, 1993
10 9 8 7 6 5

REGISTERED TRADEMARK–MARCA REGISTRADA

Printed in the United States of America

To my wife, Iwona
and to Edward, Thomas and Victoria

CONTENTS

Acknowledgments   ix

Introduction   xi

1 Camillagate   19

2 Squidgy   62

3 Dirty Tricks   95

4 Back to the Beginning   132

5 The Honeymoon is Over   166

6 Downfall of a Marriage   201

7 Spencers at War   237

8 The Way Forward   271

Update to the Signet Edition   305

Index   321

ACKNOWLEDGMENTS

I am indebted to the many friends and colleagues who helped make this book possible. Some naturally have to remain anonymous: they and I both know why. But among those I can name I would especially like to thank my former editors Richard Stott (now editor of *Today*) and Lloyd Turner, both of whom were inspirational; Tom Petrie and Charles Wilson, both great news editors; my reporter colleagues Richard Kay and Charlie Rae, with whom I have shared several crises and many good times; and the "snappers" who on tour make life worth living—in particular dear old Arthur Edwards and Mike Forster. I am bound to mention Tim and Eileen Graham, the supreme professionals, and I pay tribute to the work and companionship of my dear friend Kent Gavin (or Gavers, as Diana knows him better).

A special thank you to my masters at Mirror Group Newspapers, David Banks, the editor of the

Daily Mirror, and the group managing editor, Amanda Platell.

My heartfelt thanks to Derek Drury, the chief librarian at the *Daily Mirror,* and to his enthusiastic and very able staff.

For quite inspirational representation I applaud Patrick Walsh; and I am deeply indebted to Claudia Cragg for introducing us. To Peter Mayer in New York; Clare Alexander, Clare Harington and Judith Flanders at Penguin, I offer my sincerest thanks. Finally a grateful acknowledgement of the work of Jeanette Bishop and Frances Dow, and to Christopher Wilson, without whom this book would not have been possible.

INTRODUCTION

I first met Lady Diana Spencer at a wedding in the Guards Chapel, a few hundred yards from Buckingham Palace, in 1978. A slightly pudgy sixteen-year-old dressed in an unlovely pink dress bounced up to me after the ceremony and said, "I know you—you're the wicked Mr Whitaker, aren't you?" I felt obliged to admit it. "I'm Diana," she said, with a flash of her cobalt blue eyes. She clearly felt that no further explanation was needed. You could sense the inner self-confidence, yet at the time Lady Diana could be described as a fairly hopeless case. A three-minute conversation would have covered the landmarks in her life—child of a broken marriage, public school drop-out without a single educational qualification, a homesick young thing who came back in tears after a few weeks at her Swiss finishing school. She was an upper-crust odd-jobber who looked after the children of friends and once served in a City wine bar.

She was pretty, but not staggeringly so. She had charm, but no magic. Yet in the space of less than three years I watched her change from a homely, well-brought-up young girl into a world-famous icon, adored by the media and the masses. It was a unique transformation, unparalleled in modern history.

Her genius was to rejuvenate a tired and dusty royal dynasty. Before Diana, the House of Windsor's image was like G-Plan furniture—beguilingly revolutionary in the late 1950s and early 1960s, but now looking decidedly passé. The children of the Queen and Prince Philip—Charles, Anne, Andrew, Edward—felt safer out of the limelight and steered clear of trends. But with the arrival of Diana, the House of Windsor took on a whole new impetus. It rediscovered its glamour, and in doing so brought a gloss back to the entire nation.

She got no thanks for it. As we shall see, the choice of Diana as a bride for the Prince of Wales was as cynical a piece of social engineering as it is possible to imagine. The House of Windsor guards its blood jealously, and shares it grudgingly. The young princess was chosen to be an adjunct to her husband, never a person in her own right. She was there to provide an heir, which she willingly did within a year of marriage. She provided a spare within three years.

By the time Prince Harry was born in 1984, the few ties which held the Prince and Princess of Wales together were at breaking-point. Diana's usefulness was over, and her still-burgeoning status of international superstar was an embarrassment to Charles and the rest of his family. They had uncorked the genie and they couldn't get it back in the bottle. Jealousy has a large part to play in this story. Both Prince Charles and the Queen were jealous of Diana's instant acclaim, trained as they both were from childhood for sovereignty. Their view was that you had to earn your spurs and that somehow Diana had not. Diana, too, was jealous: jealous of the long-standing love affair which pre-dated her arrival on the royal scene and which continued virtually unabated throughout the whole of her marriage.

The crisis that now faces the world's premier monarchy is of epic proportions. The split between Charles and Diana has a direct bearing upon his future kingship, and though Diana might wish that the throne could pass directly to her son, that is not an option as far as Charles is concerned.

This was clearly laid out in a widely overlooked statement made by the Lord Chamberlain, the Earl of Airlie, at the time of the Queen's historic *annus horribilis* speech in the City of London in November 1992, in which she listed her woes and asked for clemency. In his statement Lord Airlie gave the Queen's pledge that she would join her subjects in paying taxes, and added that Charles would continue the arrangement when he ascended the throne. Though couched in diplomatic language, the message from Charles was plain and clear: I may have been unfaithful to my wife, but I will still be King.

To some it may seem strange that Charles sees no disbarment from his future role as head of the Church of England simply because he has been an adulterer throughout his marriage. Ever a keen student of history, he will have been aware from childhood of the *carte blanche* allowed his predecessors, and no doubt assumed it would be no different for him. But it is: we live in an electronic age in which eavesdroppers can listen to private conversations. And in this age, those conversations can also be disseminated, on short-wave radio, on television and in print. The wall of secrecy has been torn down, but the royals have been too occupied to notice.

The contents of the so-called Camillagate tapes were dynamite: the situation has a direct bearing on Charles's fitness to lead the nation as the head of its church, and this is an issue he has yet to address.

There was another conversation, which in the end turns out to be more explosive in content than Camillagate. The previously unpublished extracts from the so-called Squidgy tapes reproduced in this book demonstrate that Diana, too, sought solace from a cheerless marriage. I make no apology for their inclusion. Though the conversation between Diana and James Gilbey will be shocking to some, mature reflection on the circumstances in which the princess found herself can only prompt a feeling of profound sympathy.

Diana has no constitutional position, now or in the future, and it could be argued that she needs to worry less about her private behaviour. However, it is clear that she intends to play an instrumental role in bringing Prince William to the throne—and it must be remembered that Charles will be dead when King William V is crowned; Diana may be alive and still able to influence her son. She knows that from now on her behaviour must be exemplary.

The battle between Diana and Charles is being fought on many levels. First, it is a battle over the future King; and though Diana is said to take care of William's emotional growth, while Charles takes care of the constitutional side, things are not so clear-cut. In the spring of 1993, as I write, the couple are vying for the future King's affection. Photo-opportunities show Charles taking the children to church, and Diana splashing in the sea with them. Charles takes them shooting, she takes them skiing. A generation ago the Queen asked the media to leave her son and heir alone so he could grow up unharmed by their rougher attentions—yet now a royal prince appears to be being used in a not particularly sophisticated game of one-upmanship in which the press have been encouraged to play a full part.

Diana vs. Charles: Royal Blood Feud is also a battle about status. The prince and the old guard at Buckingham Palace believe that now that the marriage is over Diana has relinquished her position. And though no longer do royal wives find themselves in the Tower of London, a ruthlessness still exists in the House of Windsor: the dirty-tricks department has gone out of its way to downgrade the princess in the eyes of the population while pushing forward the less obvious charms of the prince.

In this they have been defeated. While there is little doubt that the princess's movements are being monitored closely—as much to discountenance her as to gather information—there can be little doubt that she has created a massive power base simply through her personal popularity. It is this phenomenon which uncomprehending Buckingham Palace advisers must now address: how to live on amicable terms with the princess now that she is a semi-detached royal.

So far there seems to be little indication that they are doing this, or that they have any intention of doing so in the future. Diana is regarded as the enemy. In a recent Buckingham Palace briefing, a court correspondent was told that Diana and the Duchess of York were "two bad women." This absurd comment, which brackets two quite different women in two quite different sets of circumstances, amply demonstrates the naiveté of the palace courtiers. They are so wooden-headed about guarding their masters' reputations that they end up doing more harm than good. It seems likely that the Duchess of York will soon be erased from the royal scene, but that can never be the case with Diana— and an accommodation must be reached between the warring factions. Divorce will help; so too would remarriage for both Charles and Diana.

The Archbishop of Canterbury, Dr. George Carey, who has discussed this sorry impasse with the royal family, offered the opinion that divorce would not prevent Charles from being crowned King. His view is that if the church is to retain any moral influence in the modern world, it must

INTRODUCTION

take full account of evolving social circumstances and that Charles should not be treated differently from his future subjects.

It is not a popular view within the church, but outside it people are warming to the idea of Charles remarrying. Only if Charles were to contemplate marriage with Camilla Parker Bowles would there be a problem (and in any event, at the time of writing Mrs. Parker Bowles is still firmly married to her husband). Diana, on the other hand, could marry without much soul-searching, and should. With or without a husband, a proper role must be created for her for the rest of her life. Cynical observers suggest that as Diana loses her looks she will lose popular support, and therefore her presence as a thorn in the side of the royals is only temporary. But I see no evidence to support that. She has adroitly mustered what talents she has and used them to stupendous effect. She is not going to go away willingly, and the longer the palace persists in denigrating her the greater damage they do to the whole fabric of royalty.

It is here that the Queen must play a leading role. She is, of course, advised by her private secretary Sir Robert Fellowes, a man whose family ties to Diana make little difference to his opinion of her. The Queen must listen to the advice of others and act accordingly. As head of the Commonwealth she has acted as a conciliator and healer; now is the time for her to utilize those skills closer to home.

I have never believed the Queen would abdicate. One such act half a century ago nearly put paid to the House of Windsor; she must reason that a second abdication would finish it off completely. But there is something else: she is intellectually and temperamentally opposed to giving up the reins of sovereignty and sees no reason to step aside for her son. In this she has the example of her illustrious forebear Queen Victoria. Apart from these considerations, she took an oath at the Coronation never to relinquish the throne. So accidents aside, she can expect to remain in place while the wounds are healed in the younger generation. But it is her duty to history to assist in that healing process if she wishes to leave a stable monarchy behind her. What has happened in the past year has made the royal family profoundly unpopular, and they must be made to recognize it.

In this book I have tried to set out the origins of the present crisis, and to humbly offer some solutions. I am an unashamed monarchist but not an uncritical one, and my credentials for making the few suggestions I do stem from twenty-five years of royal reporting.

The royal family give great pleasure to the country and fill a vital role, but many argue that they have lost their way. The battle between Charles and Diana is the outward and visible sign of a deeper malaise, one which we can only hope will be cured before it is too late.

London
May 1993

ONE

Camillagate

The love affair of the century was over before it began. In the hours leading up to his marriage to Lady Diana Spencer, Prince Charles lay in bed at Buckingham Palace with Mrs. Camilla Parker Bowles.

Across the Commonwealth and around the world, millions were preparing their own celebrations for the wedding of the century. Meanwhile world leaders and their representatives were gathering in London to attend a unique historic occasion.

The Charles and Diana story had struck a chord in the steeliest of hearts: lonely bachelor with the burden of kingship just around the corner; fresh, young and lovely girl who comes to his emotional rescue. Their pictures filled the pages of a thousand magazines, and drove more important news stories off the television screens.

But it was all a sham. Charles had perpetrated

the grossest deceit on his future wife, on his
mother the Queen—and on the public who, even
as he was in bed with Camilla, were beginning to
line the streets of London in preparation for the
greatest national celebration since the Coronation
nearly thirty years before.

The royal wedding cost tens of millions of
pounds. The day had been declared a holiday by
the government, closing factories and offices, but
the event the people were celebrating with such
warmth and generosity was a chimera. It was Camilla with whom Charles was besotted; Diana was
simply there to make a marriage of convenience.

But for now the world remained in ignorance.
The first marriage of a Prince of Wales for 122
years was being greeted with nothing short of hysteria: the electronic media had grown up since the
Coronation and had been waiting for decades for
just such a spectacle. Across the country street
parties and parades were organized, bunting was
hung and bonfires were lit.

In Hyde Park the night before, guns of the
King's Troop, Royal Horse Artillery, fired salvoes
into the hot, dusty sunset, followed by a massive
firework display, while across the road in Knightsbridge Barracks, officers and men of the Blues
and Royals regiment of the Household Cavalry
busied themselves preparing to provide the
mounted Sovereign's Escort. Busiest of them all
was their commanding officer, Lieutenant-Colo-
nel Andrew Parker Bowles whose job it would be

to lead the Escort next day. Meanwhile, the object of global fascination, the pink-cheeked twenty-year-old daughter of a backwoods peer was, less than a mile away, excitedly preparing for the most important event in her life—in complete ignorance of what was going on between her future husband and another woman.

The previous evening the Queen had given a dinner party at Buckingham Palace for relatives and close friends of the couple. Lady Diana Spencer's mother, Mrs. Frances Shand Kydd, was present with her second husband, Peter. So too were Diana's father, Earl Spencer, and his second wife, Raine.

The dinner party was small by Buckingham Palace standards—only forty or so—but later the party moved out into the ballroom for a huge reception and dance which went on until two-thirty in the morning. Among the guests from all corners of the globe were Colonel Parker Bowles and his wife Camilla. As the band struck up, the Prince of Wales asked Camilla to dance. Just one dance, but then she would see him again later that night.

In the run-up to the wedding Lady Diana had left her Coleherne Court flat and had been staying at Buckingham Palace in a suite of rooms next door to Prince Charles's—as no one knew about it, no tongues wagged. But after the ball that Monday night, 27 July, Diana went to sleep at Clarence House, the Queen Mother's official London residence. It was from here she would make her carriage ride to St. Paul's Cathedral, and it was here her stunning David and Elizabeth Emanuel wedding-gown awaited her.

One of two people who spoke to me of Charles and Camilla's late-night liaison was the prince's valet, Stephen Barry. Though later he became a somewhat controversial figure—he was to die of AIDS—Barry was devoted to his master and in turn was regarded with deep affection by Charles. After he left royal service he wrote two books. Instead of filling them with salacious detail, he simply painted a rosy portrait of palace life: he remained convinced of the need for royalty in Britain.

But when, in private, the royal wedding was mentioned, Barry would shake his head in disappointment. He told friends he could not believe Charles would take such a risk, carrying on with Camilla right up to the final moments of his bachelorhood. He said to me: "Sir had always been infatuated with Camilla since they first knew each other in the early 1970s. But when he took her to bed in the very week of his wedding it seemed incredible. Certainly incredibly daring, if not incredibly stupid."

Bachelors' last flings are not an uncommon phenomenon, but this was made different by the circumstances. Charles, as future King, must have been aware that virtually all his actions were subject to scrutiny, and that such an abuse of the palace and its staff would one day come to light.

Given that in the coming years he would return again and again to Camilla Parker Bowles, in the end destroying his marriage, it now seems both cruel and cynical.

Meanwhile, the crowds waited patiently outside in The Mall, the uniform hung in the wardrobe, the polished naval sword lay waiting to be buckled on.

Neighbors in Sussex remember that both Camilla and her brother Mark took to the opposite sex early on, and Camilla was widely known for her down-to-earth and energetic approach to matters of the heart. Her lack of film-star looks was more than compensated for by a vivacity and sexiness which passed some men by but ensnared others: her inner confidence carried her along. Her boyfriends after the Season was over were suitably upper-crust and included Rupert Hambro of the merchant-banking family. But she finally met the dashing Household Cavalry officer, Andrew Parker Bowles, and the couple were married in the Guards Chapel in 1973. It was one of the society weddings of the year, satisfactorily well-attended by the royal family. Princess Anne came to the service. So too did the Queen Mother—Andrew's father, landowner Derek Parker Bowles, was a close friend of hers—and though Princess Margaret missed the service, she went to the reception.

Camilla, though never likely to go down in history as a great beauty, looked lovely—"she was wearing lashings of tulle, and diamonds in her hair" recalls one guest—and sparkled at the reception held at St. James's Palace. One of her page boys was Maurice Roche, now Lord Fermoy and the Princess of Wales's first cousin.

Parker Bowles came from exactly the right kind of background. Related to the Queen Mother through the Earls of Strathmore, he is also directly related to the Earls of Derby, Macclesfield and Cadogan as well as the Duke of Marlborough. His mother, Dame Ann, was a close friend of the Queen, and Chief Commissioner of the Girl Guides. Educated at Ampleforth, the Roman Catholic's equivalent of Eton, he was a page boy at the Queen's Coronation in 1953; he went on to Sandhurst before joining the Blues and Royals, the ancient amalgamated cavalry regiment, where he launched upon a confident and successful military career.

Before Camilla came along, Parker Bowles had been going out with Princess Anne for some time, and friends from that period remember the intensity of the relationship. But his religion, and the fact that at that period she remained undecided about marriage and had other interests, most notably Earl Alexander of Tunis's brother, Brian Alexander, meant that the relationship would inevitably founder. But the two remained very close.

Meanwhile, sometime in late 1971 Camilla met Prince Charles, and for a brief moment the sparks flew. Trying to pinpoint exactly when they became lovers, some friends believe that it may have happened after a party at Annabel's, the exclusive Mayfair nightclub, six months before her marriage, when she and the prince danced the night away, oblivious of everyone else. She was never accorded the title of "official girlfriend" to the prince—because she was near to marrying Andrew—but nevertheless Charles very quickly became obsessed by her, visiting her parents' Sussex home regularly, and anonymously. It is a measure of the privacy of their early relationship that when biographies of the prince were written at the time of his engagement, and the list of former girlfriends was yet again hauled out and dusted down, the name of Camilla Shand was never among them. Their relationship can only be described as clandestine, something it remained for the next twenty years.

In any event, Charles was then a seagoing naval officer, and legend has it that he could not commit himself to Camilla when he was likely to be away for such a long time. Three points militate against this: one is that, at twenty-four, Charles was not yet ready for marriage—and besides, Camilla was not royal-bride material. Her appeal is very much in the flesh since she does not photograph well, a superficial-seeming but essential element in choosing a future Queen.

Second, her family lineage was not considered sufficiently grand. At the time it was judged that if Charles was not to marry a foreign princess, then at least he should think first of some dukes' daughters, like Lady Jane Wellesley. Meanwhile the wheeler-dealing Earl Mountbatten was angling to get him to marry one of his Knatchbull granddaughters, and all thoughts were of a great dynastic match.

The third point is that, though fascinated to have the Prince of Wales at her feet, Camilla actually was more attracted to Andrew. Like his father before him, Andrew is a ladies' man, with a swashbuckling attitude towards women that appeals to the more adventurous among them.

In the year following their marriage a son, Thomas, was born to the Parker Bowleses, and Prince Charles, who had been unable to attend the wedding because of naval duties (he was earning his ocean navigation certificate in the Caribbean aboard HMS *Minerva*), agreed to become the boy's godfather.

Soon Andrew Parker Bowles, a talented networker, was on the move in his army career. As Britain tried to extricate itself from the sorry mess of its former colony Rhodesia—premier Ian Smith had announced his Unilateral Declaration of Independence and by 1980 Britain could no longer pretend it had any influence over the country— Christopher Soames, the son-in-law of Winston Churchill, was appointed Governor of Rhodesia. With the guerrilla warfare which accompanied Britain's last retreat from Africa, Lord Soames

needed military protection and it came in the
form of a newly promoted lieutenant colonel of
the Blues and Royals.

As the orderly withdrawal proceeded, a short
paragraph appeared back home in the satirical
magazine *Private Eye* late in 1980:

> No sooner had Lord Soames been appointed Governor
> of Rhodesia than the subject of jobs for the boys arose.
> Among the lucky ones, Major Andrew Parker Bowles,
> now a colonel and in charge of British liaison in Salis-
> bury with the guerrilla forces.
>
> Andrew, 39, is married to a former (?) Prince
> Charles fancy, Camilla Shand, and if I should find the
> royal Aston Martin Volante outside the Parker Bowles
> mansion while the gallant colonel is on duty overseas,
> my duty will be clear.

It was a warning shot across the bows that gossips
in Wiltshire and Gloucestershire, where Charles
was buying the home of Harold Macmillan's son
Maurice, were aware of his continuing interest in
Camilla. But the British press failed to recognize
it for what it was, and soon forgot all about it as
the delicious new official companion of the
prince, Lady Diana Spencer, emerged from obscu-
rity into the limelight. Gossip columnist Nigel
Dempster, in his *Daily Mail* diary, recorded that
Camilla was at Plumpton races as she cheered
Charles on in his hopeless attempts to become a
good jockey. I was at the races that day and saw
the two together, but no one blinked an eyelid.

A month later attention switched back to the
absentee colonel, who had been gored by a Rho-
desian buffalo. The *Daily Telegraph* reported that
the colonel had decided to "test-drive" a buffalo
in advance of Prince Charles's visit to mark the
transition of Rhodesia into Zimbabwe. As he attempted to ride the beast bareback—it was
planned that if the experiment was successful,
Charles would follow suit to give the media a photo-opportunity—Andrew was thrown, then gored
by another buffalo as he lay winded in the dust.
He needed twelve stitches in his leg, but rose to
the occasion by borrowing a quote from Charles,
who had experienced a similar charge from a
Scottish ram: "It was damn near the end of a
dynasty."

All good British stiff upper lip stuff. But then
Andrew Parker Bowles had become a legend in
his circle not only for his eye for a pretty girl, but
also for that stiff upper lip. Like ripples in a pond,
the word was spreading about his wife and Prince
Charles—but what most people did not know was
whether Andrew himself knew.

Certainly he must have had his suspicions. It
was not the first time this couple had been, in
Stephen Barry's words, incredibly daring or incredibly stupid. Just months before the Prince of
Wales's wedding, the House of Windsor had been
rocked by the greatest scandal to hit them in several generations. It centered on the royal train.

On November 16, 1980 the *Sunday Mirror* carried a story on its front page which alleged that, ten days before, Diana had secretly joined Prince Charles on the train while it was in a siding at Staverton in Wiltshire in West England for the night. She was alleged to have stayed on board for several hours; the implication was obvious.

The story caused a furor. In the previous months Lady Diana Spencer had charmed everyone with her freshness, her innocence, her sense of fun and her unquestionable virtue. Those who had been lucky enough to meet her were charmed by her, impressed by her character and left in no doubt as to her suitability as a future Queen. The idea of her spending a clandestine night with Charles, under the full scrutiny of SAS and police minders, seemed ludicrous; if true it would have destroyed credibility with a trusting and adoring public.

Both Prince Charles and the Queen were furious. The Queen's press secretary, Michael Shea, was instructed to write to the editor of the *Sunday Mirror*. He protested in the strongest possible terms about the story and its innuendoes, which were "totally false" and "a total fabrication," and he went on to make an unprecedented request: a printed apology in a prominent position at the earliest opportunity.

The editor, Bob Edwards, clearly convinced his story was true, stuck to his guns and the following Sunday printed not only his own letter replying to Shea, but also a later exchange of letters between himself and the palace when he invited Shea to send him an official denial which he would print in full.

It takes a courageous man to fly in the face of such rebuttals from Buckingham Palace. For a time it looked, from the outside, as though Edwards would be crowning a long and illustrious career in Fleet Street (he was four times editor of national newspapers) with the sack. In fact he was totally bemused. He recalls that the story came from one of his paper's "most trusted sources," Jim Newman, a West Country journalist.

Though satisfied with the story's accuracy, Edwards ordered checks and double checks on the information: a necessary move as he was being berated by his Fleet Street competitors. Buckingham Palace—effectively the Queen—had never taken such a draconian line before, and Fleet Street smelt blood. However, he remained unruffled: Newman, apart from anything else, had been a policeman and got his best stories from police sources.

A question mark hung over the whole affair, and for every moment it remained unresolved Diana's reputation was taking a pasting. Having made inquiries myself I did not believe Diana had been on the train, but I went to see her at her flat in Coleherne Court. Her answer was unequivocal: "I am not a liar," she said. "I have never been on that train. I have never ever been near it.

"I stayed in all that evening with my three flatmates, Virginia, Carolyn and Ann. Please believe me—I am telling the absolute truth. I had some supper and watched television before going to bed early. I had been at Princess Margaret's party at the Ritz the night before and I was feeling very frail and hung over. I didn't feel like going anywhere and I never moved out of the flat. My flatmates will testify to this."

They did, particularly Virginia Pitman who supported every word, and I found it convincing: these were young, well-brought-up girls who were not used to evasion. But the rumors refused to go away. "The allegations have not put me in a very good light," a profoundly worried Lady Diana told me. "It has all been rather upsetting, but more than that, I am very disappointed that the people who printed the story in the first place won't believe me."

Resolutely determined to become Princess of Wales, she could see the issue of the royal train putting her out of the running. Of course Charles knew the truth, but she would be judged not by him but by the public. And even in the last quarter of the twentieth century it wanted its future Queen to be a virgin bride.

I reported this interview in the newspaper the next morning, but still there was a difficulty. Few of those who were connected with the arrangements that night in Wiltshire were in any doubt that a blonde woman was hurried onto the train after Charles had finished giving dinner to three Duchy of Cornwall officials. And the telephone log showed that a call had, a little earlier, been made to Bolehyde Manor, the nearby home of the Parker Bowleses.

No one at that time, in the earliest flush of Charles and Diana's romance, could imagine that the woman that night—logged by the SAS soldiers on guard duty around the train—could be any other than Diana. But they were wrong. The woman on the royal train was Camilla Parker Bowles.

This information is vouched for by several different sources, ranging from Jim Newman to a peer of the realm who is extremely close to the royal family. I have no doubts as to its veracity— and neither do senior officials and courtiers, some of whom still work at Buckingham Palace.

The reason the Queen, via Michael Shea, had rejected so strenuously the idea that Diana had been on the train was because Charles had personally told her that Diana was *not* on it. But did he tell his mother that it was Camilla on board? I would like to think he did. Certainly all denied vehemently that Diana had ever been on the train. And they were right.

The palace's iron never-apologize-never-explain policy left Bob Edwards in some confusion. At his subsequent meetings with Prince Charles the matter was never alluded to, and when a complaint was made to the Press Council by a member of the public, the palace very firmly said they had no wish to pursue the matter—and one can see why: it was not in their interests to have the incident scrutinized by an independent body.

In 1986 it was proposed that, in recognition of his lifelong services to journalism, Bob Edwards should be made CBE. The one mistake his paper had made, reporting the royal train incident, had been forgiven—not least, presumably, because the paper had never come up with the identity of the person there that night. Generously, in his memoirs Bob Edwards wrote, "How awful if I was wrong about the whole silly thing." But he wasn't. Visitors to Edwards's home the following Christmas were intrigued to see a card signed by a former politician and a close friend of the royal family. The card was inscribed with a short message. It read: "It was Camilla."

Meanwhile what was Charles's reaction to the scandal? He was in New Delhi on a tour of India, and there he hit out at the "sensationalism" of the British media, and the lack of moral values in reporting. Speaking to a thousand members of the Indian Institute of Technology he said, "Honesty and integrity are vital factors in reporting and often get submerged in the general rush for sensationalism."

No one had looked closely at the woman who was born Camilla Rosemary Shand on July 17, 1947 at King's College Hospital, London.

Her antecedents were respectable if not awe-inspiring. Her mother was the sister of Lord Ash-combe, whose Cubitt building family had constructed the Duke of Westminster's money-spinning Grosvenor estate in Belgravia during the last century. Her great-grandmother was Alice Keppel, the mistress of King Edward VII. It is said that when Camilla first met Prince Charles at a party in the 1970s her opening gambit was: "My great-grandmother and your great-great-grandfather were lovers. So how about it?"

The quick wit and dry humor were inherited from her father, Major Bruce Shand. Born in 1916, the son of Philip Morton Shand and Sybil Mary Sissons, Bruce was educated at Rugby and Sandhurst before taking his commission in a cavalry regiment, the 12th Lancers, in 1937. During the Second World War he was decorated twice for bravery, winning the MC in France and North Africa, before being captured by the Germans and spending two and a half years in a prison camp at Spangenburg. His pursuits are suitably patrician: he is a member of Boodle's, the St. James's club, a vice Lord Lieutenant of East Sussex, a former joint master of the local hunt, and for many years he derived great satisfaction from his job on the fringe of the royal household—Clerk of the Cheque and Adjutant of the Yeoman of the Guard: in other words he was the chap in the 1815 uniform who carried the royal standard on State occasions.

Camilla, according to contemporaries, was a pretty child with long blonde hair. Her first school, Dumbrells, at Ditchling, was three miles distant from the Shands' home, The Laines at Plumpton. The regime there was as spartan and cheerless as the one at Gordonstoun where Charles spent several miserable years. But Camilla was clearly made of sterner stuff: contemporaries particularly recall the cold and her ability to withstand it. There was little heating, and the children wore wellington boots all year round (in part due to the unsubstantiated rumor that there were snakes in the orchard). A contemporary of Camilla's recalls: "A school inspector came and was dumbstruck. He never knew such a place could exist. The school was so harsh I used to say that a child who could cope with Dumbrells could cope with anything."

The Shands also had a home in London, and when Camilla was ten she was sent to the fashionable Queen's Gate School in South Kensington. It has been described as a girls' school which provided "wives for half the Foreign Office."

The sixth-form English teacher was Penelope Fitzgerald, later a Booker Prize–winning author. "When I arrived the school was changing," she recalls. "It had been a place where girls were taught how to write checks and play bridge, but by then academic standards were improving." But not so much that Camilla felt the need to excel: the school records do not register her as attempting A levels. But she was interested in sport and good at fencing.

At school the quickly maturing Camilla was known as Milla. One former classmate describes her as "a complete tearaway." Another contemporary, the sixties pop singer Twinkle, recalls: "I remember her quite well and she seems to be identical today as to how she was then. She hasn't even changed her hairstyle. I always thought that she was the coolest girl in the school.

"I remember her best when she was fifteen and a half. She was a very hoity-toity little madam, and she always looked great. She was what you would call a very Sloane Ranger type. We didn't get on that well because she was very into hunting and shooting and that kind of thing. We used to have mammoth rows about all that because I was totally against it.

"She knew that I wanted to be a pop star—and she didn't have to say what she wanted to be. She had a confidence that I envied. She was someone who didn't need to be anything other than she was.

"I didn't meet Prince Charles and I don't know if Milla did then, but several of the girls went around in the circle that knew him. It was very much that kind of group at Queen's Gate."

Camilla Shand, destined to become a débutante, allowed the Swinging Sixties to pass her by—sartorially, at least. She wore un-hip twin sets and tweed skirts and appeared to be thoroughly conventional. "She didn't seem to mind being different from the others. It was odd, in a way, because girls can be cruel, but there was an inner something in Milla that others recognized as stronger," says a friend. "She was looked up to by the other girls—a lot of them wanted to be her friend. She had a certain magnetism—I think it was because she simply knew they would be a success in life. They were all going to make something of themselves, they were brought up to expect the best of everything. There was no question that she might do badly, with or without A levels. That didn't matter. She would live the life she wanted—that's what she exuded."

Though senior to Camilla, Lynn Redgrave remembers the school well, though she adds: "with nothing but disdain. I think I was the only girl who had a working mother—my mother was an actress. The idea was for us to leave as marriageable young ladies. The girls didn't think they had to learn much because all they had in mind was going to parties. Coming out and being a deb was high on the agenda."

The Season was enjoying a revival in the late sixties. Though girls were no longer presented at Court to the Queen, an influx of new money ensured that the endless round of tea parties, cocktail parties, dinners, dances and balls went on. Despite the eternal denials that the Season was simply a bluebloods' marriage market, friendships and love affairs were born, and many a union was forged between the families of this tiny self-perpetuating oligarchy. It was not that its members rejected the thought of marrying outside their set; it was just that it would never occur to them to do so. Camilla Shand could expect to find her Mr. Right somewhere among the nightly carousings in Belgravia and Mayfair and Chelsea, and without too much difficulty—a friend from that time recalls: "She'd been fooling around from an early age. Even then she was considered very sexy."

Her contemporaries differ in their accounts of Camilla's débutante year. One of her fellow debs recalls drily: "She was an insignificant little thing. There were two aspects to coming-out in those days. One was that you weren't easily impressed by other people's connections—everybody had rich and influential relations. Two, it was the girls who created the biggest splash with their looks or parties who got the best men. On the first count, there were others who were better connected than Camilla. On the second, virtually nobody noticed her. Her mother gave a drinks party for her at 30 Pavilion Road, which is a place in Knightsbridge you hire if you haven't got a sufficiently grand London address. It was one of the first parties of the year, and after that she sank without trace."

The seventeen-year-old Camilla, who had already spent a year "finishing" in Switzerland, was described by crusty social arbiter Betty Kenward, in her Jennifer's Diary in *Queen* magazine, as "attractive"—a word which in the gentle Kenward lexicon means, to insiders, the very opposite of what it says. It is only when Jennifer's Diary uses hyperbole that the beauty of her subject is beyond doubt. Camilla was frankly lost among a vintage year of fabulous girls and as a contemporary pointed out: "If you are really pretty you can be a sensation during the deb season, but if you're average, in which category I would place Camilla Shand, it can be pretty discouraging."

The escape to the real world could not come soon enough, and Camilla took a job as a secretary. She shared a two-bedroom, ground-floor flat at No. 1 Stack House in Ebury Street, near Victoria Station—on the estate her forebears had built for the Grosvenor family. Her flatmate was Virginia Carington, daughter of the former foreign secretary, who, in the way the incestuous world of London society revolves, went on to marry Camilla's uncle, Lord Ashcombe.

Her closest friends stem from this time. One is Kirsty Smallwood, the half-sister of Lord Beaverbrook, to whom Camilla is related by marriage. Another friend is Fiona Allsopp, who is married to the head of Christie's auctioneers, Charles Allsopp. Their daughter is named after Kirsty Smallwood. Another is the well-known interior designer Jane Churchill, the separated wife of Lord Charles Spencer-Churchill, brother of the Duke of Marlborough. The last is Carolyn "Chubby" Benson, daughter of the former chairman of the Guards Polo Club, Colonel Gerard Leigh.

*   *   *

It took a dozen years or so for the first concrete evidence of an affair with the Prince of Wales to surface. In December 1992 details of a tape recording of a conversation between Charles and Camilla suddenly burst upon an unsuspecting public. It was the counterpart to the notorious "Squidgy" tape of conversations between Diana and James Gilbey, which had been published in the *Sun* newspaper in August 1992.

The sources of these tapes are discussed in Chapter 3, but several important and hitherto unaddressed aspects to the couple's relationship are exposed in the exchanges. It is worth including the complete conversation because it is a rare insight into the heart and mind of the future King. The bedtime telephone call took place on the night of December 18, 1989 while Charles was staying at the Cheshire home of his old friend Anne, Duchess of Westminster (referred to in the tape as Nancy). The conversation had already been in progress for several minutes when the tape recorder picked it up:

WALES: . . . he was a bit anxious actually.

CAMILLA: Was he?

W: He thought he might have gone a bit far.

C: Ah well.

W: Anyway, you know, that's the sort of thing one has to beware of, and sort of feel one's way along with, if you know what I mean.

CAMILLAGATE

c: Mmmm ... you're awfully good at feeling your way along.

w: Oh, stop! I want to feel my way along you, all over you and up and down you and in and out ...

c: Oh!

w: Particularly in and out ...

c: Oh, that's just what I need at the moment.

w: Is it?

c: I know it would revive me. I can't bear a Sunday night without you.

w: Oh, God.

c: It's like that program *Start the Week*. I can't start the week without you.

w: I fill your tank!

c: Yes, you do!

w: Then you can cope.

c: Then I'm all right.

w: What about me? The trouble is I need you several times a week.

c: Mmmm. So do I. I need you all the week, all the time.

w: Oh, God, I'll just live inside your trousers or something. It would be much easier!

c: [*Laughs.*] What are you going to turn into? A pair of knickers? [*Both laugh.*] Oh, you're going to come back as a pair of knickers.

w: Oh, God forbid, a Tampax, just my luck! [*Laughs.*]

c: You are a complete idiot! [*Laughs.*] Oh, what a wonderful idea.

w: My luck to be chucked down the lavatory and go on and on forever swirling round on the top, never going down!

c: [*Laughing.*] Oh, darling!

w: Until the next one comes through.

c: Or perhaps you could just come back as a box.

w: What sort of box?

c: A box of Tampax, so you could just keep going.

w: That's true.

c: Repeating yourself. [*Laughing.*] Oh, darling, I just want you now.

w: Do you?

c: Mmmm.

w: So do I.

c: Desperately, desperately, desperately. Oh, I thought of you so much at Yaraby.

w: Did you?

c: Simply mean we couldn't be there together.

w: Desperate. If you could be here—I long to ask Nancy sometimes.

c: Why don't you?

w: I daren't.

c: Because I think she's so in love with you.

w: Mmmm.

c: She'd do anything you asked.

w: She'd tell all sorts of people.

c: No she wouldn't, because she'd be much too frightened of what you might say to her. I think you've got, I'm afraid it's a terrible thing to say, but I think you know, these sort of people do feel strongly about you, they've got such a great hold over her.

w: Really?

c: And you're . . . I think as usual you're underestimating yourself.

w: But she might be terribly jealous or something.

c: Oh! [*Laughs.*] Now that is a point! I wonder, she might be, I suppose.

w: You never know, do you?

c: No, the little green-eyed monster might be lurking inside her. No, but I mean, the thing is you're so good when people are so flattered to be taken into your confidence. But I don't know they'd betray you. You know, real friends.

w: Really.

c: I don't . . . [*Pause.*] Gone to sleep?

w: No, I'm here.

c: Darling, listen. I talked to David* tonight again. It might not be any good.

w: Oh, no!

c: I'll tell you why. He's got these children of one of those Crawley girls and their nanny staying.† He's going, I'm going, to ring him again tomorrow. He's going to try to put them off till Friday. But I thought as an alternative perhaps I might ring up Charlie.‡

w: Yes.

c: And see if we could do it there. I know he's back on Thursday.

w: It's quite a lot further away.

c: Oh, is it?

w: Well, I'm just trying to think. Coming from Newmarket.

c: Coming from Newmarket to me at that time of night, you could probably do it in two and three quarters. It takes me three.

---

*Lord Willoughby de Broke, a close friend of both the prince and Camilla Parker Bowles, who has a farm in Gloucestershire not far from Highgrove and the Parker Bowleses' house at Corsham in Wiltshire.

†The children of either Marita Crawley or her sister-in-law Sarah, the widows of Randall and Andrew Crawley, who died in the Turin air crash in 1988. Sarah is the daughter of a former chairman of Lloyd's, Murray Lawrence, and has a son; but it is more likely that it was Marita's two children, Aidan and Cosima, who are being referred to. Marita is the present Duchess of Westminster's sister.

‡Probably the Earl of Shelburne, who was page of honor to the Queen in 1956.

w: What, to go to, um, Bowood?*

c: Northmore.†

w: To go to Bowood?

c: To go to Bowood would be the same as me really, wouldn't it?

w: I mean to say, you would suggest going to Bowood, uh?

c: No, not at all.

w: Which Charlie then?

c: What Charlie did you think I was talking about?

w: I didn't know, because I thought you meant . . .

c: I've got lots!

w: Somebody else.

c: I've got lots of friends called Charlie.

w: The other one. Patty's.‡

c: Oh! Oh, there! Oh, that is further away. They're not . . .

w: They've gone.

c: I don't know, it's just, you know, just a thought I had if it fell through, the other place.

w: Oh, right. What do you do, go on the M25 then down the M4 is it?

c: Yes, you go, um, and sort of Royston or M11, at that time of night.

w: Yes, well, that'll be just after, it will be after shooting anyway.

c: So it would be, um, you'd miss the worst of the

---

*The family home of the Earl of Shelburne.

†A stud farm near Newmarket in Suffolk. At the time it was owned by Hugh van Cutsem, a long-time friend of the prince, and son of the trainer Bernard van Cutsem.

‡Patty and Charles Palmer-Tomkinson. Patty Palmer-Tomkinson was seriously injured in the skiing accident that killed the royal equerry Major Hugh Lindsay in Klosters in 1988.

traffic, because I'll, er, you see the problem is I've got to be in London tomorrow night.

w: Yes.

c: And Tuesday night A's coming home.

w: No!

c: Would you believe it? Because, I don't know what he is doing, he's shooting down here or something. But darling, you wouldn't be able to ring me anyway, would you?

w: I might just. I mean tomorrow night I could have done.

c: Oh, darling, I can't bear it. How could you have done tomorrow night?

w: Because I'll be [*Yawns.*] working on the next speech.

c: Oh no, what's the next one?

w: A Business in the Community one, rebuilding communities.

c: Oh no, when's that for?

w: A rather important one for Wednesday.

c: Well, at least I'll be behind you.

w: I know.

c: Can I have a copy of the one you've just done?

w: Yes.

c: Can I? Um, I would like it.

w: OK, I'll try and organize it.

c: Darling . . .

w: But I, oh God, when am I going to speak to you?

c: I can't bear it, um . . .

w: Wednesday night?

c: Oh, certainly Wednesday night. I'll be alone, um, Wednesday, you know, the evening. Or Tuesday. While you're rushing around doing things I'll be, you know, alone until it reappears. And early Wednesday morning, I mean, he'll be leaving at half-past eight, quarter-past eight. He won't be here Thursday, pray God. Um, that ambulance strike, it's a terrible thing to say this, I suppose it won't have come to an end by Thursday?

w: It will have done.

c: Well, I mean for everybody's sake it will have done, but I hope for our sakes it's still going on.

w: Why?

c: Well, because if it stops he'll come down here on Thursday night.

w: Oh, no.

c: Yes, but I don't think it will stop, do you?

w: No, neither do I. Just our luck.

c: It would be our luck, I know.

w: Then it's bound to.

c: No it won't. You mustn't think like that. You must think positive.

w: I'm not very good at that.

c: Well, I'm going to. Because if I don't, I'll despair. [*Pause.*] Hmmm . . . gone to sleep?

w: No, how maddening.

c: I know. Anyway, I mean, he's doing his best to change it, David, but I just thought, you know, I might ask Charlie.

w: Did you say anything?

c: No, I haven't talked to him.

w: You haven't?

c: Well, I talked to him briefly, but you know, I just thought I—I just don't know whether he's got any children at home, that's the worry.

w: Right.

c: Oh . . . darling, I think I'll . . .

w: Pray, just pray.

c: It would be so wonderful to have just one night to set us on our way, wouldn't it?

w: Wouldn't it? To wish you Happy Christmas.

c: [*Indistinct.*] Happy, oh, don't let's think about

Christmas. I can't bear it [*Pause.*] . . . Going to sleep? I think you'd better, don't you, darling?

w: [*Sleepily.*] Yes, darling.

c: I think you've exhausted yourself by all that hard work. You must go to sleep now, darling.

w: [*Sleepily.*] Yes, darling.

c: Will you ring me when you wake up?

w: Yes, I will.

c: Before I have those rampaging children around. It's Tom's birthday tomorrow. [*Pause.*] You all right?

w: Mmm, I'm all right.

c: Can I talk to you, I hope, before those rampaging children . . .

w: What time do they come in?

c: Well, usually Tom never wakes up at all, but as it's his birthday tomorrow he might just stagger out of bed. It won't be before half-past eight. [*Pause.*] 'Night-night, my darling.

w: Darling . . .

c: I do love you.

w: [*Sleepily.*] Before . . .

c: Before half-past eight.

w: Try and ring?

c: Yeah, if you can. Love you, darling.

w: 'Night, darling.

c: I love you.

w: Love you too. I **don't** want to say goodbye.

c: Well done for doing that. You're a clever old thing. An awfully good brain lurking there, isn't there? Oh, darling, I think you ought to give the brain a rest now. 'Night-night.

w: 'Night, darling. God bless.

c: I do love you and I'm so proud of you.

w: Oh, I'm so proud of you.

c: Don't be silly, I've never achieved anything.

w: Yes, you have.

c: No, I haven't.

w: Your great achievement is to love me.

c: Oh, darling, easier than falling off a chair.

w: You suffer all these indignities and tortures and calumnies.

c: Oh, darling, don't be silly. I'd suffer anything for you. That's love. It's the strength of love. 'Night-night.

w: 'Night, darling. Sounds as though you're dragging an enormous piece of string behind you with hundreds of tin pots and cans attached to it. Must be your telephone. 'Night-night, before the battery goes. [*Blows kisses.*] 'Night.

c: I love you.

w: I don't want to say goodbye.

c: Neither do I, but you must get some sleep. 'Bye.

w: 'Bye, darling.

c: I love you.

w: 'Bye.

c: Hopefully talk to you in the morning.

w: Please.

c: 'Bye, I love you.

w: 'Night.

c: 'Night.

w: 'Night.

c: Love you for ever.

w: 'Night.

c: G'bye, 'bye, my darling.

w: 'Night.

c: 'Night-night.

w: 'Night.

c: 'Bye-bye.

w: Going.

c: 'Bye.

w: Going.

c: Gone.

w: 'Night.

c: Press the button.

w: Going to press the tit.

c: All right, darling, I wish you were pressing mine.

w: God, I wish I was. Harder and harder.

c: Oh, darling.

w: 'Night.

c: 'Night.

w: I love you.

c: [*Yawning.*] Love you, press the tit.

w: Adore you. 'Night.

c: 'Night.

w: 'Night.

c: [*Blows a kiss.*]

w: 'Night.

c: G'night, my darling. Love you . . .

[*Charles hangs up.*]

Whatever the morality of it, there can be no doubt that Charles and Camilla love each other profoundly. By the time this conversation was recorded, the couple had known each other for seventeen years and, it can be safely assumed, had been sleeping together for nearly that amount of time—friends judge that Charles was faithful to Diana for the first two years of their marriage, but probably no longer than that. To feel as passionately towards someone after such a long time is remarkable in itself.

If there is no key here to Charles's feelings towards his wife, it is because that subject has already been thrashed out, again and again. He told

Camilla that their intimate life had collapsed quite soon after his marriage, and that he found it difficult to view Diana as he should because she had become an icon; this had put him off. But here he does not want his marital problems to impinge on a cozy late-night intimacy. However, Camilla's tart reference to her husband as "it"— "I'll be alone until *it* reappears"—is a pointer to the state of her own marriage.

A clear demonstration of Charles's tendency to blame others in life when things go wrong comes towards the end of the conversation, where he complains of a sound break-up on the line— "Sounds as though you're dragging an enormous piece of string behind you with hundreds of tin pots and cans attached to it. Must be your telephone." In fact it is he who has the mobile telephone, notoriously susceptible to such problems, while Camilla is on a land-line.

In addition he is unresponsive when Camilla mentions her son Tom—who is Charles's godson. "It's Tom's birthday tomorrow," she says, then pauses. He does not take up the bait; "as it's his *birthday* tomorrow . . ." she tries again, but still the penny doesn't drop. It is clear he has not sent a present.

Charles's underlying sense of inadequacy— which alternates with an overweening belief in the rightness of himself—pokes through. Camilla orders him to think positively, but his response is resigned and glum: "I'm not very good at that."

But perhaps the most damning indictment of the future King lies not in the intensely sexual nature of the conversation, but in a clear case of dereliction of duty. The ambulance strike of 1989 was one of the ugliest industrial confrontations in Britain since the miners' strike. It lasted six months and cost more than £35 million. The police and army hurriedly had to work out a cover system that would provide the same kind of service—and though this was finally achieved, inevitably the public suffered. Accusations rang out that people had died needlessly, because the professionals were out on strike. By the time it was resolved in March 1990 the police had dedicated an extra 1,100,000 hours to ambulance-related duties, which had necessarily taken them away from their core role of crime prevention and detection.

When Charles and Camilla's conversation took place the dispute was three months old and at its height. Andrew Parker Bowles had a key role to play in providing army ambulance backup, and the job proved demanding and time-consuming. Interestingly, it is Camilla who is apologetic about wishing the strike would carry on so as to keep her husband in London. No such regrets are uttered by the prince—"Just our luck," he says at the thought that he might have to miss his next assignation with Camilla. As a Privy Counsellor and future King he would argue publicly that the restitution of order to the ambulance service was paramount to the health of the nation. But not, it would appear, if it were to interfere with his private life.

There are echoes of his predecessor David, Prince of Wales—later Edward VIII and still later Duke of Windsor—in this inability to balance public and private duty. In the earlier Prince of Wales this trait was demonstrated on his famous tour of south Wales in November 1936, during a period of catastrophic unemployment. At Blaenavon he told the chairman of the Unemployed Men's Committee: "Something will be done about unemployment." As his official biographer Philip Ziegler pointed out: "Yet how many people remember that these words and those which followed them—'You may be sure that all I can do for you I will'—were spoken a bare three weeks before he left England for good? And how many people have ever known that when he spoke them he had already told the prime minister, his mother and his three brothers of his intention to abdicate the throne?"

Indeed, as the so-called Camillagate tapes demonstrate, there are other similarities between the successive Princes of Wales. David confessed to his mistress Freda Dudley Ward: "In my own childhood I never knew love. There were servants who seemed to love me, but I could not forget that it might be because I was heir to the throne."

Compare that to Charles's plaintive demands for love from Camilla Parker Bowles, and the essence of her attraction suddenly becomes plain. Friends of the prince who know Camilla remain surprised that she holds such power over the prince because, though it is offensive to pass such judgments, she is not universally perceived as an attractive woman and as one friend put it, "Charles could have his pick, married or unmarried. There are well-born women all over the land who'd love to fall into bed with him." But the secret lies partly in the fact that Camilla mothers him. That, and the strange, almost animal-like attraction he gets from the way she lives her life. "She's frankly not the most pristine of women— you're not sure whether they're today's knickers she's got on," said one acquaintance cruelly. "Her house is a bit of a mess, I don't think she goes to the hairdresser and most of the time she can't be bothered to dress up."

This is the very antithesis of everything Charles is used to. Compared to the almost glacial attractions of his wife, Camilla is earthy and unbothered. Though virtually the same age as Charles, she can offer a mother's refuge to a man with a troubled childhood who is easily downcast—Diana, with problems of her own, cannot. Indeed, it often seems that Charles never thought of Diana except as a child. Certainly he never discussed his speeches with her, preferring to take them to Camilla. And certainly Diana never asked to see a copy of one. It could be argued that between Charles and Camilla there was, and is, a meeting of minds—but it is something more fundamental than that: she is both mother and mistress, adviser and advised.

One more thing binds them, and that is the thrill of the chase. As royal author Suzy Menkes says: "I believe that Charles gets a tremendous sexual thrill and charge from hunting, which many people do." Diana, of course, is hopeless on a horse after an early childhood accident. Camilla on the other hand is fearless. "She's a ruthless horsewoman—aggressive, shouting on the hunting field," a member of the Beaufort Hunt says. "To use the word assertive would be an understatement. You often hear her screaming as you approach a fence. She's shouting, 'Bloody hell, get out of the fucking way!' She steamrollers people and it can be quite frightening."

The hunting field has been an ideal place for the couple to meet, and members of more than one hunt have described how Charles and Camilla will start the day far apart in the field, but will eventually meet up for discussions in a wood. Camilla, too, took up some of Charles's other passions—water-color painting and fishing. For a time the pair were both under the tutelage of the Wiltshire portrait painter Neil Forster, and of course Camilla has spent much time at Birkhall, the Queen Mother's house on the Balmoral estate, where she accompanies Charles salmon fishing.

But what of Camilla's relationship with her husband, now a brigadier? One friend of the family characterized it thus: "They row a lot. Not necessarily about Charles, but about lots of things—money, what they should do, who does what job, whether they should be together—and there is much shouting when they are at home. They are an ongoing irritation to one another and not at all cosy. She shouts at him more than the other way round. When he's at home Andrew likes pottering around in the garden and if the phone goes for him she will come out and yell for him rather than go over and talk gently to him—that makes him very cross. And she will regularly nag him about doing chores."

After the Camillagate tapes were published, they were both prepared to admit that their situation was "pretty hopeless," but with their children still at school—they also have a teenage daughter, Laura—they were not prepared to separate or divorce. However, it is an open secret among their friends that until Commander Timothy Laurence came on the scene, the brigadier had once again been spending time in the company of Princess Anne, taking her to the cinema, the theatre and out to dinner at a number of restaurants. She visited him at his home, then Bolehyde Manor near Chippenham, and saw much of him when he was commanding officer at Knightsbridge Barracks.

It was suggested that there was, at times, too little discretion and that Andrew and the princess had resumed their friendship. Despite Andrew's popularity with staff and royals alike, there was some concern at Buckingham Palace as to where this relationship would lead. But upsetting the princess is not something people do willingly, so little was said. As Anne became more and more interested in the man who would ultimately become her second husband she saw less and less of Andrew Parker Bowles. Ever the cavalier, Parker Bowles is said to present former fancies with a mascot for their car when a relationship comes to an end. He then switched his attentions to Charlotte Soames, daughter of his former boss in Rhodesia, Lord Soames. Some thought that after Charlotte's marriage to banker Rick Hambro collapsed, Andrew might leave Camilla to be with her—but in the end she married a Yorkshire landowner, Earl Peel. A friend remarked, "If Charlotte hadn't married Willie Peel, Andrew would have divorced Camilla and asked her to marry him. But he kept messing Charlotte about, and she lost patience in the end. Camilla hated the intensity of the relationship with Charlotte. But even if it did go on for quite a long time, she was really in no position to complain."

The brigadier has been characterized in the press as the perfect English gentleman, steadfastly supporting his wife and brushing aside the ever more blatant hints that he has been cuckolded. But he has had to endure far harsher criticism from within his own world, the army, where brother officers have complained that he turned down postings abroad so he could stay close to Buckingham Palace. This broke into an open row when he was made the first non-medical director of the Royal Army Veterinary Corps in its 203-year history. Colleagues said he had turned down so many foreign posts justifying the rank of briga-dier that it was all the army had left.

So disgusted was the corps's Colonel Comman-dant, Brigadier Robert Clifford, that he resigned—though not before putting his feelings in a stinging letter to the military secretary at the Min-istry of Defense, Lieutenant-General Sir John Learmond. Threading through the criticism was the fact that Parker Bowles was merely using the army to stay close to the royal family, and that eventually he would be making his career in the royal household.

In 1987 he was given glittering and official rec-ognition when he was made Silver Stick in Wait-ing to the Queen. Dating back to the seventeenth century, the position was created at a time when the sovereign's life was believed to be in danger from Roman Catholic plotters. Historically, Silver Stick would attend the monarch "from rising to going to bed." Now, although the position is purely ceremonial, it carries enormous kudos.

None the less, some polo friends remember asking Andrew to umpire matches for them at the Guards Polo Club, only to be met with an embarrassed response from the soldier: he had to go home, he explained, to make preparations because the Prince of Wales was coming to dinner. The impression he left was that he would be providing the food for the occasion. Polo wags asked behind his back whether his wife would be provided as well.

Strangely, though the brigadier—seemingly the more vulnerable character of the two—has managed to steel himself against the greater excesses of a prurient public, Camilla has found it more difficult to do so. On several occasions she felt it necessary to step out of the public gaze and seek refuge at the spacious Breconshire home of former Life Guards officer and merchant banker Nicolas Paravicini.

Paravicini, the grandson of Somerset Maugham, was married to Andrew Parker Bowles's sister Mary Ann until they divorced in the mid-1980s. Though his house provided a respite from the public gaze—and, according to some locals, another meeting place for Camilla—she has nevertheless forced herself to appear in public from time to time, experiences that have been ill-chosen and have left her feeling hurt and vulnerable. At a service for El Alamein veterans in Westminster Abbey she turned up on the arm of her father, Major Bruce

Shand. But the Princess of Wales was there too—and the press photographers had a field day. "She was appalled by the way she was chased that day," says a friend. "Serves her right," was Diana's tart comment.

On another occasion, in the summer of 1992, just as her name had been firmly linked to Prince Charles, Camilla turned up to polo at Windsor, defiantly wearing a Prince-of-Wales-check suit in front of the Queen. "No one could be sure whether this was Camilla making a forceful point, or whether it was the only thing in her wardrobe that was pressed," joked one member of the Guards Polo Club. The photographers weighed in again, to Camilla's disgust.

Both Charles and Camilla have complained bitterly and often to their friends about what they consider to be malicious press intrusion into what they see as essentially a private matter—and no doubt they would prefer the self-imposed moratorium on reporting that occurred when Charles's predecessor was Prince of Wales. Then, in the mid-1930s, Britain's national press decided they would not print *any* material relating to the prince's relationship with Wallis Simpson—even though newspapers around the world, especially in Mrs. Simpson's native America, were running stories on the romance virtually every day. In fact national newspaper editors *did* take the view that anything Charles did in private was his own affair, until the matter became too pressing. They were almost prepared to believe the repeated protestations of Andrew Parker Bowles, who publicly denied Camilla and Charles had had a sexual relationship. "It's not true," he said. "It's fiction." But it wasn't.

In the end, though, it was Charles's own team that shot him in the foot. A member of his staff when interviewed by the *Daily Mirror*, admitted that Charles had had an affair.

"So what?" he said. "So the prince has had an affair with this woman—it happens in France all the time. Politicians and famous men in all walks of life in France have mistresses and nobody turns a hair." After two decades, after all the secrecy and all the denials, it was a staggering admission, although oddly enough this man remains in employment with the royals to this day. Charles and Camilla were beleaguered. The marriage of the Prince and Princess of Wales—though it was now clear that it had barely ever been a marriage—was over. An official separation was announced, and the world's press camped on the doorstep of the Parker Bowleses' Wiltshire home. The couple were forced to change their telephone number.

Through the early months of 1993 the pressure continued to grow—until one person could take it no more. Major Bruce Shand, now nearly eighty, demanded a meeting with the Prince of Wales at Buckingham Palace. His tone was bewildered and sad and sometimes very angry. His wife, he said, was an invalid. His daughter's life had been ruined. It was all Charles's fault.

The Prince of Wales responded to the old man's poignant but feeble complaint by bursting into tears.

TWO

Squidgy

It is generally agreed among the Prince and Princess of Wales's circle that the conjugal side of their marriage was over by 1986, a mere five years after the royal wedding. Certainly that is what Charles told his polo manager, Ronald Ferguson. Friends put this schism down to a number of factors, principal among which is the goddess syndrome. Within a very short space of time Charles discovered that the pink-cheeked teenager he had married had turned into a goddess, her picture splashed across magazine covers from London to Tokyo, her every move documented by reporters and cameras and gossip columnists.

For someone who had spent every day for thirty-four years being constantly reminded by courtiers that he was the most important person in the world after his mother, Diana's instant eminence was hard to swallow. Having dedicated himself to his preparations to become King, studying history, philosophy, ecology, politics, fine arts and the environment, he suddenly found himself being overtaken in public acclaim by an "airhead" with a passion for Dire Straits and the novels of her stepgrandmother, Barbara Cartland. Or so it seemed to the prince. You could almost feel the temperature dropping between the two.

On a tour of Australia and New Zealand in 1983, the couple were still in the first flush of married love. At a reception at the High Commissioner's residence in Auckland which I attended, Charles was continually patting her on the bottom and she squealed with delight at the attention. It was a repetition of the scene at a polo match when he'd given her a pinch in full view of the cameras—a most uncharacteristic dropping of his guard. Earlier in the tour the couple attended a dance in Melbourne and got lost in the lift trying to find the correct floor. The lift finally stopped and as the doors opened they found themselves face to face with the Press Association's veteran photographer Ron Bell. Charles stepped out, his eyes shining, and, turning back towards Diana, he said, "Ron, isn't she absolutely beautiful? I'm so proud of her." It was the only public pronouncement of adoration for his wife he ever made. When asked by Anthony Carthew, ITN's royal correspondent, on the day of his engagement whether he was in love with Diana, his answer had been stilted, half-embarrassed: "Whatever in love means." Nevertheless, those first two years of marriage were acceptable enough—until it started to hit home that his child-bride was getting equal billing in the press, and, increasingly, top billing. His reaction, at first puzzlement, started to become resentment.

But even on the Antipodean tour of 1983, those feelings started to surface in public. The couple had undertaken a number of highly successful walkabouts, where they established a routine that involved getting out of the royal car and, each taking one side, walking down the lines of adoring spectators before swapping sides after twenty yards or so. Noting the crowds' reactions, Charles started to preface his remarks to them by saying: "I'm sorry you've got me—if I were you I'd ask for my money back." And though it was delivered in a jokey way, there was a growing irritation in his manner, as if he were hurt that people were disappointed when he appeared. That, after all, had never happened in his life. Where once there was universal joy when he came over to speak to members of the public, now he saw them looking over his shoulder for Diana. Their frustration was plain, and quite quickly he came to hate it.

At the same time a multi-million Diana industry had started up. Her clothes were copied and sold, and magazine editors the world over discovered a very simple fact: if they put a photograph of Diana on the cover, sales went up. If in the next issue they put another photograph on the cover, sales went up again. Within two years she had become a phenomenon unequalled in world history, adored by the masses but untainted by commercialism, and therefore purer than the other twentieth-century icons, who all had products to sell—the Beatles, Marilyn Monroe, Michael Jackson, Rudolph Valentino. It took Charles some time to wake up to what was happening. Instead of providing himself and the nation with a charming but shadowy helpmeet, a compliant mother for his children, he discovered instead that he had unleashed a demon. He found it unmanning.

It was clear that Diana, who was gradually discovering the extraordinary power she could exert over individuals and crowds alike, found Charles's patronizing tone increasingly difficult to swallow. It was his belief that she couldn't learn overnight what had taken him thirty-four years to absorb; she, on the other hand, realized that when it came down to the showbiz aspect of royalty, much of his knowledge and prejudice was simply superfluous baggage. She deduced this from her own experience—every time she stepped out of a car, the crowds would draw in their breath in an audible whoosh, then they would cheer and cheer. The energy from their serried ranks would flood over her in waves, and she took strength from it. But if she came to recognize the joy she could give simply by turning the public's dreams of fairy tale princesses into reality, her poor bemused husband just didn't understand. Jealous and cross, he could not bring himself to admit that, without a single O level exam result to her name, she had something in her own right. And something very powerful at that. It was explained to me like this: men who reach a certain eminence view women in a strange way. Wives are there to be mothers of their children, not sex objects.

But at the same time, Diana's combination of unhappiness and new-found inner confidence led some friends to ask whether this was the moment when she, seeing the example set by her husband, would embark on a full-scale love affair. But those closest to her felt differently. One told me, "It's unthinkable. Diana has wanted to be Princess of Wales since she was fifteen, and the position means more to her than anything else in the world, apart from her children. There's no way she would risk being caught having a silly fling. And anyway it's just not in her nature."

By 1987 Diana was ready to test the boundaries of her marriage. No one who knows her would dare claim that she has been unfaithful to her husband but, to borrow a phrase from the former US president Jimmy Carter, it may be that she would acknowledge that she has sinned in her heart.

The first young man to catch her eye was the tall, dark-haired, Old Etonian godson of Princess Alexandra, Philip Dunne. Described as a man with an appreciation of his own good looks, he strode onto the scene during the Wales's skiing holiday at Klosters in 1987. Although involved with international banker Lord Grenfell's daughter Katya, Dunne at twenty-eight was nevertheless the twenty-six-year-old princess's cup of tea. It was noted that Diana, naturally flirtatious, had become increasingly aware of her ability to interest handsome men. One evening after skiing, everyone joined in an after-dinner party which ended with Diana lying in the bottom of a large chest of drawers pretending to be asleep. One observer reported that she called out that the first person to kiss her would become a prince. Dunne stepped forward.

This was followed up by an invitation back in England to Dunne's family home, Gatley Park, in Herefordshire. Quite soon it emerged that Diana had spent the night there without Charles, and that Dunne's parents—Thomas Dunne, the Lord Lieutenant of the county, and his wife Henrietta—weren't there either.

A major scandal looked likely to erupt until the young merchant banker defused the situation by pointing out—in extremely forceful terms—that a dozen friends had also been present. So that was all right, then.

Soon after that came the wedding of the Duke of Beaufort's son, the Marquess of Worcester, to actress Rachel Ward's sister Tracy. At the reception Charles danced with the woman he had first proposed marriage to—and who had turned him down—Scottish landowner's daughter Anna Wallace. As if that weren't enough to infuriate Diana, he then locked himself in conversation with Camilla Parker Bowles, to the virtual exclusion of all others. Charles left early, but Diana stayed behind, dancing furiously into the night and not stopping until six o'clock the next morning, "pausing only long enough to wipe her forehead with the hem of her gown," noted one guest. During those long hours on the dance floor, one of her partners was Philip Dunne.

It is many people's belief that Prince Charles's angry withdrawal to Balmoral on September 22 that year was a direct result of this friendship. The prince was not to see his wife for thirty-seven days, nor did he see his children. Instead, he sat in the Scottish estate, fishing, painting, stalking— and sulking—in the company of his friends Lord and Lady Tryon, and the ubiquitous Camilla. The news of Diana's weekend with Philip Dunne at Gatley Park had surfaced in one of the gossip columns, and Charles had wrongly assumed the worst —that his wife had been unfaithful. He was beside himself with mortification and rage that he had apparently been so publicly humiliated. Without pausing to inspect his own double standards, he instead flew to Scotland, unclear what to do next.

Meanwhile, back in London, the newspapers were counting the days the couple were apart in bigger and bigger type, and Diana's friend Major David Waterhouse sprang to her defense. "There has been a lot of talk about the princess and

Philip," the Household Cavalry officer said. "It is absurd to say they are having an affair. The allegation is totally untrue." Waterhouse was in a position to know. Very similar in age and background to Dunne, the two men were close and had been in the Klosters skiing party together. Diana found his personality "magnetic" and before too long he escorted her to a David Bowie concert at Wembley. When the inevitable photographs appeared in the newspapers the captions wrongly described Waterhouse as Dunne, which the major laughed off with characteristic good humor.

But during her grass widowhood curious behavior was noted. Diana went out one evening to a cinema near Kensington Palace with Waterhouse and her friend Julia Samuel, the sister of one of Prince Charles's former girlfriends, Sabrina Guinness. When photographers emerged from the night to let off their flashguns, Waterhouse leapt over a pedestrian barrier and raced off, leaving the two women to fend for themselves.

And that was not the only incident involving Waterhouse. One night he, together with Diana, was visiting the London mews house of Kate Menzies. As the couple emerged in high spirits, they found themselves confronted by a freelance photographer, Jason Fraser, who started taking pictures of them. Fraser was immediately approached by one of Diana's detectives, who asked him to hand over the film. Well, what he actually said was, "Give me that film, otherwise your life will be fucking hell. You know what hell is? I can make it hell for you if I don't get it." Despite this, the photographer was reluctant. But then the princess herself came over and caught hold of his sleeve, saying, "I must have that film—you don't know what this could do to me. I feel so trapped. Please, please . . ." Fraser admits that her apparently heartfelt personal approach was more than he could resist. "She was very red in the face. I felt sorry for her and handed over the film. She said, 'Thank you very much,' but as soon as I gave her the film she stopped blushing and her tone became clipped. Her tears were turned off and I had the distinct feeling it had all been an act. She said to her bodyguard, 'Shall we go?' then she got in the car and drove off without even saying good-bye. The transformation was remarkable. I realized I'd been taken for a ride. She got what she wanted—that was all that mattered to her."

Whatever the relationship, Waterhouse's cousin, the Marquess of Blandford, as recently as early 1993 was telling acquaintances that he believed that Waterhouse was still "the one."

By 1988 the royal marriage had reached a new level of detachment. It was inevitable that a young and healthy woman, married to a detached and unphysical husband, would experience feelings and desires which found no outlet.

Things were to change when, that summer, she arrived at Combermere Barracks near Windsor with her sons for riding lessons. In retrospect, it could be argued that if the Prince of Wales had taken upon himself the perennial fatherly chore of teaching his children how to ride—after all, with hunting, polo and racing under his belt he was one of the country's more experienced horsemen—Diana's brief and controversial liaison with Major James Hewitt of the Life Guards may never have happened.

But William needed to be taught to ride, and since Charles wasn't providing the lessons, they would come from the army. Hewitt, who according to brother officers has a dazzling charm hidden only when talking to social inferiors, was considered the right man for the job. A fine horseman and an excellent polo player, it was thought he might be able to guide the notoriously horse-shy Diana back into the saddle. In no time he had become a firm favorite of the princess and a popular "uncle" figure to the princes, and the lessons moved to Highgrove when Diana and the boys were in residence. There was an instant rapport. Hewitt, though coming from a distinctly less refined background than Diana, had all the social skills, and they found they had friends in common—not the least of them his brother officer, David Waterhouse. The age gap was negligible and Hewitt's educational plane—he had attended the ruinously expensive public school Millfield, generally held to be an institution for "rich thickos"—allowed for conversation uncluttered by the need for an analysis of life's conundrums. Also

Diana, I have always noted, is a sucker for a uniform—and there is no finer military sight than a Life Guard in his plumed helmet and shining cuirass. Lunches and suppers followed, and the bond was forged. Hewitt was young, sexy, adventurous. He adored Diana, and she responded positively—and the friendship moved to fast-forward.

Soon the instruction at Combermere Barracks was stepped up to twice, then three times a week. Generally Diana would arrive, dressed in silk shirt, hacking jacket, tight jodhpurs and boots, at around eight in the morning. She would mount up in the riding school with Hewitt, then head on out into Windsor Great Park with him.

In a lengthy interview Lance-Corporal Malcolm Leete, Hewitt's personal valet and groom between 1988 and 1990, recalls the intensifying of the relationship:

> One particular morning I got a call at three-thirty a.m. to say that Diana was coming to ride at seven. The usual happened: she arrived, gave Hewitt a peck on the cheek and said hello. But I remember from that day on they became much more friendly toward each other and Princess Diana's visits changed from once a week to three days a week, regularly—Mondays, Wednesdays and Fridays.
>
> They always went into the Park, but this particular morning there was no lady-in-waiting. They went out by themselves—I thought it was quite peculiar. She should have had someone with her like a detective, who she usually arrived with at the barracks.

Leete went on:

> They were becoming closer and closer to each other.
> She started sending him presents and buying him
> things, always in a flash carrier bag—Harrods or other
> big stores. I never paid much attention to it all, but I
> always had to press the clothes before he wore them,
> and that made me think that whenever he wore them,
> he was always going to see her.

Leete recalls that when the cold weather came
in the autumn of 1988, the riding tactics changed.

> It would have been horrible and wet for her to go riding
> outside, very unsuitable, so Hewitt started giving her
> lessons at seven a.m. (in the riding school).

One day in November, Leete fetched the princess's horse as usual, and the couple disappeared
inside the riding school. Later Leete could contain
his curiosity no longer and, standing on a mount-
ing-block, he looked inside the school. He reported: "The pair of them were in the corner. I
wasn't quite sure what I saw, but they were certainly cuddling." At that moment the camp's commander appeared and Leete moved away.

Leete acknowledges that he has had his differences with Hewitt, but justifies making public
these claims by saying, "I believe people in Britain
are entitled to know about their future Queen."
How much they are entitled to know is a matter of
hot debate, but in the relationship between James

Hewitt and the Princess of Wales there was one other person involved who felt the nation should know more—and that was Hewitt's girlfriend, Emma Stewardson.

In March 1991 she decided to go to the *News of the World* with her story about Hewitt's crush on the princess, no easy decision for a well-educated girl from a privileged background. But in the interview she suggested that the soldier had become disoriented by the new milieu in which he was moving. "I remember after one of his trips to Highgrove he came back raving about the solid-gold dinner service. He liked things like that—he liked the high life. I was worried he might become a bit dazzled by it all."

On one occasion Hewitt maintained he was unable to come to lunch because of work, but later Miss Stewardson saw him driving his TVR sports car out of Highgrove. Their four-year relationship—which she had expected to end in marriage—cooled, said the *News of the World,* after he made "personal remarks" about Diana after a "passionate bedroom session" with Emma.

Diana showered Hewitt with presents, including a diamond-studded tiepin and a gold-and-silver clock from the royal jeweller, Asprey. According to Malcolm Leete, the gifts included "suits, ties, shoes, socks—you name it." This was confirmed when in the Squidgy tapes Diana was heard to say, "Well, I've decked out people in my time . . . James Hewitt. Entirely dressed him from head to foot, that man. Cost me quite a bit."

Diana signed the accompanying cards "Dibbs"—the name she used when she wrote letters to Hewitt while he served as a tank commander in Kuwait during the Gulf War. Whatever his intellectual prowess he was a valiant soldier, leading the Royal Scots battle group in a hundred-hour dash into Kuwait, tales of which kept Diana enthralled in the days and weeks following the allied victory. She later admitted to staying up night after night to watch the progress of the war on television "to check on how my friends were doing."

Though some of this information emerged via Emma Stewardson's interview, Diana and Hewitt were still sufficiently close in the summer of 1991 for him to be invited to spend the evening of her thirtieth birthday at Kensington Palace. Charles was, as usual, absent.

However, the two men met a fortnight later, and in very public circumstances. Charles had agreed to play at a charity polo match at the Royal Berkshire Polo Club near Windsor, in aid of families of soldiers killed in the desert. Charles lined up with the 7th Armored Brigade while opposite him was Hewitt, playing for the 4th Armored Brigade. Before too long both men were clashing in a series of encounters that were as unedifying as they were enthralling to the crowd. After one shoulder charge on Charles by the major, the commentator gasped, "Oh, I say, that was a bit rough." And after another closely fought tussle he declared, "There's a real battle going on there." Hewitt emerged the victor as his Black Rats beat Charles's Red Rats 4–1, and he later bragged, "I ran rings round him. He's a brave player but he's getting a bit long in the tooth. He was very aggressive—it was supposed to be a friendly."

After the match Charles exploded at his polo manager Major Ronald Ferguson, "Why didn't you tell me that man was playing?" Ferguson, astounded, replied, "I thought you knew. It's been in the newspapers for days." But he had forgotten—Charles had given up reading all newspapers apart from the pro-royal *Daily Telegraph*.

The nature of the princess's relationship with Major Hewitt should, in all conscience, be a matter for them alone. But for Prince Charles's own intimacy with Camilla Parker Bowles, it probably would be. But the question arises, and must be answered—if Charles was unfaithful in his marriage, was Diana?

The answer has to be no. The relationship, by Hewitt's own account and that of his servant, was physical but stopped short of full sexual intercourse. Moralists may argue that infidelity takes place in the heart and head and needs no physical act to accompany it. But the fact remains that Diana maintained a psychological advantage over her husband by practicing self-restraint.

Mere males would interpret that differently,

and some did. Ronald Ferguson, hugely partisan to his polo boss, and depressed because he saw parallels between his own and Charles's marriage, said, "Diana is the biggest tease I have ever known." In the old days, teenagers might have described Diana's behavior as "heavy petting."

In the end, the relationship faded simply because there was nowhere for it to go, though it may be that Hewitt hastened its demise by his own behavior. Apart from his boasts to Emma Stewardson, he was accused of talking indiscreetly elsewhere, and the relationship ground temporarily to a halt in 1989 when he told a friend about his relationship with Diana and claimed, perhaps jokingly, perhaps not, that the princess was obsessed with him. When a friend of Diana's mentioned over lunch Hewitt's comments, she is said to have returned to Kensington Palace where she initiated a deadly telephone call to the soldier. Later the relationship was resumed, but by that time the person who was taking center stage in her affections was a used-car dealer, James Gilbey.

Gilbey, sometimes described rather more glamorously as a motor-trade executive, shares with Hewitt the same jejeune view of the world that is the very opposite of Prince Charles's agonized soul-searching. Not for nothing was he once named "Car Salesman of the Year." Educated at Ampleforth, the same Roman Catholic public school as Andrew Parker Bowles (where the younger man was known as Fatty), Gilbey is a scion of the wealthy gin-distilling house—though little of its massive fortune accrued to his particular branch of the family. In fact his father Ralph is a retired wine merchant—as indeed is Major Bruce Shand. Gilbey senior lives with his wife Barbara in an inherited Somerset farmhouse.

In 1988, aged thirty-one, James Gilbey acquired a company called Plusquick and turned it into the Holbein Motor Company plc. His plan was to sell up-market Saab cars from the slightly less up-market environs of Battersea, south London. It was short-lived. Within two years, liquidators had been appointed to the company with the monies owed assessed at not less than £500,000. In the first eighteen months of trading Holbein had managed to make a recorded loss of £128,138. This and James Gilbey's heavy involvement in Andrew Morton's book about the Princess of Wales caused his great-uncle, one of the most eminent Roman Catholic priests in Britain, to deny his existence. In the wake of Gilbey's revelations of Diana's bulimia and "suicide attempts," Monsignor Alfred Gilbey, a legendary figure and the only priest in Britain sanctioned by the Pope to say Mass in Latin, told the *Daily Express*'s columnist Ross Benson: "I don't know who he is. I have a great-nephew of that name, but his description doesn't correspond to anything I've heard about this person."

None the less, this was the man in whom the

Princess of Wales chose to put her trust. He had known her since the Coleherne Court days, where they met at a party given by Julia Samuel, but it was not until they were re-introduced by Lady Carina Frost, daughter of the Duke of Norfolk and wife of television personality Sir David Frost, that the friendship began in earnest. Carina's brother, the Earl of Arundel, had been at school with Gilbey and married his ex-girlfriend, Georgina Gore.

Possibly part of Gilbey's appeal for Diana, apart from his looks and his legendary capacity to listen to women's woes, was that after leaving Ampleforth he had spent a year as a trainee farmer on the Sandringham estate, arriving just as the Spencers were packing up at Park House to move to Althorp after the death of the 7th earl. The two did not meet at that stage, but in the year he worked on the royal estate Gilbey met many of Diana's friends and neighbors as well as becoming well-versed in the arcane ways of the royal family. In a nutshell, he learned to speak the same language as Diana.

But the rigors of farming were not for him. While at school he had made plans with his friend Thomas Noel, son of the Earl of Gainsborough, to go together to the Royal Agricultural College at Cirencester. Noel did, Gilbey didn't. Instead he became a BMW salesman before having a stab at the property world—he established a small residential-property company called Haldon Investments at a time when a host of blue bloods who would never dream of describing themselves as estate agents were making quick killings around fashionable London in the booming property market.

But by 1989, when he suddenly hit the headlines, Gilbey was back in the motor trade. One night in October, just a few weeks before the Squidgy tapes were recorded, the princess was photographed coming out of Gilbey's rented one-bedroom flat in Lennox Gardens, Knightsbridge, at one-fifteen. Earlier she had dismissed her detective, Sergeant Dave ("Razors") Sharp, for the night, but he returned two and a half hours later. He sat outside for another two hours before she finally emerged.*

The Buckingham Palace press office tried to deny that Diana had even been there, but later, after it became clear that Gilbey had already admitted she had been with him at the flat, it was implied that Diana had been playing bridge. "I suppose it wasn't that wise for Diana and me to meet in those circumstances," Gilbey said, a shade smugly, at the time. "It's hard for the princess to keep up old friendships." In fact their friendship was a mere four years old.

*Royalty protection officers have rejected the suggestion that Diana was left unguarded that night. One told me at the time, "Do you really think we would have left her alone? The commissioner himself would have had us fired if we had gone. What happened was that one person stayed outside the front and two more went round the back. Nobody could have got near her without us knowing."

For some time the two Jameses ran parallel in Diana's affections, but in the end it was the fey, ballet-loving Gilbey who won over the essentially macho Hewitt.

An early pointer to the essentially clandestine nature of Diana and Gilbey's relationship might have been gleaned from two paparazzi photographers who, one night, were to be found standing outside San Lorenzo, the fashionable restaurant in Beauchamp Place just off Knightsbridge. The photographers were hanging around in the hope of catching a celebrity or two—the likes of Joan Collins, Mick Jagger and Eric Clapton are regulars—as they came out after dinner. In addition they were aware that Diana's car was parked nearby and there might be an opportunity to get a fresh shot of her—even though they knew she had been photographed at the Royal Opera House earlier in the evening.

Suddenly they saw emerging from the restaurant a detective, who approached them and, with his not inconsiderable charm, asked if they would do him a favor. Would they, just on this occasion, be kind enough not to photograph the princess? She'd faced a barrage of cameramen at Covent Garden and just wanted to go home without any more flashguns popping off in her face. It was late and she was tired, he explained. What persuaded the two men to agree was that the detective, a man who keeps his word, promised they would be "looked after" in the near future. This might mean a chance at an exclusive shot of Diana—which could be worth many thousands of pounds on the international market—and with that promise they were content.

Shortly afterward Diana stepped out of the restaurant followed by a young man in evening clothes; he had a receding hairline and a furtive look. "I now know that man was James Gilbey," one of the photographers told me, with bitter regret at missing the only opportunity to take a picture of the two together. At the time, though, the paparazzi thought no more about the incident and were duly "rewarded" at a later date.

Over the next few months San Lorenzo became the headquarters for Diana's increasingly passionate relationship with James Gilbey. This was mainly due to the friendship and assistance of Mara Berni, the Italian-born proprietress who, with her husband Lorenzo, had built the establishment up over thirty years. A motherly figure, whose sympathetic personality has encouraged the rich and famous to bare their souls to her, Mara gained Diana's confidence through a mutual interest in astrology. An expert in Tarot cards, she gave readings that left the restless princess more at ease with herself—although it is not clear whether this was due to the way the cards turned or, more likely, the way Mara had of letting people hear what they wanted to hear.

But when Diana confessed to the emptiness of her marriage and her interest in a new young man, Mara was able to provide a number of solutions. First she suggested that the restaurant could be used as a dead-letter drop so James Gilbey and others could write to Diana without her post being monitored by Kensington Palace staff. This ruse had already been tried elsewhere with a measure of success: Diana had sent her lady-in-waiting Anne Beckwith-Smith to a rented mailbox outside a newsagent's in Seymour Place, near Marble Arch, to retrieve letters. But San Lorenzo was considered to be a more secure address.

Mara Berni also provided Diana with a private area in the restaurant where she could sit and talk without being overseen. Sometimes she would be with friends like Millie Dunne, Julia Dodd-Noble, Kate Menzies or Carolyn Bartholomew; sometimes with Gilbey. On other occasions the princess and her companions would sit out among the other lunchers. The restaurant's motto "Labyrinth" is from a quotation from Jorge Luis Borges—"When you enter the labyrinth, time stops." For Diana, casting aside her roles as wife, mother, princess and public figure as she entered the canopied portals, it was an apt enough metaphor.

But the most crucial assistance Mara was able to offer was to lend Diana the key to the Berni family home around the corner in Walton Place. In the Squidgy tapes—so-called because of Gilbey's pet name for Diana—which were to blow apart their relationship, the couple talk about Mara:

> GILBEY: Darling, just forgetting that for a moment, how is Mara?
> DIANA: She's all right. No, she's fine. She can't wait to get back. [*Mrs. Berni was on holiday.*]
> G: Can't she? When's she coming back?
> D: Saturday.

Later the conversation returns to the restaurant:

> G: And I cry when you cry.
> D: The rate we are going, we won't need any dinner on Tuesday.
> G: No, I won't need any dinner actually. Just seeing you will be all I need. I can't wait for Ken [*Wharfe, Diana's detective*] to ring.

It is clear from the tape that the couple only went to San Lorenzo when Mara was there, and that Diana was in touch with the restaurateur on her holidays and waiting for her return. Diana not needing any dinner was less to do with her eating disorder, and more to do with the fact that she and Gilbey would be able to pick up the key and disappear round the corner to Mara's house. Since the disastrous night when Diana was discovered coming out of Gilbey's flat in Lennox Gardens, the couple needed somewhere else to be alone together. Anyone in their circle would have been happy to provide such a rendezvous, but that would involve their knowledge—and the resultant fear that the information might inadvertently slip out elsewhere. One thing Diana learned early on was to cover her tracks, and Mara deftly solved the problem for them.

And there it might have remained, out of the public spotlight, had it not been for the publication of the tapes. The origins of this tape are discussed in Chapter 3, but when the *Sun* finally published them in August 1992 they were already two and a half years old. Diana and Gilbey still enjoyed a close relationship, though by this stage he was also in a relationship with Lady Alethea Savile.

The contents of the tapes have already received worldwide exposure, and therefore a verbatim transcript of the conversation is unnecessary here. But what is most remarkable in the thirty-minute conversation is the way "shy Di" has been transformed into a tough nut. She, quite accurately in my view, assesses her value to the image of the House of Windsor—"After all I've done for that fucking family," she says angrily at one point in their conversation—and wonders why she is still treated like an outsider. And though at the time the shock value of the tape obliterated it, on reflection it becomes clear that here is a woman who is desperately crying for help.

But if for a moment we were able to gaze on the private face of the Princess of Wales, would it be so very different from the public one? One of the most telling passages in the conversation is when she tells Gilbey that, while at Sandringham, she went to see her old home, Park House, now a Leonard Cheshire home for the disabled:

D: There was something really strange. I was leaning over the fence yesterday, looking into Park House, and I thought: "Oh, what shall I do?" And I thought, "Well, my friend would say go in and do it." I thought, "No, 'cos I'm a bit shy," and there were hundreds of people in there. So I thought, "Bugger that." So I went round to the front door and walked straight in.

G: Did you?

D: It was just so exciting.

G: How long were you there for?

D: An hour and a half.

G: Were you?

D: Mmmm. And they were so sweet. They wanted their photographs taken with me and they kept hugging me. They were very ill, some of them. Some no legs and all sorts of things.

There, in a nutshell, is the Princess of Wales: the care and concern she demonstrates with AIDS victims and lepers, old people and the poor, is utterly genuine. She is clearly moved by the experience and seems ready to talk more about it, but Gilbey hastens her on to another subject.

Gilbey throughout adopts a supplicatory tone, and early analyses by pop psychiatrists suggested that while he was expressing love and affection for her, she managed to remain aloof. But what the psychiatrists and others did not know was that the tapes had been edited. Fuller versions of the telephone call reveal the extent of the relationship between the two, and provide the final evidence that Diana and Gilbey were sexually involved. By exercising an uncharacteristic self-censorship the editor of the *Sun* actually managed to mislead as well as shock.

To the unworldly and the critical, what follows may seem shocking in the extreme. But it must be remembered that by the end of 1989 the princess had been without physical affection from her husband for over three years. She was young, fit, attractive and full of all the natural feelings and desires of a woman of twenty-eight. She had devoted herself to charity work and to the further glorification of the House of Windsor. She had never been known to let down either the family or her husband publicly. She had won adoration and respect in Britain and far beyond—and she was left in no doubt, wherever she turned, that men saw her not only as a contemporary icon but also as a desirable woman.

Yet she was not about to commit adultery. Arguments vary as to whether this was because she enjoyed the power her continued fidelity gave her over her unfaithful husband; because she took to her role as future mother of the King with almost religious dedication; or simply because she was morally opposed to stepping over the line into adultery. As the tensions within her grew, some-

D: Did you just get my hint about Tuesday night? I think you just missed it. Think what I said.

G: No.

D: I think you have missed it.

G: No, you said: "At this rate, we won't want anything else to eat."

D: Yes.

G: Yes, I know, I got there.

D: Oh well, you didn't put the flag out.

G: What?

D: You didn't put the flag out.

G: What, the surrender flag?

D: Oh.

G: Squidge, I was just going over it. I don't think I made too much reference to it. Because the more you think about it, the more you worry about it.

D: All right. I haven't been thinking about a lot else.

G: Haven't you?

D: No.

G: Well, I can tell you, that makes two . . .

Diana's anxiety as to where the physical nature of their relationship may lead verged on the paranoid. After Gilbey tells her about a vivid dream in which Diana featured, she responds with guilt:

D: I don't want to get pregnant.

G: Darling, that's not going to happen. All right?

D: Yeah.

G: Don't think like that. It's not going to happen, darling. You won't get pregnant.

D: I watched *EastEnders* today. One of the main characters had a baby. They thought it was by her husband. It was by another man.

G: Squidgy, kiss me. Oh God. It's so wonderful, isn't it, this sort of feeling. Don't you like it?

D: I love it. I love it.

G: It is absolutely wonderful. I feel about twenty-one again.

D: Well, you're not, you're thirty-three.

Inevitably, the difficult circumstances in which they find themselves—Diana at Sandringham, unhappy and claustrophobic in the post-Christmas royal house party, and Gilbey in his car, in the dark, in an Oxfordshire lay-by—lead to the inevitable conclusion. The very matter-of-fact way in which the two discuss self-gratification, sandwiched in between conversations about whom they had seen and whom they had lunched with, makes the level of their intimacy plain. Gilbey, in these regular late-night conversations, was clearly providing an outlet for Diana.

One can only feel deep sympathy for a woman who finds herself in such extreme circumstances. It is a measure of the dedication Diana had and has for her job and family that, rather than walk away from the marriage, she sought whatever solutions she could to ease her miserable private life. Daily challenged by the infuriating, and not at all concealed, fact of Charles's on-going sexual relationship with Camilla Parker Bowles, she simply did the best she could. In an ideal world such solutions remain a private matter: but in sanctioning a biography of herself which discussed matters that previously would have been considered *verboten* by the press, Diana unwittingly opened the floodgates which have led us to where we are today. Once opened, it is difficult to close them again.

When discussing her personal needs, people in the outer royal circle would jokingly remind each other that it is an act of treason for the Princess of Wales to be unfaithful to her husband. I am certain that no such consideration would have entered Diana's mind. While in need of some gratification, she sought to minimize the contact she had with other men, and I doubt that in recent times those particular circumstances have been repeated. I do not know of another royal princess in the present House of Windsor who has exercised such exceptional self-restraint.

But the publication of the Squidgy tapes put an end to the intimacy between Diana and Gilbey, and some might argue that was no bad thing. The scandal came as a complete shock to Gilbey's girlfriend (some said fiancée), Lady Alethea Savile. The twenty-nine-year-old Oxford-graduate daughter of the Earl of Mexborough was apparently barely conscious of the strength of the relationship between Gilbey and Diana, and certainly totally ignorant of its quasi-sexual element. Lady Alethea and Gilbey had been together for more than two years and had planned to marry. Just as Emma Stewardson had, for a time, been shielded from the intimate details of James Hewitt's relationship with Diana, so too was Lady Alethea. It is safe to assume that Diana was still enjoying her quasi-sexual relationship with Gilbey when he first started courting Alethea Savile.

One can make what judgments one likes about the quality of escorts Diana chose for herself: after all, both men were single, well-brought-up and personable. It would be unkind, though not necessarily inaccurate, to say that both had their heads turned by the fact it was a princess they were courting, or that they'd succumbed to what at Buckingham Palace is known as "red carpet fever." But if Prince Charles was not an ideal consort for Diana, neither, for very different reasons, were these men.

The effect on Lady Alethea and Emma Stewardson was, in both cases, shattering. Emma Stewardson told her story to the *News of the World*, a wholly uncharacteristic lapse of judgment. Lady Alethea took off for America to undergo fringe psychotherapy, about which she later wrote amusingly and self-deprecatingly for another newspaper—though few were in any doubt that the piece was not really written for the readers of the *Mail on Sunday*; it was written for Gilbey. She wanted him to know what she'd been through, but was far too well-bred to admit it personally.

Their relationship shattered, Gilbey—whose family motto is "Honor and Virtue"—moved on to pastures new. In December 1992 he was linked with a model, Lisa Butcher, who is married to the chef, Marco Pierre White. Subsequently he was seen with another model, now a freelance TV director, Emma Pounds. Emma's father Harry made a fortune from scrap military hardware, a refreshing change from the blue bloods Gilbey normally preferred to dance attendance upon.

No doubt it was with the best of intentions that Gilbey cooperated with Andrew Morton in his biography of Diana, but the damage he inflicted on the woman he claimed to love was immense. To promote the idea that the Princess of Wales had made successive suicide attempts was foolish, harmful—and not particularly accurate: when Diana was said to have hurled herself down the stairs at Sandringham while pregnant with Prince William in 1982, the rather more mundane truth of the matter was that she actually slipped.

In some respects, though, the information he imparted was essential for a fuller understanding of the deteriorated state of the royal marriage. He told the author, "Their lives are spent in total isolation. It's not as though they ring each other and have sweet chats each evening and say, 'Darling, what have you been doing?' It simply does not happen." He also pointed out that the Buckingham Palace machine was less than complimentary about what Diana was doing for the royal family and for the nation. But unworldly in most things apart from the world of the motor car, he went too far: Diana was shattered by the extent of the revelations in the book, prompted as they were by misplaced enthusiasm, or something worse.

In fairness to Gilbey, Diana did not distance herself from him when the storm clouds burst; it must be assumed that any indiscretions were forgiven if not forgotten. But their ardor had cooled and, with a new job in the motor trade—working in the promotions department of Lotus Cars—Gilbey was effectively removed from London and daily access to the princess.

But the damage had been done. There was little time between the publication of the Squidgy tapes in August 1992 and the announcement of the separation of the Prince and Princess of Wales four months later, in December.

THREE

Dirty Tricks

It took some time for the country to wake up to the unthinkable idea that members of the royal family were being bugged by the security services. Indeed, it seems that the family members themselves were not aware that they were being spied on. At a lunch at the Duke and Duchess of York's home, Sunninghill Park, in the spring of 1992 a discussion arose over MI5's clandestine activities. The duke, a serving naval officer and knowledgeable about military security, queried whether MI5 would dare bug his family. His attitude, according to those present, was that it was impossible, both as a notion and as a reality.

The publication of the Camillagate and Squidgy tapes—and also the disclosure of a low-shock but fully detailed row on the telephone between Andrew and Sarah—made him change his mind. That forces were at work to destabilize the royal family suddenly seemed to be distinctly possible, in fact very probable. But the public's response to these successive revelations was slow to gather force. The facts that were coming out of the woodwork were so completely shocking that it was some time before Parliament started to ask: How did these tapes come into being, and who is responsible?

At the time of writing the prime minister has yet to satisfactorily answer those questions. At the end of March 1993 he published two official reports which cleared MI5 and other intelligence agencies of spying on the royals, to the almost universal scorn of the House of Commons. Members of Parliament immediately demanded powers to control the activities of the spymasters, spurred on by the admission of government officials that there had been no specific inquiries into allegations of involvement in the royal tapes scandal.

John Major published one report on phone-tapping and another on the security services generally. In the first, the Master of the Rolls, Sir Thomas Bingham, said a tribunal had found no evidence of breaches. In the second, Lord Justice Stuart-Smith said he could see no reason why the security services would shoot themselves in the foot by bugging the royals. But Conservative MP Richard Shepherd spoke for many when he declared contemptuously, "All we have here is two old buffers saying that in their opinion the security services act with integrity."

The reality is that conversations of the Prince

of Wales, the Duke of York and their separated wives—as well as other key royals—have been closely monitored for some years. MI5, which is split up into small cells called IGUs (intelligence-gathering units), has a specific group that concentrates on monitoring the royal family. Its existence was confirmed by former MI6 officer James Rusbridger in 1993, and other sources suggest that it is made up of six men who mount a round-the-clock surveillance of calls passing through all royal switchboards.

But it does not stop there. Technological breakthroughs in surveillance techniques have made comprehensive monitoring far easier, principally because it is now no longer necessary to enter people's homes to fit bugging devices. Conversations can be picked up from long distances, often from the vibrations off a window or wooden floor. This means that the eavesdroppers can station themselves and their equipment miles away from their targets. These conversations are recorded and sent on to the government's GCHQ listening center at Cheltenham for inspection and analysis. Any very sensitive information should be passed on to relevant ministers and the prime minister.

Though they never feel the need to justify their actions, MI5 had the perfect excuse following an incident in 1987 when Diana, after receiving a call at Kensington Palace, jumped into her car and sped off without police backup. Within minutes she became involved in an alarming high-speed chase with a car full of Arab men who had recognized her. Eventually she shook them off in Pimlico, driving up and down three streets in a grid pattern to establish that she had finally lost them. She then stopped, parked, switched off her lights and used her mobile phone to call relieved protection officers to let them know her location. The spymasters argue that this demonstrates there must be effective monitoring of the royals if they are to discharge their security duties properly.

It has become routine for them to filter the results of their cloak-and-dagger work to GCHQ, where it is briefly held in the Discarded Information (DI) file for material that is still highly sensitive and top secret. When telephone calls or private conversations are monitored, key words are given a numeric value; if the cumulative value is high enough, the authorities will read carefully the whole conversation. Information which has once been sifted or has failed to have a high numeric value will be wiped from the GCHQ computer.

What follows below is an extract from a conversation reported to have taken place between the Prince and Princess of Wales at their country home, Highgrove, in 1992, before their official separation was announced. It should be stressed that this is not a telephone conversation, but a discussion in a private house between a man and wife who have agreed to part but have yet to make it public. The conversation, which concerns the family's Christmas arrangements and the future of the two princes, comes from GCHQ'S DI file.

CHARLES: To be honest I have never really thought about it.

DIANA: Well you wouldn't, would you?

c: Is there any reason why I should?

D: Should what?

c: Think about it.

D: Do I have to?

c: Is this really getting us anywhere?

D: Not particularly, no.

c: Shall I just go?

D: I don't think that would solve anything.

c: It may allow us to get some sleep tonight.

D: I couldn't sleep on this!

c: Quiet, you'll wake the children.

D: They know anyway.

c: Look, three days is hardly a lifetime. Three days . . .

D: My first reaction is—what do you mean by three days?

c: You know full well what I mean.

D: Would you like to explain?

c: Circles, circles, round and round we go. I haven't seen anyone for days. God knows when I last picked up a newspaper or watched the TV. You make it sound as if this is all my fault personally. How can I explain something I don't even know?

D: Well, there we are. Would you like to explain further?

c: Not now. Not here. Why?

D: I want to know. I think it needs to be resolved.

c: But I keep saying—why here? Are you looking for a

confrontation? Honestly, I don't want or need one, I just don't want or need one.

D: Have you considered the implications of a custody battle?

C: For what?

D: The children.

C: Oh, don't be so silly. No, no, I haven't.

D: Well, that's what would happen, the children would suffer. You know that?

C: No, no, I don't. This is so silly, talking like crazy people, talking about custody. It won't come to that.

D: No?

C: No.

D: Well, as long as you are sure.

C: Please, let's not argue now. Not now.

D: But that's what we are getting to because we are resolving nothing. Nothing is being decided. None of us will make a firm decision—a firm decision.

C: Is there really one needed, now? We've spent all night going over the same thing without getting anywhere and now you're making demands for a decision? Please be sensible.

D: No, no, no, no, no. Let's decide it now and then we can start afresh tomorrow morning. If nothing is decided now we'll be in the same position tomorrow, next week, next month as we are tonight. If there's just one Godforsaken thing we can do, let's decide tonight.

C: I am trying to see things your way. I just can't. It's too late.

D: Well, for once could you put yourself out and think of me?

C: Don't you dare to sit there and tell me to think of you. How the hell do you have the nerve to say that? I've done nothing but think of you and the children ever since this thing started. You . . .

D: No, no, I don't believe that at all. For once stop being so self-centered. You still think of me as the person you married.

C: I stopped thinking like that years ago.

D: Yes, I suppose that would be a good indication of why we drifted apart, my dear.

C: Can I say anything right? Tell me what it is you want me to say.

D: Say something I want to hear.

C: I'm leaving.

D: Oh, don't be so bloody childish.

C: Oh God.

D: Must you always run when the pressure gets too much?

C: I'm not running. Unlike you I want to deal with this like adults.

D: I think I am. It's just that I want to get it done now rather than later. I don't want it to run on like a silly soap opera.

C: I'm going to bed.

D: But why? You can sleep tomorrow, you can sleep any time, but think of me for once, yes, think of me for once.

C: I'd rather think of the other parties involved. I don't know why, but right now I feel they are more important. You'll take care of yourself, you know that.

D: How dare you be so presumptuous?

C: I'm tired. Good-night.

D: Look, you are doing it again. Come back, for Christ's sake come back! How can you leave it like this?

C: I'll speak to you tomorrow.

D: Oh no you won't.

C: Good-night.

D: Can you come in here please?

The content of this conversation is, in itself, of little moment—which is why the transcript ended up on the DI file. But its very existence demonstrates that the royals are being bugged, and that MI5 is not particularly worried if they know they're being bugged. A security source tells me: "For obvious reasons the royal family are closely involved with the security services, but I feel it will come as a great shock to them to realize the extent to which their private lives are being secretly monitored."

That does not mean that the royals are themselves suspected of being traitors, or security risks, but it is thought that they are such an important part of the social fabric that no risks can be taken. My security source adds: "MI5 see it as their duty to defend the realm and will go to any extremes to maintain the status quo. Of course people will be shocked at the extent to which the royal family is spied upon—what could be more personal and private than a conversation with your wife in your own house? But at the end of the day the intelligence services are not directly answerable to anyone. They are virtually a law unto themselves." They claim as justification, "We do this for the Defense of the Realm."

To defend the realm, they claim, it was necessary to be "inside the princess's very mind." To show the extent of this, here is another example of a conversation at Highgrove, again in the weeks leading up to the separation, when Diana was there alone with a girlfriend. It shows clearly that she was just waiting for the announcement to be made.

D: Now don't call me stupid or anything, because classical music is most definitely not my bag, but was the music written for the film or was it already a tune?

F: I think it was written a long time ago. They just used it for the film.

D: It's so beautiful, so sad. I love tunes like that. Did you see it?

F: Brilliant film. You didn't go to the first showing, did you?

D: No. I think Anne Diamond got the job.

F: Play it again then.

D: I got this as well.

F: Oh, that's great.

D: Just turn this thing here and I think we've got a show.

F: Would you go?

D: No, never. It's not the sort of thing I like at all. I remember seeing this really bad war film once and it was like, oh, terrible. I just can't stand violence. That film with Richard Gere, that's what I love.

F: Ah, he's married.

D: I know. Did you see to who?

F: Aah, no way.

D: Is she an actress?

F: No, I don't think she's even a model. Just a celebrity.

D: Trust House Forte. I should be in movies.

F: Oh, what experience have you got? On the . . .

D: I've been acting the biggest role of my career for ten years. That must put me in line for something.

F: A film about Princess Diana?

D: Huh, who do I play?

F: Put the other one on.

D: Did I tell you about William's song?

F: Not like that . . . other way . . . Go on.

D: He listens to songs and makes his own words up. The latest is, "We all live in a yellow submarine, in a pub in Aberdeen, in a tub of margarine."

F: Do you sing with him?

D: Yeah, all the time. I can't figure this thing out at all . . .

F: Just turn it . . . no, other way.

D: What time are you going?

F: Soon. Are you still going out tonight?

D: No, Charles is coming down.

F: How's it going?

D: Bad.

F: What will happen now then?

D: It makes no difference. I'm going, so are the boys. It's an impossible situation. Everybody thinks they know everything about us, and yet nobody . . .

The recording ends here, but the message is clear. That Diana had had enough was already known by those who needed to know from other bugged conversations over the preceding months, so this tape went, along with the others, on to the Discarded Information file.

Those in government departments who are keen to preserve the status quo see an independent Princess of Wales, freed from the day-to-day strictures of court life, as a growing threat. The theory has been aired that hardliners within the security services have deliberately targeted her because they fear she has the power to undermine the House of Windsor. The argument is that when Diana married Charles she boosted the royal family's wilting image, but that while her popularity has grown theirs has diminished. Their thinking was summed up to me in this way: "She is now viewed by the mandarins at Buckingham Palace as a rogue royal who threatens the very existence of the constitution of this country. She holds all the trump cards—she has outmaneuvered Charles and his advisers and she is in a no-lose situation. That bugged conversation at Highgrove bears out her hard-bargaining skills.

How conscious Diana is of this twenty-four-hour surveillance is anyone's guess. But it is a fact that she has had her Kensington Palace home swept for electronic bugs on at least one occasion, and when she started discussions with Paul Butner, the lawyer who was to guide her through the official separation, their meetings were deliberately held away from the palace, in the flats of friends and in a series of French and Thai restaurants. Charles too has had his rooms and cars swept for bugs by Ian Johnson Associates, a company run by an ex–army intelligence officer recommended to him by the former British Airways boss Lord King. The operation was said to involve "electronic counter measures" to disable bugs. But both these operations were useless. An intelligence unit can set up their equipment up to six miles away and listen in as and when they want.

While many may find it shocking that the royals are being overheard by the security services, within the service itself it is taken as a matter of course. Anthony Sillitoe, a former intelligence officer whose father, Sir Percy Sillitoe, was director-general of MI5 from 1946 to 1953, said, "I know from personal experience at MI5 that Edward and Wallis Simpson were taped. It would be surprising if the conversations of the royal family were not being taped today."

In fact it was Charles's predecessor as Prince of Wales who opened up the hitherto unthought-of idea of eavesdropping on the royals. In the run-up to the Abdication the friends, contacts and past history of his mistress—later wife—were a cause for considerable alarm among the Establishment. Agents were dispatched to bug the New York home of Mrs. Simpson, and they continued to keep a close eye on the Duke of Windsor in his post-Abdication exile.

In the dark days of 1940, as the duke was preparing to take up his wartime post as Governor of the Bahamas, it became clear to the intelligence services that clandestine contacts were being made with the enemy through "neutral" intermediaries. There seems little doubt, notes Philip Ziegler, that the duke was convinced the British would lose the war and that, in such circumstances, he hoped to have a role to play. An intelligence report noted:

Germans expect assistance from Duke and Duchess of Windsor. Latter desiring at any price to become Queen. Germans have been negotiating with her since June 27th. German purpose to form Opposition Government under Duke of Windsor, having first changed public opinion by propaganda. Germans think King George will abdicate during attack on London.

Once the principle was established, the security services saw no reason to withdraw their scrutiny of Britain's first family. The next royal to come under their gaze was Earl Mountbatten, not only for his supposedly leftist leanings and ambiguous sexuality, but because of his increasing influence over his great-nephew, the future King.

With the raising of the Iron Curtain and with a by now uncontroversial royal family, there became less and less for the security services to do. Maybe that is why a retired bank manager, Cyril Reenan, suddenly found himself one night listening to a conversation between the Princess of Wales and a former car dealer. Intercepted on his £900 scanner linked to a twenty-foot aerial at his home in Abingdon, the conversation was to break new ground in the public's perception of the royals. Mr. Reenan later explained that he was an amateur radio enthusiast and that he used his equipment to tune in to police and air-traffic messages. On one occasion, he said, he had eavesdropped on a private call between a trainer and a jockey about a horse that was "sure to win" at Newbury races.

Early suggestions that Mr. Reenan had recorded the conversation "live" were proved false as it became clear that the tape was in fact a compilation of two separate telephone calls. Expert opinion was that it had been cleaned up by a communications specialist before being rebroadcast with the express intention of it being picked up and recorded by someone like Mr. Reenan. In fact a second radio ham, Jane Norgrove, also recorded the conversation in Oxford. An ITV program broadcast in April 1993, which specifically set out to debunk the conspiracy theory, signally failed to do so. It seemed instead to have been merely a cynical excuse to broadcast the Squidgy and Camillagate tapes for the first time on British television.

Though no doubt a very efficient bank manager, in matters of the world Cyril Reenan was not so sophisticated—and there can be no doubt that he was used. He swore quite convincingly that his only copy of the tape went into the hands of a national newspaper, but other copies turned up in Fleet Street and elsewhere. Richard Kay, a talented royal reporter for the *Daily Mail*, was sent one anonymously in a plain brown envelope: it did not come from Mr. Reenan. And, though it took some months, the truth finally dawned on him. Six months after the contents of the tape were published in the *Sun*, Cyril Reenan revealed that he now realized that he'd recorded the intimate telephone chat four days after it had actually taken place. Also, the *Sun*'s transcript did not match Mr. Reenan's tape. "I think now I was being used by someone, somewhere," he said ingenuously. Miss Norgrove, on the other hand, revealed that she'd recorded the conversation on the night it actually took place—New Year's Eve, 1989.

An authority on sound who designs systems for Sony, Martin Colloms was given the tape for analysis. He concluded that Mr. Reenan's tape recording was not the original, but that the tape had been made first from a direct wiretap onto a telephone line, and that afterwards the recording had been processed so that superficially it sounded like a mobile-phone broadcast. This meant that it was the princess's land-line, not Gilbey's mobile phone, that had been tapped. Lord Rees-Mogg, a former editor of *The Times*, stated in an interview given to *Four Corners*, the Australian Broadcasting Corporation's current affairs equivalent of the BBC's *Panorama* or *60 Minutes* in the USA, that he believed the security services must have been monitoring the royals and that the tapes made by the security services were then leaked.

As rumor and counter-rumor spread among the corridors of Westminster—MPs are often the last to know what their security forces are up to—another theory was tossed into the espionage stew. Instead of GCHQ or MI5 it could be—the

Americans. This is always a neat get-out when little progress is being made in tracking down wayward agents, and so in the spring of 1993 it was suggested that two American listening posts operated by the American National Security Agency (NSA) were hard at work bugging the royals. The NSA illegally tap large numbers of private conversations from their posts at Morwenstow, Cornwall, and Menwith Hill, Yorkshire. One pundit explained it this way: "By getting the Americans to do it, the British government is able to say truthfully, though misleadingly, that GCHQ does not tap domestic telephone calls. The reason the government is resisting an official investigation into the tapping of royal conversations is that it would be forced to admit publicly that these American-owned and -controlled listening stations exist on British soil."

Whether or not this rather far-fetched notion is true, there were a number of other tapes of royal conversations in circulation, though none so contentious as the Squidgy and Camillagate tapes. At one stage the count was thought to be as high as twenty-five.

But then perhaps the Squidgy tapes might never have been published had it not been for me. I wonder whether the *Sun*'s editor, Kelvin MacKenzie, would ever have printed the transcripts, had he not been desperate to strike back in the traditional circulation battle between his newspaper and mine. Certainly he was badly in need of something to give his paper a boost after I brought off a royal "scoop" in August 1992.

Earlier in the year I had been visited at my London home by John Bryan, at that time masquerading as merely a consultant to the Duchess of York. Cocky and determined, he maintained he was acting as a broker in the negotiations between the Queen's solicitors, Farrer's, and the Duchess of York's over the financial terms of her separation from the duke. He described Farrer's and their senior partner Sir Matthew Farrer as "a bunch of assholes," and he claimed to be playing a central role in the negotiations. "They can't do a damn thing without me," he bragged, "and the Queen has said I have got to be involved at every single level of negotiation. My word is final." It was a bravura performance, if not a particularly pleasant one. Bryan had been telephoning me on a regular basis from the Yorks' marital home—though whether Prince Andrew ever knew he made such free use of his house I don't know. Despite his insistence that evening that his relationship with Sarah was purely business, I felt it necessary to ask if he were her lover. He told me he knew people were saying that, but it was absolutely ridiculous. I remained unconvinced, but had no firm evidence to the contrary.

By mid-August, however, it was becoming plain that there was something more to the relationship. The couple flew to the South of France, arriving at La Mole airport near St. Tropez in their private plane. There was no secret about their arrival, because two local photographers, having been tipped off by the police, were there, standing with their cameras ready, as Fergie came off the plane. One of the Scotland Yard bodyguards who flew in with the couple came over to the photographers and told them to get lost. So, from the moment they touched down, John Bryan and the Duchess of York were conscious of a press presence. Indeed, the duchess had even gone so far as to don headscarf and dark glasses before getting off the plane. Next morning the pictures were in *Nice Matin*, the local newspaper, the final evidence of press interest in their holiday. I mention all this because what happened next was a thunderbolt for the House of Windsor.

I had just returned from covering a trip Charles and Diana had made to Greece when I received a call from a photographic contact in Paris who told me he had photographs of the Duchess of York holidaying in the South of France. Some of them, it turned out, were of Sarah topless. But when I got to Paris to inspect them I discovered there were also pictures of Sarah with John Bryan that gave the lie to what he had told me several weeks earlier. The couple were kissing and cuddling by the poolside and, with the Queen's grandchildren, Princess Beatrice and Princess Eugenie, playing nearby, John Bryan was lying on top of the duchess.

Despite a wide-of-the-mark piece in one of the London papers that weekend that claimed that the photographs must have been taken just a few yards away (the implication being that the photographer trespassed in order to get them), they were taken from a distance of between 400 and 500 yards. The villa is easily accessible, set as it is in a natural bowl in the countryside. The couple were open to public view and should have known it—and so, too, should their bodyguards. One of them was subsequently transferred, though as a senior Scotland Yard officer told my newspaper, "You can hardly blame them for what Fergie got up to. They were there to look after the little girls. We protect their lives, not their morals."

The fifty-five photographs were published in the *Daily Mirror* and created a worldwide stir. The reaction in Britain was one of amazement and disbelief. John Bryan had succeeded in convincing everyone that his relationship with the duchess was perfectly proper. The topless pictures meant nothing in themselves—it was the photographs that uncovered their shabby deception which were important.

The royal family followed the story as closely as everyone else. The morning of publication, every member of the family at Balmoral was to be found poring over half a dozen copies of the *Daily Record*, the Scottish version of the *Mirror*, at breakfast. They were clearly taking some delight in the duchess's impending discomfiture. Suddenly Fergie herself entered the dining room. I was told, "There was a mad scramble to turn the pages over and everybody pretended to be reading some other story. But the duchess knew. She was very close to tears, poor thing. She just hadn't known the photographs would be as explicit as they were. She knew she had been photographed in France, but until the moment she actually saw the paper in the dining room she didn't realize how near the knuckle they were." Five days later Fergie left Balmoral to return, upset and sad, to London.

In the next two days the *Daily Mirror*'s circulation increased enormously, and later I found myself being fêted by the respected former national newspaper editor and media pundit Brian MacArthur. In an article for the London *Sunday Times* summing up the journalistic successes of 1992, he wrote:

Journalists often get scoops because they are lucky—but their strokes of luck usually involve years of dogged work as well.

James Whitaker, the doyen of Fleet Street's royal ratpack, has been reporting the royals since 1974 [in fact since 1968]. All those years of ratpacking paid off handsomely in August.

On Thursday, August 20, when the story was published, sales of the *Daily Mirror* were boosted by 482,000. There was so much demand for the newspaper that the presses had to be started up again at 10 a.m. the next day. The 27p *Mirror* was changing hands in Covent Garden for up to £2. Next day sales rose by

573,000 compared with Wednesday, and on Saturday by 583,000. Over four days the *Mirror* put on extra sales of 1.9 million.

My story was greeted by different people in different ways, but significantly what many of the *Mirror*'s readers objected to was not the publication of the pictures, but the fact that, in front of the little princesses, the duchess should openly make love to a man who was not their father. A sense of outrage pervaded the country and Kelvin MacKenzie clearly believed he had lost the initiative in bringing shock-horror stories to the nation's breakfast tables. It was then—and only then—that he pulled out some audio tapes that had been gathering dust in his safe for two and a half years. His reason for not publishing up to this point was "because of possible damage it could cause to Di and the royals." How, suddenly, Diana was no longer going to be damaged by their publication Mr. MacKenzie failed to explain.

On August 24, 1992 he started to publish extracts from the Squidgy tapes. It was a scoop, of course, but one in very questionable taste. I felt that while the Fergie pictures made a very good journalistic exclusive, they also served to alert the Queen and Prince Andrew to the behavior of the Duchess of York and her financial adviser. Until that point, I was informed, Andrew believed that there was nothing improper in their relationship and he had every hope that their broken marriage might be repaired. According to his father-in-law, Major Ronald Ferguson, he was so devoted to this idea that he had even argued Sarah's case to the Queen.

To add insult to their injury the *Sun* ran a pay phone-line number; members of the public could ring in and listen to the tapes. There followed a merciless hounding of all those associated with Diana—from her close friends like Carolyn Bartholomew and Gilbey himself to bit-part players like Mara Berni.

If MI5's intention was to split Diana from the mainstream of royal activity and leave the core, represented by Charles and the Queen, intact and unsullied, then it failed. The conspirators, and there can be no doubt that there was more than one, had reckoned without the extraordinary love which the public has for the Princess of Wales. But then in the summer months of 1992 the destabilizing maneuvers were coming from the inside as well.

Back in January of that year things were not going smoothly for the Duchess of York. Marooned in what she perceived to be a loveless marriage, she was not behaving well. She had already had an affair with the Texan Steve Wyatt and was embarking on a second one with his fellow American John Bryan. Suddenly the front pages of the tabloid newspapers were covered with compromising photographs from a holiday she had enjoyed with Wyatt at Somerset Maugham's old home,

Villa La Mauresque at Cap Ferrat. There once again were the princesses being cuddled by a man their daddy didn't even know. The photographs had been found by a cleaner in an empty London apartment that Wyatt had once rented, they were published in full color, and the world went mad.

Though the pictures offered no direct evidence of anything untoward, the scenario they conjured up was all wrong for an English princess, and Sarah's public image took a severe dent. Nobody listened when Wyatt laconically pointed out that he had not left any photographs behind when he quit the flat; and media attention was somehow diverted elsewhere when it was revealed that the photographs had originally been in Sarah's possession, and were believed to have vanished from Sunninghill Park. Scotland Yard was asked to investigate, but mysteriously nothing ever came of their inquiries. Barely two months later the *Daily Mail* leaked the announcement that Sarah was seeking an official separation from Andrew, had approached lawyers and was saying she wanted their advice. Within twenty-four hours a full-scale row developed which embraced the Queen, her private secretary, the world's press and the House of York.

The leak to the *Mail* caused immense fury within Buckingham Palace, not least because it was forced to hold a press briefing *after* the event. Palace officials blamed the duchess because they could not believe the information could have come from any other source.

That morning, March 19, BBC Radio's court correspondent, Paul Reynolds, and five other court correspondents were summoned to the palace and given a statement announcing Andrew and Sarah's official separation. The journalists made notes, then rushed off to file their stories. Charles Anson, the Queen's press secretary, told them to come back to his office if they wanted more guidance. Forty-five minutes later Reynolds did just that, and spent five minutes alone with Anson. The briefing he received so shocked Reynolds, a seasoned and highly respected journalist, that he immediately went on air on the BBC's *World at One* radio news program. A massive audience heard him say, "The knives are out for Fergie at the palace." He went on to say that the palace believed Fergie to have had a PR firm brief the paper, and that in retaliation they were discussing how unsuitable she was for public life in terms no public official had ever been heard to use before. Reynolds added that the palace was saying that the rift between Andrew and Sarah had begun the previous year, and he went on to name public relations guru Sir Tim Bell as the man retained by the duchess to leak the story. In fact, as in other aspects of the briefing, this was wide of the mark. Andrew and Sarah had both consulted one of Bell's employees, David McDonough, some time previously. He was known

to the couple because his first wife Kiki was an
old friend of Sarah's. But this had nothing to do
with the *Mail*'s report. Someone else was to blame
for the leak. And when both Sir David English,
then editor of the *Daily Mail,* and his proprietor
Viscount Rothermere denied that they had been
spoonfed the story—they had got it by "journalistic enterprise"—Sarah began to get an inkling as
to just who could have been behind this latest
example of the work of the dirty tricks department.

Meanwhile, more poison seemingly was poured
out behind the scenes to justify the attack on the
duchess. The *Sunday Telegraph* reported that the
Queen's private secretary, Sir Robert Fellowes,
was thought to have confided to others his fears
that the duchess was not in control of herself, and
it suggested that both the Queen and the Queen
Mother had "attempted to calm the duchess," but
that the entire family now felt it was "time to
wash their hands of her." That last sentence,
straight from the mouth of an anonymous palace
source, said it all—we've done our best, but
frankly she's just not up to it. Temperamental,
hopeless in public, you can quite see why she's
got to go.

The briefing, unprecedented in its candor, was
by way of a thank-you to the *Telegraph* group,
who alone had stood by Charles Anson when he
had made his shocking denunciation earlier in the

week when he had spoken so unwisely to Paul Reynolds.

There was more. Sir Robert Fellowes, it was said, had put the duchess "on probation" because of her behavior. "The trouble is people were reluctant to be too heavy-handed with her. Maybe they should have been more so," said a royal whisperer. "The duchess is a tough, headstrong person, good company, inspiring. But she is not an easy person to tell things to." The Queen had consulted Fellowes and the Lord Chamberlain, the Earl of Airlie, about the possibility of a separation, but they were convinced nothing would happen before a general election. The article finished with the assertion that the palace was convinced it was a set-up job, an orchestrated campaign by unspecified individuals, and they were "deeply upset." This unctuous self-justification was an attempt at patching up one of the worst own-goals scored by courtiers in living memory.

During the whole of this episode the *éminence grise* standing well back in the shadows was Sir Robert Fellowes. For a long time the irony escaped most people's notice, but it appeared to me there was on occasion something deeply personal in the attacks on Fergie, for Sir Robert— "Bellows" as she called him—was her father's first cousin. As can happen only in families, the two men despised each other. Sir Robert's mother Jane had married Ronald Ferguson's uncle, Brigadier-General Algernon Ferguson, but all the two cousins had in common was their Eton education, and even that had been spent ten years apart.

At a lunch in April 1992 at Sunninghill, Sarah was furious about her cousin's behavior. Her father's anger was just as deep. "He's part of my family. How can he do this to us?" roared Ronald. "I'm going to do something about this." He did. He rang Fellowes at home and shouted, "How dare you behave like this toward Sarah? You're cousins!" Sir Robert is said to have answered quite coolly, "It's my job to protect the family, and particularly the Queen. I have to." Major Ferguson replied, "You don't have to go that far. I want an apology and the situation put right." Fellowes reluctantly agreed to do something, and a day or so later there was an apology from Sir Robert to the Duchess of York. Charles Anson offered to resign, but the offer, unsurprisingly, was refused. Ferguson was left in no doubt as to his cousin's ulterior motives: "Even with this apology Robert is out to get Sarah," he alleged bitterly. "He's an enemy in the camp." And the question still lurked in Sarah's mind—if she didn't leak the story of her separation to the newspapers, who did? For her there seemed only one answer—Diana.

A guest at Sunninghill recalls: "I heard Sarah claim, 'Well, you know who did that—that woman.' And Prince Andrew felt that she was probably right. He said, 'I can't be sure, but I wouldn't put it past Diana.'"

At this period Major Ferguson's closest confidante was Lesley Player. She comments: "Diana was immensely competitive where Sarah was concerned—she never wanted Sarah to have more attention than her. She doesn't want anyone to be more important than her. It sounds childish, but that sort of thing really does happen in the royal family."

The duchess's father told Lesley that Diana and Sarah had discussed the possibility of separation and divorce together, and had made a pact that they should both leave their husbands at the same time. But, Sarah believed, Diana had "done the dirty" on her by not separating when she said she would—and, at the same time, shopped her to the press. Diana's motive, according to Sarah, was to gain the upper hand, to move into a more favorable position with the Queen, and to appear the more responsible. The duchess felt that it had occurred to Diana that if Diana walked out on her marriage before Sarah did, there was an outside chance that Andrew in certain circumstances, like the premature death of his elder brother, could be made Prince Regent. "That would make Sarah more important than her, a situation Diana could not face," observed Ronald Ferguson to Lesley Player. "She couldn't bear to be usurped in that way."

Whether this was true or simply a maggot in the mind of a distressed and disoriented Fergie is a question that might not have been resolved had it not been for a further earthquake hitting the young royals at the beginning of 1993. Its beginnings lay in a luncheon two years before, between the ubiquitous Sir Robert Fellowes and members of the Press Complaints Commission, the industry's regulatory body. Sir Robert complained that "tabloid journalists" were writing about the growing chill between Charles and Diana. He described these stories as "rubbish" and sought the help of the commission and its sympathetic chairman, Lord McGregor of Durris. With one of the commission's members, Lady Elizabeth Cavendish—sister of the Duke of Devonshire—he went to lunch at Buckingham Palace, where again officials spoke about media intrusion.

So the media were using the royals. But were the royals using the media? Evidence seemed to be mounting that the traffic was not all one way. According to one analyst it was Prince Charles who had opened up a media offensive against his wife, on the occasion of her thirtieth birthday in July 1991. It was only ten years after their spectacular wedding, but the couple spent the day apart. Fed up with a press that was universally sympathetic to his wife no matter what, it was arranged for a story to be given to the *Daily Mail* that claimed that Diana had snubbed all the prince's attempts to organize a party for her. Unnamed "close friends" were quoted as saying, "The prince is being made to look bad through no fault of his own." But though the story was undoubtedly true, the ploy backfired badly—next day, other newspapers slammed the prince for over-stepping the mark in an attempt to improve his public image.

Diana was furious, and it was at this crucial point that she decided that her friends could talk to the journalist Andrew Morton. She felt belea-guered in her marriage and increasingly held the belief that people did not understand her posi-tion—that she was in a loveless relationship with a man who had a mistress who pre dated her own arrival on the scene. She felt used and abandoned, and decided to turn her not inconsiderable powers of media manipulation to greater effect. Close friends and members of her family were soon giv-ing Andrew Morton more than enough ammuni-tion to create a climate of sympathy for Diana to bask in.

The publication of his book, with its details of bulimia and suicide attempts as well as accusa-tions of her husband's infidelity, marked a water-shed in royal candor. It was accompanied by a deluge of press and television coverage. The Press Complaints Commission and its chairman Lord McGregor began to feel increasingly uncomfort-able. It was at this point, in June 1992, that he decided that enough was enough. He issued a statement condemning Fleet Street for its "pruri-ent" interest in the royal couple, and damning the newspapers for "dabbling their fingers in the stuff of other people's souls." He rang Buckingham Palace and read over his savage indictment to

Sir Robert Fellowes, to the latter's evident gratification.

But he had been duped. Diana herself was responsible for the information that had been seeping out into the public domain—hugely responsible. Not yet knowing this, McGregor wrote in a letter to Sir David Calcutt, the lawyer charged with introducing tighter press controls: "The impression that the Princess of Wales and her friends had cooperated with Andrew Morton in the writing of this book was denied by Charles Anson and Sir Robert Fellowes." And before issuing his statement, McGregor had sought further assurances from Sir Robert Fellowes that Diana was not assisting in this outflow of information. Fellowes obliged, but the next day McGregor was told by Andrew Knight, chief executive of the News International group, that Diana *had* helped Morton, and to underline her support for the book was going to be photographed arriving at the house of Carolyn Bartholomew, one of Morton's acknowledged sources. This was Diana at her media-manipulative best, and McGregor was appalled. The Lord Chancellor, Lord Mackay of Clashfern, the Leader of the House of Lords, Lord Wakeham, and the Prime Minister were all immediately informed. Though hidden from the public gaze, this was a major constitutional crisis. Fellowes, who was with the Queen in Paris, was fetched to the telephone and apologized for causing McGregor to make his condemnation of the press. He claimed his assurances had been given in good faith and, said Lady Elizabeth Cavendish drily, "We had to accept that." Later she was to add her own version of events. "They did mislead," she said. "The palace did mislead us. I have read the serializations [of Morton's book] in the press. It is obvious that, whether directly or through friends, the princess had been talking to newspapers."

Her anger was contained, but visible. She had helped draft the Press Complaints Commission statement that accused the press of "odious intrusion," and at the time she had spoken publicly of Morton's claims of Diana making suicide attempts, saying: "It is a terrible thing for a child, no matter whose, to read that your mother tried to kill herself five times."

She added that she knew of nothing that implicated Charles in briefing the media. But if she didn't, others did. In July a lengthy article appeared in *Today* newspaper, entitled "Two Faces of a Princess." It was by Penny Junor, billed as "the royal author closest to the Prince of Wales, who was contacted by his circle and asked to write this article." In the many eloquent words that followed, a different picture of the princess began to emerge. She was "paranoid" in her suspicions about Charles's "innocuous" relationship with Camilla Parker Bowles, "jealous" when he spent time on royal duties and prone to "petulant tantrums." Charles was a "doting father thwarted at every turn" by a scheming Diana. As one observer put it, the anecdotes were so detailed they could only have come from a source right at the heart of Charles's most intimate circle. Significantly, there was no attempt by Charles to distance himself from the article or discredit any of it.

Charles and Diana had taken on the great and the good of their nation, people of eminence and distinction, and embroiled them in their petty marital differences. Three of the country's leading statesmen had been drawn into the row, only to find themselves sullied by the underhand attempts by both sides to discredit the other. The dirty tricks manipulators were working overtime—but it wasn't over yet. Throughout this whole period I had been told that Charles himself would not stoop to criticize his wife—privately, publicly or through his friends. This message was delivered to me forcefully and often by courtiers who seemed determined to play down the scandal attached to Morton's book. But after Penny Junor's article appeared in *Today*, I had a conversation with Charles's private secretary, Commander Richard Aylard, in which I pointed out that the piece attacking Diana was exactly the sort of thing Charles had said he didn't want. Aylard agreed: "No, the prince didn't want to do anything. He is worried by her volatile and emotional state and therefore he thinks it is totally unfair to attack her." This was pretty destructive, but it was clear from the briefing that Aylard meant the information to be used. So I wrote a story for the *Daily Mirror* which duly reported what he had said without naming him as my source.

Soon the information machine went into reverse and a vain attempt was made to pour oil on troubled waters. The Waleses had an important joint engagement coming up in late 1992: a tour of South Korea. By then the damage had been done by Morton's book and to all intents and purposes the marriage was over. Yet for some reason Prince Charles felt that there was still a chance to paper over the cracks, and maybe the public could be fooled into thinking that all was well—and if not well, then just about tolerable. And in that he may not have been wrong: part of the magic of royalty is that people *want* things to be normal and are quite happy to rearrange the facts in their minds to make it so.

This, then, was in Charles's mind when he sent Commander Aylard out on his last Mission Impossible, to prove to the public that as far as the House of Wales was concerned, it was business as usual—a favorite and well-worn Buckingham Palace phrase. But as the *Sunday Times* reported on November 8, Diana refused to cooperate, bringing down the whole sham edifice. She put out a statement denying that there was a rift between her and the Queen, but tacitly admitting that there were problems with her marriage. This destroyed Buckingham Palace's plan to bill the

South Korean trip as a tour designed to mend
the marriage.

The *Sunday Times* then reported that Sir Nicholas Lloyd, the editor of the *Daily Express*, had
been visited by Aylard on the morning of October
28. The next day the paper had carried a sympathetic three-page analysis of the marriage by
Christopher Wilson, headlined "Why Charles and
Diana are back together." The thrust of the piece
was that they were putting their differences behind them and going out to work for "Great Britain plc"—a phrase that put the accent on a
working partnership rather than a love match. In
the circumstances it was all Aylard *could* stress,
given the flood of personal and intimate material
that had been printed over the past few months.

Colleagues say that when Sir Nicholas directed
his feature-writer to do the piece, his instructions
came with a wry smile and a raised eyebrow: the
Daily Express had been fed an exclusive line from
inside the palace and was not about to throw it
away. But the rose-tinted spectacles were to be
donned only for as long as it took for the article
to be written. On the same day the *Daily Mail*,
said to be acting on "special inside knowledge"
ran a picture of the princess with the headline:
"From Diana, the look as hopes rise of a marriage
on the mend."

But from their arrival in Seoul, the tour was a
fiasco. If Fleet Street was prepared to give the
prince and his spindoctors the benefit of the

doubt—and it was a massive doubt—it was not prepared to turn its back on the evidence. And when Charles and Diana walked down the steps of their jet at Seoul airport, we knew what we were in for. The couple had evidently had a blazing row within minutes of touchdown. They came out angry, and stood fuming on the tarmac as the national anthems were played.

Diana, it was clear, could not bear even to look at her husband: when she went off on solo duties she was relaxed and friendly and smiled for the camera. Charles, if he had ever had any intentions of trying to keep up the charade, soon forgot them and appeared equally cold and uninterested in the presence of his wife. Newspaper headlines back home started to refer to them as "The Glums." I felt sorry for Peter Westmacott, the court official who accompanied them. Nothing could be further from Commander Aylard's Togetherness Tour. I was waiting at the British Embassy in Seoul when the royal car pulled up, and I saw Diana visibly flinch as Charles reached out between them to pick up a piece of paper—she clearly thought he was going to touch her and the expression on her face signaled just how repugnant that possibility was.

Within forty-five minutes of touchdown they had established separate walkabouts, and when Charles headed toward the Embassy's hospitality house he did not even bother to turn round to see where his wife was: so much for togetherness.

Diana was as chilly. When the royal couple visited the Imjun River where the Glorious Glosters fended off hordes of Communist troops during the Korean War, she barely showed interest as a senior regimental officer explained how the battle was fought and won. But as Charles turned to leave for the car, clearly expecting Diana to follow, she suddenly developed instant interest in what the officer had to say, engaging him with animated conversation and flirtatious behavior. Charles was left standing and fuming while she made him wait. It took at least a minute for her to join him while the crowds looked on at his discomfort.

By the time the Togetherness Tour reached the Great Lovers' Temple on the fourth day, the two camps were not speaking to each other. They now appeared to be on separate tours, with one huge entourage surrounding Charles and another around Diana. There was no conversation or cooperation between the two sides and the pair were only visibly happy when they were apart.

It was a very public, and very humiliating, end to the love story of the century.

FOUR

Back to the Beginning

Even if they go wrong in the end, most marriages start out in a spirit of hope and cheerful optimism. In the case of the Prince and Princess of Wales, there is little evidence to support the idea that any enduring passion, let alone a grand passion, ever existed. The "fairy-tale love affair" was a calculated act by two people who both thought they knew what they wanted, and went after it, without considering the long-term consequences. By the time the couple announced their engagement in February 1981 Charles had, for the best part of a decade, known that he had found his soulmate in the person of Camilla Parker Bowles. Diana knew it too, and went along with it. Put in its crudest terms, it came to this: he needed someone suitable to produce a future King, she desperately wanted to be Princess of Wales. History is littered with many such examples of cynical opportunism, but when presented with a dashing prince and a beautiful young bride, the public—and even hardbitten journalists—were prepared to suspend disbelief.

In the weeks leading up to the engagement an "authorized version" of Diana's early years, her upbringing and the royal romance were laid out for public inspection. The details were sometimes right, sometimes wrong and sometimes downright lies. What was wanted was a palatable and romantic story, and that was produced. No one was in the mood to learn, for example, that Diana was at least Charles's *fourth* choice as a bride—he had already unsuccessfully proposed marriage to Jane Wellesley, to Anna Wallace and to Earl Mountbatten's granddaughter Amanda Knatchbull.

Nor did Charles first meet the young Lady Diana Spencer in a field at Althorp when the prince was part of a shooting party hosted by Earl Spencer. In December 1980, in a memorable hour-long conversation on the steps of her Coleherne Court flat, Diana told me about their first encounter. Or, at any rate, as much as she could recall. The truth, she told me, was that the first time she looked into the pale blue eyes of her future husband she was gurgling happily and padding around the floor on all fours. She was just a few months old and the location was her then family home, Park House, at Sandringham. "I don't remember a great deal about it," she laughed. "But I do know that it was when I was still wearing nappies." This recollection was followed up by a remark that seemed curious coming from a nineteen-year-old: "It's funny, but a lot of the best things happened to me when I was in nappies. It just seems to have been a good time in my life."

The love affair, such as it was, was not a *coup de foudre*, because the people who lived at Sandringham were like one large extended family and she and Charles had been "constant, regular friends ever since. I have known him all my life. He was just somebody who was always around."

Her acquaintance with the prince was necessarily at arm's length because of the difference in age—he is twelve and a half years her senior—and their differing lifestyles. By the time she was ten he had already been around the world. On her engagement day Diana said that the age difference was unimportant: "The gap just does not matter." But at the same time she revealed that her closest male friend in the royal family up till the romance had been Prince Andrew. This public statement was at variance with what Diana's flatmates and friends had been telling me privately. Ann Bolton said that the age gap *had* slowed the official announcement down; Diana was concerned about it. And who can blame her? It is my belief that toward the end of their courtship Diana deliberately put away all thoughts of this in a conscious effort to keep the relationship as strong as possible. But the memory of him, so much older when she was a tiny child, never quite went away.

One such occasion was at Sandringham in the mid-1960s, when the five-year-old Diana was to be found playing with the six-year-old Prince Andrew and a grown-up. Diana's nanny Janet Thompson recalled walking into a drawing room after hearing a voice urgently calling out, "Where are you?" only to discover the Queen playing hide-and-seek with her son and his guest. "It was all so normal really—it wasn't the Queen playing with the children, just a mother having fun with them, a lovely sight."

Diana remembers Charles for the first time at that tea party. Just as Prince Edward had covered himself in honey, his eldest brother walked into the nursery after a day's pheasant shooting. Janet recalled: "There was a lot of noise going on. I remember Charles called out, 'Everything all right? It looks like a good party to me.'" At the time the prince was not yet eighteen, but he behaved as if he were much older, a habit he never succeeded in discarding and which was to infuriate Diana in the years ahead.

Though these tea parties did not happen every day, they were not unusual, and go a long way to explaining why Diana was never shy in the company of the royal family when she and Charles started to see each other regularly. So many of

Charles's previous girlfriends had frozen on first meeting the Queen in a family environment that I asked Diana if she would be concerned at entering a room in which the Queen, Prince Philip and other royals were sitting. "No, why should I?" she replied, and there was no affectation in her answer. Almost from birth, she was ready to join their number.

Her father had been a royal equerry. Her sister Sarah has the Queen Mother as a godmother, her other sister Jane has the Duke of Kent as a godfather, and her baby brother Charles has, as his godmother, the Queen. Ironically, the only Spencer child who does not have a royal godparent is Diana herself. Though her father's family were Spencers, with a peerage going back to 1765, her mother's family were from the peerage as well. The Lords Fermoy came from Ireland, though they have long been established in the royal enclave of Norfolk, at King's Lynn.

But this rarefied and privileged life was not without its darker side. When Janet Thompson first started to work at Park House, Diana was just over three years old, her eldest sister Sarah nine, her next sister Jane seven and brother Charles a tiny baby. Diana wanted constant reassurance and looking after in the dark. The former nanny recalls: "She would call out to me to bring her a glass of water or to take her to the loo in the middle of the night. Sometimes she would wake up after a bad dream and would cry. I would have to talk to her gently. Then in the morning she would come into my room and sometimes creep into bed with me to keep warm and for a cuddle." When Janet had a weekend off, or was on holiday, Diana's mother would leave the bedroom she shared with her husband to sleep in the nanny's bed in the nursery.

Even in those days Diana loved two things that have remained favorites to the present day—clothes and sweets. Says Janet: "Diana was very fond of pretty clothes and kept them neat. She loved floral dresses and used to go shopping with her mother for party outfits. They were a very sociable family and were out all the time at tea parties, so Diana needed a good choice."

The idea that Diana is shy or hesitant, as she is so often described, makes Nanny Thompson laugh. She says: "Diana could not be called a difficult child but she could be obstinate. Even in those days she knew what she wanted and how she wanted things done—she wouldn't necessarily go along with what you would tell her, and she never did anything straight away. She would think about what you had asked her and then—slowly—do it.

"She wasn't easy. Some children that young will do as they are told immediately, but Diana wouldn't—it was always a battle of wills. She was full of spirit. But she was a lovely child and after she had been reasoned with she would usually cooperate . . . eventually."

The princess, who has been known to smack her own children on occasion—I once saw her whack William at the end of a sports day at Wetherby school—was never subjected to corporal punishment by Nanny Thompson. "I just don't believe in it," she says. So when Diana really misbehaved she would be sent to her room to think things over. She was, however, devoted to her baby brother, Charles, and loved mothering him, a habit which continued into adulthood when she would regularly drive to Eton when he was a pupil there to take him out to lunch.

On Sundays the whole family would go to church at Sandringham to pray together alongside the royal family when they were in residence. In the afternoon, children's television would be allowed briefly, but oddly Diana's favorite program was the weather forecast. She would mimic what the forecaster was saying, quite accurately.

Horses and dogs were never of any great interest to her. Her eldest sister Sarah was horse-mad and put Diana on her pony Romany, but she derived no pleasure from the experience and just before her tenth birthday, while out riding with Sarah, Diana's horse bolted and she was thrown off and broke her arm. Following her marriage the princess desperately tried to please the Queen and her husband by trying to relearn, but she not only looked a picture of misery as she hacked around the Norfolk estate, she also looked inelegant. I remember a colleague commenting that she "looked like a sack of spuds" while riding. She knew this, and turned her back on it as a pursuit. The charms of James Hewitt persuaded her once more back into the saddle, but only briefly.

The departure of Nanny Thompson coincided with the deterioration of Viscount and Viscountess Althorp's marriage. Staff working at Park House remember vividly how, after his wife left, Lord Althorp locked himself away for weeks on end, refusing to speak to anybody, including the children. Said a member of staff: "He wouldn't see anyone but Mr. Smith (the butler and chauffeur) for ages. It was all very sad." The atmosphere that prevailed at the time had a lasting effect on all the children. But somehow it affected Diana and Sarah most. Given the sometimes brutal circumstances surrounding the end of the Althorps' marriage, it comes as no surprise that later in life Diana adopted as one of her favorite causes, along with AIDS sufferers, the plight of battered women: she has a special affinity with their cause, understanding their problems and fears. At event after event she attended, particularly during the period when her own marriage was breaking up, she spent extra time dispensing kind words and understanding. It does not need a psychologist to explain why.

At the time of her mother's departure Diana started her official education at school, having already had lessons from her governess, Gertrude Allen. Often children from a broken home "adopt" their alma mater as the one place where they feel safe, and Diana was no different. She told me she adored her schooldays, even though she hardly shone as a scholar: I asked her once to give me an accurate figure for the number of O levels she had, as there had been so much speculation on the subject. At first she wouldn't answer.

"Well, do you have more or less than Sarah?" I asked. "Because she has six."

"About the same," Diana said, laughing.

"Does that mean four or five?" I replied. She laughed louder and started to blush, the area just below her neck going blotchy, which always happens to her in times of difficulty or stress.

"I'm not going to answer that," she said. "I'm sure you'll find out soon enough."

It rapidly became clear that our about-to-be Princess of Wales did not have a single O level to her name—not that this has been a serious setback to her life as a member of the House of Windsor. In fact the princess turns her lack of academic attainment to good use: I've been with her on several occasions when she's put herself down by making comments like, "Brain the size of a pea—that's what I've got," or, "I'm as thick as a plank." When one meets her and watches her exert her flawless charm on old men, young girls, disadvantaged teenagers — even animals — one soon acknowledges that her skills far outreach any mere booklearning.

Diana didn't make any attempt at further education. After attending West Heath school in Kent she left, aged sixteen, to go to a finishing school in Switzerland, the Institut Alpin Videmanette, at Château d'Oex, near Gstaad. She joined after the school year had begun, she spoke far more English than she was allowed to (French was the prevailing language), she felt homesick and, after six weeks, she was allowed to return home. The only positive thing to come out of this unhappy period was that she began to learn how to ski.

At about this time Sarah Spencer received an unexpected invitation which was to change the lives of both sisters—she was asked "out of the blue" if she would care to join the royal house party at Windsor for Ascot week. Sarah later told me that the invitation was a complete surprise because "all I had done was make an application to go to Ascot through the usual channels." The deputy master of the royal household rang to ask whether she would like to stay at the castle. She would, and did.

She recalled later, "I drove myself to Windsor but did not see Prince Charles that evening—he wasn't feeling well—and met him for the first time the next day. We were introduced by Prince Andrew whom I knew from children's parties at Sandringham."

That first meeting, which took place on the opening day of the Ascot race meeting, occurred at a very unhappy time of Sarah's life. In an echo of her sister's later problems Sarah was suffering from an eating disorder, in her case anorexia nervosa. Unlike his chilly response when faced with Diana's bulimia, Charles showed sympathy and understanding. Sarah told me: "Almost as soon as we had greeted each other the prince said to me, 'Do you have anorexia?' I said that I didn't. But although I knew I hadn't fooled him, he didn't persist."

It is not surprising that he asked. In the weeks running up to her Ascot invitation Sarah was more existing than living. A few months earlier, standing 5 feet, 7 inches tall, her weight had gone from eight stone (112 pounds) down to a skeletal five and a half (seventy-seven pounds). She confessed that her vital statistics at this time had gone down from 34–24–34 to 27–20–28. "I looked like something out of a concentration camp—I couldn't find any normal clothes to fit me, and I did my shopping in the children's department of Marks and Spencer—the section for ten-year-olds.

"In such circumstances you behave like an alcoholic. You will just not admit that there is a problem. Worse, you end up believing you are beautiful, looking so thin. You really believe that if a man says you should put on more weight he just prefers fat women. And if other women say something you think they are jealous."

It could have been Princess Diana speaking. Lack of love, once again, was at the root of it. Sarah's parents' marriage breakup had played a part, as had a broken love affair. "The combination of the two things was catastrophic. I bust up with my boyfriend and then just stopped eating. I would toy with a couple of pieces of lettuce but if I forced a meal down I would just bring it up again. Naturally I was worried to begin with, but after being taken into hospital to be 'cured' in May 1975 things got worse. Instead of losing weight slowly, I lost half a stone in two weeks and by then I was really in a mess although of course I wouldn't admit it."

The illness had stripped the enamel from her teeth, and her situation seemed even worse than after her early departure out of West Heath for drinking. ("I used to drink because I was bored. I would drink anything: whisky, Cointreau, gin, sherry, or most often vodka because the staff couldn't smell it.")

While Sarah was struggling with this illness her father married Raine, the former Countess of Dartmouth and daughter of the romantic novelist Barbara Cartland. This was a bleak time not only for Sarah but for Diana too. Publicly Sarah would say little about "Acid" Raine except the terse comment: "She has been an all too frequent visitor." Privately, she summed up the feelings of herself and her youngest sister with an extraordinary viciousness. And though Raine was credited with saving the life of Earl Spencer following a severe cerebral hemorrhage, she got few thanks from Sarah and Diana.

When the hemorrhage struck, Spencer was rushed to Northampton hospital where doctors feared there was little they could do to save him. He was moved to the Brompton Hospital in South Kensington, London, where doctors still talk about how Raine would play opera loudly as she sat at her husband's bedside, willing him back to life. She subsequently said, "people forget I'm a survivor at their peril . . . Nobody destroys me and nobody was going to destroy Johnnie so long as I could sit by his bed and will my life-force into him." She added that some of her husband's family had tried to stop her sitting with Johnnie so often.

This may or may not be true, but I knew from Sarah that while her father was battling for his life there was also a battle going on between Raine and the Spencer girls. The countess had left instructions that none of the children were to be admitted to the hospital without her permission. Sarah recalled: "We were not going to stand for that. He was our father, we loved him very much, we knew that by going to see him we could help him recover and we were not going to stop because of Raine."

There were false stories, following the recovery of Earl Spencer, that Raine was reconciled with the children, but Sarah denied this to me. She and Diana were completely unforgiving, she said, and Raine knew it. The countess later commented: "I could have saved my husband's life ten times over, and spent all my money doing this, and it wouldn't have changed anything in his children's attitude toward me."

At about this time, with Sarah in improved health, she headed for Klosters in Switzerland very much as the girlfriend of Prince Charles. The official line was that she was an excellent skiing partner for the prince, but it wasn't the full story: Sarah was very keen on being the woman in Charles's life—not only because she liked him but because, like Diana a couple of years later, she was in love with his title and wanted to be associated with it.

She told me at the time: "He makes me laugh a lot and I really enjoy being with him." They also had quite a lot in common, both keen on riding and horses, both enjoying historical books. Charles, ever the romantic, went along with the idea that they might one day marry and the two did discuss the possibility. On their skiing holiday Charles's bodyguard John McLean, a tough and likeable Scotsman, slept in the corridor outside the bedrooms to keep intruders away.

During the week I went up to the chalet late each afternoon to check that none of the party, particularly the prince or Sarah, had suffered any broken limbs. McLean would normally answer the door and I and another colleague would get a briefing on the day's goings-on standing in the small hallway. Sarah, who loved everything that was happening, would usually join in this meeting, sitting on a radiator, swinging her legs as we chatted. More than once Prince Charles, with a towel wrapped around his waist and carrying a radio, would wander through our gathering, saying, "Sorry, but can I break up this press conference to get through? I want to go and have a bath." But he was happy with Sarah, an extremely attractive woman with glowing red hair and an effervescent character. She was attentive, courteous and did her best to fit in with the prince's wishes as he tried to balance his public life with a growing urge to find himself a suitable bride. And she was available.

That summer Sarah made strenuous efforts to holiday in Deauville when Charles flew there to play polo, but she discovered she was just one of four girls vying for the prince's attention. The opposition was made up of Jane Ward, the witty and attractive blonde secretary of the Guards Polo Club at Windsor, an American admiral's daughter, Laura Jo Watkins, whom Charles had met in the United States a few years earlier, and a French girl called Chantal.

As the week approached, Lady Sarah more and more obviously let it be known that she wanted to be taken to Deauville. "She kept going on and on about how she would love to go, how she could speak almost perfect French and how she knew so many people who would be there, including the prince's polo patron at the time, Guy Wildenstein," I was told. But Charles went alone,

was introduced to Chantal in France and the two
hit it off splendidly. I remember particularly the
evening they went bopping at a discothèque in
nearby Trouville. She was not the kind of girl who
was likely to become Princess of Wales, however.

Soon after this, Charles's romance with Sarah,
or what was left of it, petered out. But the link
between the Spencers and the royal family was
immeasurably strengthened by their liaison, and
as it became clear that Sarah would never get
Charles to the altar, she passed on what advice
she could to Diana. The whole family was very
supportive. Earl Spencer's other daughter, Jane,
now married to the Queen's then deputy private
secretary Robert Fellowes, arranged for Diana to
travel to Balmoral during the summer holidays to
look after their newborn daughter Laura. And she
encouraged Diana to be around and available as
Charles moodily strode about the nearby moors
and fishing pools as he thought over the breakup
of his latest romance, this time with the fiery
Anna Wallace. Their relationship had always been
peppery, and in August, as Diana, gentle and
sweet, spent long days with the prince, she helped
soothe the pain.

There had been a sharp intake of breath among
his friends when Charles started escorting Anna.
She was rich, uninhibited, very attractive and a
woman who was not in the slightest bit overawed
by having the Prince of Wales pay court to her.
She also had a hot temper when upset, and in the

early summer of 1980 the prince twice managed to cross her, first unintentionally at the Queen Mother's eightieth birthday ball at Windsor Castle. On this occasion he danced diplomatically with a wide range of guests, but it drew a sharp rebuke: "Don't ever ignore me like that again. I've never been treated so badly in my life." Charles, who can be extremely sensitive, was horrified as Anna, known to her friends as Whiplash, went on: "No one treats me like that—not even you." Soon after this came a polo ball at Stowell Park, the Gloucestershire home of Lord Vestey. Prince Charles, still irritated at being rebuked by Anna, was out to show who was boss. I noted at the time that Anna watched with mounting fury as her lover had dance after dance with his favorite married woman. Not even Lady Vestey—who was, after all, his hostess—was asked to dance. Anna looked on with a mixture of anger, disbelief and horror as the prince, who was clearly besotted, spent the evening holding Camilla Parker Bowles close.

It took some years for the mists to part, but at last it has become clear that not only did Camilla have a hand in destroying the relationship between Charles and his wife Diana, but she also put paid to the relationship between the prince and Anna Wallace. With Anna out of the way, the route was open for Diana to stake her claim to the most eligible bachelor in the world. She knew what she had to do to get him, and when she was overheard commenting at her sister Jane's wedding that the Guards Chapel wasn't good enough for her—"It will be Westminster Abbey for me"—it was clear she wasn't joking.

In September 1980 I found Diana, aided and abetted by her two sisters, at Balmoral. Certainly I had seen her before with Charles at Sandringham and, I suddenly remembered, watching the prince playing polo at Cowdray Park in Sussex at the end of July. But if there was anything between them, it had happened quickly and away from the public gaze. I was given "guidance" by the palace: "Don't get too carried away with what you write. The prince likes her but she's just a baby." I had found the couple on the river bank where Charles appeared to be fishing, but the lengths to which he went to conceal his companion implied there was more to the outing than mere pursuit of the salmon.

The following day I came across Diana again, this time at much closer quarters: we were both booked on the same flight back to Heathrow from Aberdeen. She was accompanied by Nicholas Soames, now Minister for Food in the Conservative government, and Andrew Parker Bowles, the husband of the woman whom Diana would learn to loathe with passion. Camilla was not on the flight and at the time I assumed that she had not been at the castle as part of the weekend party. I have since been told, "Of course Camilla was there. She stayed on to be with the prince for a few days as his guest." Only in the light of recent discoveries have I understood the significance of this.

The outside world still knew nothing of Lady Diana Spencer. The Prince of Wales's profile at that time was a man who was not so much unlucky in love as plain disastrous. There had been rumors circulating that after the Anna Wallace débâcle—whatever actually transpired, it looked as though *she* dumped *him*—the prince's friends had got together over lunch and drawn up a list of "known virgins." The idea was that it would be shown to Charles and accompanying it would be some stiff advice to sort himself out with a wife. Whether any of this ever happened, I remain doubtful. But the pressure was increasing on Charles to make his choice and get married; into this scenario Lady Diana fitted perfectly. She was the most likely candidate to be future Queen that I had seen in some years, but if there was a relationship, things were clearly at a very early stage.

That evening I returned to London and my photographer and I headed for Coleherne Court, which was to become world famous over the next few months. After establishing that the apartment we wanted was No. 60 we returned early the following morning to await Lady Diana's appearance. Fifty minutes later Diana, tall, slim and wonderfully pretty, came out of the front door and headed for an Indian-run delicatessen to buy milk and bread, before crossing the road to buy newspapers.

The following morning we were back at the flat again, this time to take pictures. More were taken on September 17, outside the Young England Kindergarten in Pimlico, where I discovered Diana worked as a helper—not as a teacher, as most newspapers described her. The photographers loved what they saw and snapped happily away for some time: obligingly she waited while they finished, unaware that, with the low angle of the sun and the fact that she was not wearing a petticoat under her flimsy Liberty-print skirt, it was possible to see her legs through the fabric. The result was sensational if somewhat upsetting for the young innocent: she certainly cried when she saw what the newspapers printed, but it was an early and relatively harmless lesson in media tactics. Diana never had to be told twice when it came to the media, and it didn't happen again. Charles, I later learned, was extremely amused. His reported comment was, "I knew your legs were good, but I didn't realize they were that spectacular." Teasingly, he added, "But did you really have to show them to *everybody*?"

Following that day, the prince and Diana decided to keep their meetings even more low-key, and at this they were highly successful. For a whole month they were not once found together until they attended a race meeting at Ludlow, in the West Midlands. Charles was riding in a race,

Diana was there as a spectator. Charles finished second on his own horse, Allibar, and Lady Di, as she had come to be known by the public, became so excited she openly revealed just how much in love with the prince she had become. There was, however, still a certain reticence at the time, which I put down to the excessive curiosity she attracted wherever she went. But there was another explanation. The couple were not alone that day to enjoy Charles's success and Diana's excitement, for they had brought a chaperone with them. Her name was Camilla Parker Bowles. Even then the wife of one of the Queen's senior cavalry officers was making sure that whatever the prince and Lady Diana might be planning with each other she would know about, and would make sure her interests were fully protected.

Diana desperately wanted Camilla out of the way, but at the time was too young and inexperienced to take the necessary action: "She had to swallow her feelings, and just bide her time until she became the fiancée of Charles." The couple had engendered such press excitement that they anticipated great trouble in getting away from the racecourse without being followed. Somehow they managed to effect an escape and headed for a house that Diana came to regard with hatred— Bolehyde Manor—where they spent the next two days. It is easy to understand now her dislike for her rival since, from the beginning of the relationship, when she wanted to spend time alone with the man she was going to marry, they somehow ended up with Camilla in tow.

The chances of Charles and Diana making a proper love match barely stood a chance. Charles didn't seem to care who he was with as long as Camilla was nearby; Diana didn't have the presence to say no. I was told by a family friend, "She had to keep going in the way she did, fitting in with everything that Charles—and Camilla—suggested. The alternative was that she would be ditched. Can you imagine how awful it all was for her?" But Lady Diana was nothing if not persistent; her determination to marry Charles transcended everything and she kept going, smiling through the humiliation of the older woman's patronage and always being available for the prince whenever he called. At the time it was remarkable how little courting was done: Charles never once went to her flat to pick her up, he never sent flowers or chocolates, and arrangements to meet were made via his bodyguards John MacLean or Paul Officer, or his valet Stephen Barry. And all the time he told her that he "couldn't stand her silly flatmates."

One person who saw danger in the situation was Diana's mother. She saw how Camilla was an ever-present force in Charles's life and cautioned her vulnerable and ambitious youngest daughter. On the weekend that Charles first showed Diana round his newly bought country home, Highgrove, Mrs. Shand Kydd said drily, "I have three daughters and the Queen has three unmarried sons. My daughters have all been invited to stay at Balmoral and Sandringham. Diana has recently been invited back for the fourth time—so she obviously hasn't blotted her copybook." But there was no excitement in what she was saying.

The then Lord Fermoy was Frances Shand Kydd's younger brother, and I approached him to talk about his niece. His response was quite extraordinary, as he launched into a monologue about Diana's virginity. Granted, this was extremely important to her chances of becoming the prince's wife, but it was more than a little surprising to hear Lord Fermoy say, "Diana, I can assure you, has never had a lover. Purity seems to be at a premium when it comes to discussing a possible royal bride for Prince Charles at the moment. And after one or two of his most recent girlfriends I am not surprised. To my knowledge Diana has never been involved in this way with anybody. This is good."

Well-meaning he may have been, but Diana was horrified at what her uncle had said. But the word was that Fermoy had always been a bit of an eccentric who said and did strange, unpredictable things.

Soon after this interview the prince celebrated his thirty-second birthday at Sandringham. Having said in his mid-twenties that the age of thirty seemed like a good time to get married, the pressure on him to become engaged was building furiously. Apart from the efforts of his well-meaning friends, Fleet Street was also imploring him to "do the decent thing with Diana." She had become, in the space of a few short weeks, the most popular woman in the country.

It was in this context that the royal train scandal erupted. The pressure on Diana to voice her suspicions—if it wasn't her on the train then it must have been Camilla—must have been immense. But she was still young, still inexperienced and, most important, still doggedly determined to marry the Prince of Wales. She had seen him slip through her sister's fingers, and she would not allow history to repeat itself.

It was at this point that a bond developed between Lady Diana and myself that I have cherished ever since. One day, with a horde of photographers popping flashguns in her face, Diana turned to them and said, "Please leave me alone for a second. I want to speak to Mr. Whitaker in private." We talked for some ten minutes on a number of subjects, and it turned out to be the first of several intimate chats I had with her over the next few weeks: from mid-November until the day of the engagement on February 24 I spoke to her either in person or on the telephone virtually every day.

In early December Charles flew to India on an official visit. There was still no indication from Buckingham Palace that this relationship was any different from the scores of other girls who had trailed around after Charles. That day I found Diana, sitting on a bench in Kensington Gardens, the park which adjoins Kensington Palace. She had her head back and to one side and she was lost in thought. I asked her the question everyone by now wanted her to answer: "Are you going to marry Prince Charles?" She thought before answering deliberately, "I really don't know." This was not a "No comment" or a "Get lost"; clearly she and Charles had discussed marriage. I believe that he had made a formal proposal of marriage but, despite her ambition to become Princess of Wales, Diana was thinking the offer over.

It was hard to see at that juncture what she was hesitating about; I now know that not only was she worried about the age gap, she was also terrified she could not deal with the omnipresent Camilla. She knew that the prince was still involved both mentally and physically with her, and Diana's nerve was failing her as she wondered whether she could beat off the older woman. I asked her another question—"Is it true that the prince has already asked you to become his wife?"— and she replied, "I can't say anything. I just can't say anything." Things were about to happen.

Shortly after this, Diana's mother wrote to *The Times*, complaining of press harassment. It was a strange letter, written from the heart but sadly lacking in accuracy as to what had really been going on between her daughter and the press.

That same day, during one of our telephone conversations, Diana told me that she disagreed with what her mother had written. "There are times when people upset me," she said, "but that's rare, and I like to think I get on very well with most of you. The only thing that really annoys me is when my children (at the kindergarten) get frightened by things like flashguns." Already she had learned to deploy one of the most powerful assets in her armory—how to handle the press. It was something her husband would never be able to do.

The prince returned from India and, apparently, did not see Diana for a whole week. I could not understand this at the time, but there was a simple answer, if one had looked for it. The prince did not rush to Diana's side, as one might expect, because he was with Camilla Parker Bowles— before his death Stephen Barry confirmed to me that no sooner did he return than he was with Camilla. He added, "The prince explained to Diana that he was busy for a day or two, but she did not know with whom."

On the night of December 17 I was once again outside Coleherne Court, because I had heard that there might be an announcement of Charles and Diana's engagement in *The Times* shortly. Diana had been out to dinner with a friend—not Charles—and I awaited her return in the cold and dark.

After exchanging pleasantries I asked if her engagement was to be announced the following Friday, but she made no reply. I mentioned *The Times*, but there was still no response. I then said, "This is just about the most important question I have ever asked anybody in my journalistic life. I wouldn't be bothering you at this time of the night unless I was in earnest." Finally Lady Diana replied, "I know. Obviously this is all very serious." She then suggested we go inside her block of flats "where we can talk." We then started to discuss the situation, sometimes standing, sometimes sitting on the stairs. We talked for nearly an hour. To begin with, Diana was giving away very little, but when I said that if she would not deny there was to be an engagement announcement on Friday I was going to write a story immediately, she was concerned. "Please, Mr. Whitaker, do be careful," she said urgently. "There is so much I want to explain to you but I can't. This is very, very difficult for me. I want to help you so much but I mustn't. You must understand how hard this is for me. I want to help you . . ." and she stopped speaking. Clearly she was in a dilemma. But I was forced to place her in a bigger one—I told her that I was intending to write the story on the basis that she wouldn't deny it because in all the weeks we had been talking she had never lied to me. She said, "Wait a moment. Look, please go and check your information more. This is so difficult but be careful." After talking quietly for another half hour or so—it was now approaching one in the morning—I said I wouldn't write a story for the time being. She sighed with relief and said, "Good, people have got excited too soon."

Following this evening things went very quiet. One weekend Diana slipped away to spend some time with the prince at Birkhall, at Balmoral, instead of following the increasingly grating routine of going to stay with Andrew and Camilla Parker Bowles in Wiltshire.

Two days later I caught up again with Lady Diana, once more at her apartment. I went to wish her a happy Christmas, but I found her in red pajamas with a blue dressing-gown on top. And for a change she didn't look so good. "How are you?" I asked as she leaned against the door. "Not too well," she replied. "In fact, I feel awful, I've got flu." Since she was on her own and with no help in sight I asked if there was anything I could do, but she said she thought she would be all right if she just stayed in bed. When I asked if she had called a doctor she said, "No, it's not that bad." It was now that I introduced Diana to homoeopathy. "Do you believe in it?" I asked. "Homy ... what?" she responded, laughing. "What on earth is that?" "If you are going to become the daughter-in-law of the Queen you had better learn about homoeopathy. It's her favorite form of medicine." I told her a bit about it, and she was intrigued. I said I would arrange for some homoeopathic medicine to be sent round to her. When I saw her after Christmas I asked how she'd got on with it, and she replied, "It was terrific for about twenty-four hours, but then when the effect had worn off I think my cold was the worst one ever."

The new year of 1981 was chaotic. Reporters swarmed up to Sandringham in the hope of finding Diana staying there, and the Queen, clearly rattled by the extra attention, abandoned her customary sang-froid to shout at me, "Go away. Can't you leave us alone?" Charles in another outburst added his own unseasonal greeting. Relations had sunk to an all-time low—the nation wanted the royals to deliver them a future Queen, but the House of Windsor was not yet ready to play.

A couple of weeks later Diana joined the prince at Sandringham, originally planning to stay for two or three days. In the event she stayed just twenty-four hours because of the enormous media interest, choosing to return to London because she felt that she was causing the family's holiday to be spoilt.

A few days later Charles went off alone to Klosters to ski. He returned on February 2 and, two days after that, according to the couple on their engagement day, he formally proposed and she accepted him. The news did not creep out for another three weeks.

During this period Diana herself went off on holiday, to a place as far away as possible so she could hide and "think it all over." She accompanied her mother and stepfather to New South

Wales in Australia. I found out almost immediately what was happening and wrote a story saying where Diana had gone, but when Mrs. Shand Kydd was tackled about the story at their farm in Yass she denied it and said Diana was not with her. Later explaining that she had no regrets about doing this, Mrs. Shand Kydd said that they had had a fun holiday, swimming and surfing. She added, "Of course we talked about Diana's future. I enormously approve of my daughters marrying the men they love." Ringed around that comment was a barely veiled and continuing reservation over the whole arrangement.

Shortly after Diana's return from Australia there was an accident on the gallops belonging to the prince's racehorse trainer at Lambourn in Berkshire. Charles was out exercising his horse Allibar with Nick Gaselee when suddenly the horse, without warning, collapsed and died of a massive heart attack. The prince jumped off to cradle the head of the chaser and Diana, crying, rushed to their sides. But there was nothing either could do.

Two days later, on February 22, I rang Diana at her apartment to say how terribly sorry I was about the death of the horse. We went on to talk about her Australian holiday, but just as I was putting the telephone down I sensed something in her tone which told me that this was the last time I would ever be able to ring her at home, and find her picking up the telephone herself. Her final words were different to her normal goodbye. Having said that she would be back at the kindergarten on Tuesday and would see me there, she concluded, "Goodbye, Mr. Whitaker, and thank you."

It was a friendly farewell. With the prince about to embark on a lengthy tour of Australia, New Zealand and the United States, I think there was a sudden decision to get the engagement announcement out of the way. Certainly when I talked to Diana's flatmates later they had not anticipated the engagement was being made official quite so soon. But by announcing their plans in February there was time to arrange a summer wedding, something that the prince badly wanted. The previous royal marriage—Princess Anne to Captain Mark Phillips in 1973—had been in "dreary" November. So two days after we spoke for that final time, the engagement was officially announced from Buckingham Palace. Considering that the tabloid press always came in for criticism in the way that it handled the royals, it was ironic that it was *The Times* which broke the embargo. William Rees-Mogg, then editor of the paper, chose to publish the scoop of the century in a small box, halfway down the front page. The news had been given him off the record by, it was said, the former prime minister Edward Heath. Charles was furious but gradually resigned himself to the situation.

During their interviews with television and the

Press Association later that day there were some interesting comments made, remarks that did not bode that well for the future. Describing how he felt they both had a lot in common, the prince said, "Diana is a great outdoor-loving sort of person." Lady Diana chipped in, "We both love music and dancing and we both have the same sense of humor." To which Charles added quickly, "You'll definitely need that." Coupled with Charles's statement about love—"Whatever that may mean"—it was not quite the joyous moment many had hoped for. Most put this maladroit performance down to the couple's nerves. But even now Diana was concerned about outside influences on her husband-to-be: she had been told that the prince's two confidantes, Australian-born Lady Tryon, known by Charles as Kanga (short for kangaroo), and Camilla Parker Bowles, had "approved" the engagement. Diana didn't particularly care what Dale Tryon thought—though she quite liked her and subsequently bought dresses from her Knightsbridge shop—but she was concerned about Camilla. However, with the confidence of youth and her newly acquired status as the fiancée of the Prince of Wales she believed she could get Camilla out of Charles's mind. And for the next few months until the wedding day—July 29—this was what she set out to do.

As a result Diana began to suffer. She lost weight at an alarming rate, she started to sleep badly, she didn't see her former flatmates as much as she wanted. On the day she left Coleherne Court she begged them to keep in touch—"I'll need you more than ever now"—but somehow it didn't work out like that. While Charles toured the world she was incarcerated inside the palace and had the added burden of a police escort shadowing her everywhere. She was nowhere near the happy young woman the nation fondly pictured her to be.

She moved from her flat to Clarence House, the official London home of the Queen Mother. There, popular belief has it, she was taken under the wing of the kindly Queen Mother and coached by her in the ways of the royal family. "This," Diana told me a number of years later, "just wasn't true. When I started carrying out official engagements I hadn't got a clue what I was meant to be doing. It was dreadful. I know that people think that all sorts of people gave me lessons, instructed me on what I should or shouldn't be doing. But they didn't. Just nobody helped me at all."

Her confidence was further undermined by constant phone calls to Charles from Camilla. One particularly unsettled her. It came a few hours before the prince left for his trip to Australia and New Zealand. Diana was talking to her fiancé in his study when the telephone rang and she realized who it was. She said later, "I didn't know whether to stay or leave. It was awful." But another incident, heavily reported in the wake of recent revelations, gave her the spur to fight back. A parcel for the prince arrived at the palace and

Diana decided to open it herself. Inside was a gold chain bracelet with a blue enamel disc attached to it with the initials "G" and "F" intertwined. It has been said that these initials stood for Fred and Gladys, pet names the prince and Camilla had for one another. In fact the initials stood for "Girl Friday," which is how Charles referred to Camilla.

Diana desperately wanted Camilla excluded from the wedding guest list, but Charles hardly bothered to discuss this before dismissing it. But then she won the next battle—she said that she could not bear to have "that woman" at the official wedding breakfast given by the Queen at Buckingham Palace. And so while 120 royal relatives and intimate friends of the couple drank Krug champagne at the reception, dined on quenelles of brill with lobster sauce, chicken breast stuffed with minced lamb, and strawberries with clotted Cornish cream, Camilla and Charles's other confidante had to make other arrangements.

Said Lady Tryon at the time, "I was not invited on to the palace. I know Mrs. Parker Bowles wasn't invited either. She is holding her own party for friends. Obviously I can't comment on why I wasn't invited. I do not feel offended."

Neither did Camilla: she knew that she had a hold on the prince that Diana would find hard to prise apart. She also had the perfect excuse—if ever she needed one—for always being able to call Charles, or be called by him. The prince was godfather to her son Tom.

FIVE

The Honeymoon Is Over

The pattern of what was to follow was set from the moment the Prince and Princess of Wales began their honeymoon at Broadlands, the home of Charles's "honorary grandfather," Earl Mountbatten. The prince went trout fishing while his new bride spent a short time watching him before walking off on her own, spending the time trying to adjust to her new position in life. Despite everything she was deliriously happy to have achieved what she had. With the resilience of youth Diana had complete faith that she could win her husband round to loving her, but what she failed to understand from the very beginning was that Charles regarded her as a child, a person who should be shown respect—as long as it didn't interfere with his own personal arrangements—and as a highly suitable person to be the mother of his children. That was all.

She learned quickly that, in all things, she had to fit in with him. If she didn't particularly like fishing—which she didn't—that was too bad, because that was what he liked doing and that was what he was going to do. Broadlands was a second home to him, and he was a creature of habit. Having a wife along made no difference to the rituals he so enjoyed. The same applied to hunting and, to a degree, polo. If Diana, out of loyalty, wanted to attend any of these activities, she was not discouraged. But at the same time Charles was not going to go out of his way to make her welcome. She was irrelevant to a very large part of his life and, self-questioning though he may be, it never occurred to him that maybe his life should alter when he married.

One incident, following the birth of Prince Harry, amply demonstrates the chilly vacuum Diana had experienced for the first time during the latter months of 1981. After giving birth in the Lindo Wing of St. Mary's Hospital, Paddington, there was a happy get-together between the newborn child, Prince Charles and Prince William. Charles stayed for ten minutes, then went home for his lunch. He came back, collected his wife and their new son and drove them back to Kensington Palace. Then he went on to polo where—new baby or no new baby—he spent the rest of the day.

As with all newlyweds, there were flashes of warmth and shared jokes, and certainly in the early days the prince demonstrated his feelings for his wife by touching her in public—an embrace or a kiss became the norm, and as I mentioned one photographer took an amusing picture of the prince pinching his wife's bottom at polo.

Soon after returning from Egypt, where they ended the second stage of their honeymoon on board the royal yacht *Britannia*, Diana made her first public appearance in Scotland as Princess of Wales alongside Charles. It was at the Braemar Gathering, exactly one year after I had first found her sitting on the river bank, hiding behind a pine tree and watching Charles fish.

Suddenly, the full reality of what she had done in giving away her privacy was brought home to her. For the first time, in full public view, she incurred the wrath of her mother-in-law. As she sat beside the Queen and Prince Charles in the royal box, the same one that has been used since Queen Victoria's time, the band started to play the national anthem. They all stood, but as the first words—"God save our gracious Queen"— were sung, the prince leaned over to Diana and whispered something in her ear. What he actually said was, "They're playing our song . . ." and Diana burst into a lengthy giggle. The prince then forgot the training and iron discipline of the previous thirty-three years and joined Diana in silent laughter. The Queen was furious. A member of

Diana's family told me the following week, "That was a definite *faux pas*. But though the Queen was annoyed with Diana, she was furious with Charles. I can assure you neither will make that mistake again."

The Queen's chilly reaction to a moment of innocent amusement was a sobering reminder to the novice princess that although millions around the world would bend the knee to her, she was now the servant of a rigid protocol. Certainly in public she never made such gaffes again, but she was far from being a conformist. As people were soon to learn, particularly those courtiers who were supercilious or overbearing, she took pleasure in debunking their petty rules.

This became apparent on her first tour as the Princess of Wales—appropriately enough, in the principality from which her title derives. During three hectic days her spirits were undampened by torrential rain, and she shunned the offers of umbrellas so as not to impede her hand shaking with the adoring crowds. Soaking wet but with a perpetual smile on her face, she soared in the nation's estimation as they watched her début on television.

In the euphoria that surrounded her arrival on the public stage, there was general agreement that she was going to save the royal family from its dowdy, boring self. Princesses are quite illogically expected to have certain magical qualities, most of which seemed to be absent from the House of

Windsor's complement of royal highnesses. Anne and Margaret and Princess Michael all now looked long in the tooth and dull by comparison with this sparkling newcomer. But what no one saw in this moment of high excitement was what the princess was doing to Charles. For the first time in his life he was upstaged and, no matter what public face he put on it as he stood by Diana's side, he did not like what was happening. As a Prince of Wales, the twenty-first English one since the title was created in 1301, Charles had been used to being the center of attention all his life, with staff everywhere to open and shut doors for him. He has never traveled by bus, nor has he ever stood in a queue, although he probably knows what one is. The only moments in his life when he was outfaced were at his school, Gordonstoun—and that was long ago.

If Diana was a more popular draw than he was, it was a passing phase, he reasoned. For the time being he was complimentary about his wife and treated her with extreme courtesy. It was suggested to me that he was prepared to be this way because he considered himself the ringmaster and Diana his number-one act—the implication being that she was only a star because he had made her one. It was to be another few months before disillusionment and consequent signs of irritation began to creep into their joint public appearances.

But Diana's début had been a remarkable success, and she was exhilarated. Less satisfactory, however, were her domestic arrangements: she and Charles were having to delay moving into their own home, Highgrove, near Tetbury in Gloucestershire, because furniture needed to make the place habitable was still on display to the public. It was part of an exhibition at St. James's Palace to raise money for charity. Diana's sister Sarah told me, with more than a trace of diplomacy, that although it was no great hardship to stay on at Balmoral Castle, the new bride was "absolutely dying to move into her own home with Prince Charles."

Diana had slipped away from Scotland for a couple of days in secret, had gone to the exhibition at St. James's to remind herself what was available, then driven down to Highgrove to see where everything would be put. Sarah also told me that the prince and princess had resigned themselves to the fact that they would have to stay up at Balmoral until the end of October, making their three-month honeymoon one of the longest in the royal record books.

Explaining her sister's longing to get into Highgrove, Sarah said, "Diana is a very home-loving person and it is important to her that everything is just right. When she went to check the place out she went through it like a dose of salts, checking on this, questioning that." In the same conversation Sarah denied that Diana was suffering from the strain of married life. She said, "She is absolutely adoring what is going on. She could have been born into the role. She loves all the adoration and attention she is getting and the way people are looking and reacting to her."

Whatever stress she was under in those early days, and it seemed to me to be considerable, there was a brief lull when, on November 5, it was announced Diana was pregnant. The announcement was made to "stop speculation," but it did not stop the relentless pursuit of the former kindergarten helper who, even in this short period of time had become the most photographed woman in the world. In the second week of December the Queen's press secretary, Michael Shea, arranged a meeting between Fleet Street editors, TV and radio people and the Queen. It was made clear that although the princess was the main subject of the gathering, she had not asked for it to take place. After the formal briefing and a request to leave Diana alone, the Queen made her appearance, a rare interface between sovereign and the Fourth Estate. If she had any doubts about the wisdom of meeting with the jackals who were relentlessly pursuing her pregnant daughter-in-law they were confirmed when she was confronted by Barry Askew.

Nicknamed "The Beast of Bouverie Street," Barry Askew was the editor of the tabloid *News of the World* and he had every intention of showing he was not overawed in the Queen's presence. Remembering his conversation earlier with Shea, when the press secretary had complained that photographers had even pursued Diana to the village shop in Tetbury when she went to buy sweets, he asked, "Would it not be better to send a servant to the shop for Princess Diana's winegums?" This was too much for the Queen. Drawing herself up to her full height of five feet, four inches, she replied, "Mr. Askew, that was a most pompous remark." A month later Mr. Askew was relieved of his editorship.

Just six months after the wedding, I set off for the Bahamas where the Waleses were having a holiday with their friends Lord and Lady Romsey. Contrary to reports published recently that even by now—February 1982—Diana was desperately unhappy, to the point of attempting suicide, there were no signs that the couple were anything other than blissfully happy. In fact, the couple behaved like all newlyweds, standing in the water for ages with their arms around each other's necks, kissing constantly. All of which makes suggestions that only a couple of weeks earlier Diana had thrown herself down the stairs at Sandringham completely laughable. At the time, I spoke to a contact who was on the scene almost immediately Diana had fallen, and far from Prince Charles walking away as she lay there, as has been intimated, he was extremely concerned and called a doctor right away.

Nor did Charles go off riding as has been written, but after the princess had been pronounced fit, he took her for a picnic lunch at the royal family's beach house on the Norfolk coast, near Wells-next-the-Sea.

My newspaper published photographs from the Bahamas trip showing the still-shapely Diana in a red bikini. The Queen was unamused, calling it "a black day for British journalism," and I wrote to Diana saying that I was very sorry if I had upset her in any way. Via one of her staff I learned that she had not minded, so the black day suddenly appeared a great deal sunnier.

Prince William of Wales, the future King, was born in June. The following months started in a state of contentment and fulfilment for Diana—after all, besides having a healthy baby boy, she had, first time around, provided the nation with an heir to the throne—but suddenly things began to deteriorate.

In early November, just before Remembrance Day, there was an extraordinary scene at London's Albert Hall on the occasion of the annual British Legion Festival of Remembrance. This event is attended each year by the Queen and other senior members of the royal family as a matter of course. This year, the year of the Falklands conflict, the princess was to be there to remember the living as well as the dead. Everybody was thrilled.

But things went terribly wrong. Minutes before the evening was due to begin a doorman was told that, after all, Her Royal Highness would not be attending. Immediately there was a hurried shuffling of chairs in the royal box, with Diana's being removed. Five minutes later, and with the Queen already in her seat, the princess astonished everybody by turning up at a side door, accompanied by her bodyguard Alan Peters. The princess looked "grumpy and fed up" according to an eyewitness to her arrival. By the end of the evening she was "radiant and happy" once more, responding to the audience and their applause. But no one is ever late for the Queen, so I set out to find out what was the matter.

In truth this sort of unpredictable behavior had started to become a way of life for Diana in the preceding weeks. A month or so before, Diana had swept out of Balmoral in a fury, leaving Prince Charles and their three-and-a-half-month-old son behind. She just wanted to get out of Scotland, I was told, she couldn't bear the cozy smugness of the other royals all around her. Most particularly she objected to the way that Charles would always side with his mother in any disagreement. She was also beginning to be extremely irritated with the Queen Mother continually "helping" her. She had been given no assistance by the Queen Mother on her introduction into royal circles, despite popular myth, and she felt that by now she could cope perfectly adequately without little lectures. At the same time Charles said nothing, and this infuriated her even more.

I also started to get reports that her personal staff were becoming frightened of the princess. Her press officer, Vic Chapman, explained that there was "a little problem" which meant, of course, that there was a major one. "What sort of 'little problem'?" I asked. "Nothing much," said Vic, "but she's become a bit obsessive. When, for example, her shoes are cleaned, she wants them put back in precisely the straight lines they were in when they were taken away. She is obsessed that everything and everybody around should be perfect. She feels that so much is expected of her, she should be able to command the same." I wrote at the time, under a headline saying, "Is it all getting too much for Diana?" that this sort of behavior had aroused deep fears that the princess had been put under too much stress, that too much was being asked of her and that she was suffering badly trying to satisfy everybody.

Then, to howls of horror, I ventured the suggestion that all these pressures could lead to irrational behavior which could manifest itself in the form of the slimmer's illness, anorexia nervosa, or obsessive dieting. I went on to say that there was concern that Diana was beginning to show some of the symptoms of the disease. I wrote that from my own observation she looked painfully thin, and kept telling everybody that she had to watch her waistline. Since the birth of William the princess had lost weight alarmingly. She had also become obsessive about what she ate, as well as how much. I mentioned a lunch she had attended with Duchy of Cornwall tenants the week before. She first rejected the main dish of tenderloin pork, and subsequently refused to eat the substitute meal of salmon. Prince Charles, mindful of the anorexia of Diana's sister Sarah, had started to try to have lunch with his wife "just to make sure she eats properly."

I pointed out that everybody should be vigilant. No one should lose sight of the fact that the princess was still only twenty-one. When my story appeared on 15 November there was outrage. The London *Evening Standard* talked about the Princess of Wales being affected by stresses and strains caused largely by "grossly exaggerated" reports of her health. "Claims that the princess is suffering from the slimmer's disease were unsubstantiated speculation," an unnamed Buckingham Palace source was quoted as saying. "For God's sake, leave her alone."

That same day I appeared on the Radio Four program *Today,* which is listened to regularly by Prince Charles. The presenter, Brian Redhead, described as "outrageous" the suggestions that the princess was anorectic. I defended what I had written by saying that I had been speaking to a member of the princess's family who had admitted there was a problem. I said that this person had told me, "We would like to have a chat with her about it, but she doesn't take advice kindly." What I did not say, however, was that my informant was a deeply anxious Lady Sarah McCorquodale, Diana's sister.

It took another nine and a half years for my

story to be confirmed. It was Diana herself who finally made the admission. The illness, exacerbated by so many pressures and by the perpetual attention of the outside world had one root cause: her husband could not come to terms with his wife's obsessions and problems. Some might argue that he did not love her enough, but since he queried at his engagement press conference the definition of the word love, it was clear to me that he did not love her at all.

He discovered that the woman he married so cynically was quite impossible to talk to. "We just can't ever have a reasonable conversation," he would complain, and he began to view Diana with increasing distaste. He thought of her as a woman who reveled in the personal publicity and attention she received from the media and the public, and he confided to his family that he was unable to cope with her moods and her constant demands for support. Charles's view was that she had known what she was doing when she had married him and that by now she should have started to get the hang of things. It was time she grew up. There appears to have been no attempt to look beyond the tantrums and the tears to the root cause of the problem. For Charles, the symptoms were the problem—tears meant trouble, and when the tears flowed, he fled.

It was at this time, in the spring of 1983, less than two years after his marriage, that Charles took the decision to resume his sexual relationship with the one person in the world who had always understood him, Camilla Parker Bowles. But it didn't happen immediately.

There was a major tour of Australia and New Zealand to be undertaken first, followed almost immediately by a similar visit to Canada. As I covered both these trips my feeling was that they were a triumph for both the prince and princess, but at a cost. As I have already discussed, for the first time in his life the prince was upstaged and he displayed irritation at the fact. In a speech at a farewell banquet in Auckland, he appeared to be in jocular vein when he declared, "I have come to the conclusion that it really would have been easier to have had two wives. Then they could cover both sides of the street and I could walk down the middle directing operations." In private he was not so relaxed about the switch in emphasis from him to his partner, but manfully he tried to steel himself against his disappointment and burgeoning jealousy. In the same speech, the prince then went on to refer to their son William, who a few days earlier had given his first photo-opportunity on the lawn of Government House. The inclusion of the young prince on this month-long visit to Australia and New Zealand had gone down badly among older members of the royal family and, even more so, with their senior staff. They pointed to the days when the Queen had gone off on tour, leaving the infant Charles and Anne behind at home—"the right and proper

place for them." Change has never been popular
with courtiers, as it implies the passage of time
and with it their advancing years.

Diana recalled being told by her husband that
when the Queen returned home after being away
on a months-long tour, Charles was expected to
behave formally, holding out his hand to his
mother for her to shake it. There were no hugs,
no kisses. With her own bruised childhood still
very much in mind, Diana was determined that
that was not going to happen with her and William. In the teeth of heavyweight opposition, she
won the battle to take her son with her, but, as
Charles pointed out, it didn't work.

The couple had to travel much more than
would otherwise have been necessary, because
William was based at a farm at Woomargama in
the Outback. This meant that they returned there
every three or four days. Charles enjoyed these
breaks, but thought that his son's presence was
distracting them from the real job in hand: per-
suading the people of Australia that continuing to
have a royal family was a good idea.

By the end of the tour Diana also had doubts
about the wisdom of having William there, although her maternal instincts tended to take precedence over her royal ones. The boy slowed the
tour down and diffused its focus, but she delighted in returning to Woomargama for an extra
dose of kisses and cuddles. However, this format
was never again allowed by the palace tour orga-

nizers: when Charles and Diana followed up this tour with one to Canada, William was left behind. The courtiers pointed out the difficulties of having small children around when there was serious business to be done, and ordained that from now on children were not to be included on royal tours.

Diana responded swiftly to this dictum, saying that in that case she would never again undergo such lengthy tours as they had endured to Australasia. Her explanation to Charles was simple: "Children cannot be left for that length of time at their age." Her attitude hardened as she matured in her job as Princess of Wales, and her invariable rule on foreign tours today is that all overseas travel must be contained within one week. She also insists that she will not travel abroad if it means missing her children on a weekend exeat from their boarding prep school.

These two momentous tours of 1983 turned Diana from an object of fascination into a world-class megastar, but they appeared at that stage to have had little effect on her natural charm and outward modesty. The princess returned home and settled into a reasonably cozy existence, purposefully training herself into the job and in so doing becoming more self-reliant. By now she realized that if her life was to have any purpose, it would have to come from within. Her relationship with Charles, though companionable, was not a meeting of equals. He did not discuss affairs of state with her, and at difficult moments he would turn to one of two women—and she wasn't either of them. First he would consult Camilla then, on occasion, the Queen.

I can find no evidence that he consciously rejected his wife, but with too many other calls on his time and loyalty, he never seemed to be able to focus fully on the uncomfortable situation she was in. She had been drawn into his family and by a withering process had been forced to drop most of her contacts with the outside world. And yet there were few compensations within the royal compound—she regularly met and talked with people who regarded her either as an outsider or as someone who could not be taken seriously. Charles, born inside the compound, could not—or would not—understand the justifiable complaints she made. If one word characterizes his attitude toward her at this time, it is aloof.

However, in September 1983 she became pregnant—maybe it was the daughter she has always longed for; we will never know. Certainly at Balmoral that month she told the Queen in the presence of Princess Margaret that she was expecting her second child. The Queen called for champagne and the child's health was drunk, but within a week Diana suffered a miscarriage.

By the end of 1983 the princess was pregnant once more. Whether both were thrilled at this prospect, it is hard to judge—but it emphasized Diana's *raison d'être* as a provider of children, and

Charles was content with the idea that he might possibly have a "spare," as well as an heir.

The problems experienced by the couple were sufficient in number to be aired to a wider audience now, and friends of the couple started talking about life for the princess and prince as they approached their third wedding anniversary. Most agreed that the young, untutored girl and the much older man had had a struggle learning to understand each other's needs—needs that too often were in conflict. They had, it was becoming clear, very little in common. Their sleeping arrangements, for example, did not tally: if Diana was doing nothing in the evening (which in those days was often the case) she would go to bed at Kensington Palace at around nine o'clock. She had no television in her room; her bedtime companions were a Paddington Bear and an even scruffier Teddy. Charles on the other hand would be extremely irritated as she went off after an early supper. Reported one member of staff, "He would go to his study most nights and stay up until all hours, listening to opera at full blast, watching videos or, when he couldn't put it off any more, ploughing through a mountain of paperwork."

Conjugal relations were not high on his list of priorities: the servant was even more categoric that at this early stage of their marriage the couple rarely slept in their four-poster bed together. He reported, "When he had finished what he was doing each night, the prince would creep upstairs and without disturbing his wife slip into his dressing room, which adjoined the master bedroom, from an outside door leading off the corridor. There he would get into the bed which was always made up for him. Whether this was out of consideration for his wife or because he just wanted to be on his own I couldn't say. But it did happen frequently."

The sad truth of this arrangement—which was instigated by the prince—is that Diana didn't seem to mind. The member of staff explained, "Diana has learned to accept her husband's absences, to enjoy them even, and the two have reached an understanding that they will never have many joint hobbies or recreations." They did enjoy opera and they loved playing with William, but that was about it. Charles's friends bored Diana and vice versa: despite only a twelve-year gap they were from two different generations, and they could find no common meeting-ground.

By this stage the princess had learned to live with the permanent security surrounding her, and she soon began to realize that her "shadows" could be fun and were certainly attractive. It was their duty to be with Diana constantly (even when she went to the loo) and such proximity bred a certain warmth. In the twelve years that Diana has had a Scotland Yard protection officer she has formed friendly relations with three of them— Sergeant Barry Mannakee, who sadly died in a car

Prince Charles with Lady Sarah Spencer (*Tim Graham*)

Prince Charles and Lady Diana Spencer during their
engagement (*Tim Graham*)

The moment before the kiss (*Tim Graham*)

Honeymoon on the Royal Yacht, leaving Gibraltar
(*Tim Graham*)

The pose that used to irritate her husband (*Tim Graham*)

When they were best friends (*Glenn Harvey*)

Prince Harry goes home from hospital (*Glenn Harvey*)

Waltzing Diana, in Australia (*Glenn Harvey*)

The young family in Venice (*Lionel Cherruault*)

How a fairy-tale princess
should look (*Glenn Harvey*)

A mother and her sons
(*Lionel Cherruault*)

On holiday on Richard Branson's island,
Necker (*Robin Nunn/Nunn Syndication*)

Diana with her mother-in-law (*Glenn Harvey*)

Diana, all heart with Wills at polo (*Lionel Cherruault*)

Fergie and Diana against the world (*Lionel Cherruault*)

Diana with the Queen Mother at the Epsom Derby
(*Glenn Harvey*)

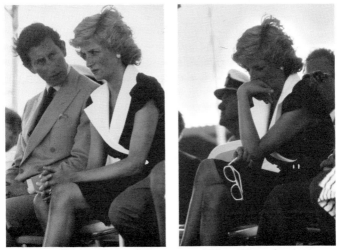

By now, beyond persuasion (*Glenn Harvey*)

The winner and the loser (*Glenn Harvey*)

The prince and his former polo manager, Major Ron (*Glenn Harvey*)

One still has to put on a show (*Glenn Harvey*)

When they still kissed, June 1986 (*Lionel Cherruault*)

The day we knew it was all over, February 1992
(*Rex Features*)

Camilla – the look that Charles could not resist (*Robin Nunn/Nunn Syndication*)

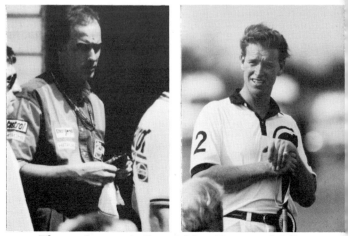

The two Jameses in Diana's life—Hewitt and Gilbey (*Glenn Harvey Empics/Nunn Syndication*)

Up in the air with William and Harry (*Lionel Cherruault*)

Fun and games in the snow (*Glenn Harvey*)

Brigadier and
Mrs. Andrew Parker
Bowles (*Dennis James/
Nunn Syndication*)

Charles and Camilla sneak away for a picnic at Balmoral
(*Jim Bennett/Nunn Syndication*)

The outdoor look (*Glenn Harvey*)

Diana with her mother,
Frances Shand Kydd
(*Tim Graham*)

The 8th Earl Spencer at
Althorp (*Tim Graham*)

The funeral of the
8th Earl Spencer
(*Tim Graham*)

The four Spencer children (*Kelvin Bruce/Nunn Syndication*)

Action-woman (*Julian Parker/Nunn Syndication*)

Why she's the world's top glamour girl (*Glenn Harvey*)

accident a few weeks after being transferred away from her (at one stage a baseless rumor circulated that he had been bumped off by MI5); Inspector Graham Smith, known as Smudger, who had to stop work in 1991 when it was found he had contracted cancer (He has since died from the disease.), and her current number-one bodyguard, Inspector Ken Wharfe, who was previously protection officer to the little princes.

But despite this ease and even friendliness, Diana could never readily accept the restrictions on her life created by these people, although she needed their unwearying attention as from time to time she would find herself confronted with quite the strangest circumstances. I remember in her very early days as a princess, when she first started carrying out engagements, there was a man in a raincoat who always seemed to be around when she emerged from wherever she had been. He would get very excited whenever he saw the princess and his coat would jump up and down rapidly. On closer inspection I could see what he was doing and it wasn't very nice: my colleagues and I had to call the police over to him more than once before some particularly rough sergeant persuaded him not to come back.

There were also constant intruders into Kensington Palace. Because of the security ring around royal residences, particularly following Michael Fagan's break-in at Buckingham Palace, when he reached the Queen's bedroom, they were usually caught within minutes. But with the threat ever present there were panic buttons located all over the prince and princess's apartment, including at the side of every royal bed. At the same time both Charles and Diana, along with their drivers and bodyguards, would go on special training courses at the Hereford headquarters of the SAS. There they would learn survival techniques—how to brace themselves in the event of being tied up so that the knots could later be worked loose; how to drive a car backwards at forty miles per hour; how to use a .38 Smith and Wesson, and even a Heckler and Koch machine pistol. They were also given intensive lectures and live demonstrations on how to survive terrorist attack. Thunderflashes and smoke bombs would be thrown at them to add reality to what they were being taught. "In fact," one SAS officer subsequently admitted, "Charles and Diana enjoyed these days out. And she would flirt like mad with the lads."

But any contentment that Diana derived was mainly from her new pregnancy. She told her sisters that "only when the baby is a lot older will he realize how lucky he is to not be born the eldest." Desperately close to William because of lack of affection from her husband, Diana added, "The second child will never have the same sort of pressures or problems that poor William will always have to put up with." And she told a friend, "I just want my children to be happy and normal.

I will do everything I can to help them achieve these very ordinary feelings." It is clear, in hindsight, that Diana was also talking about herself and how she felt then, but at the time few people were privy to the royal love-triangle which had once again been established: the prince, the princess and Camilla Parker Bowles.

Family friends of Camilla say that by the time Harry was born, again in St. Mary's, Paddington, and in the same room as the future King had been born, Charles and she were regularly seeing each other once more. Following the birth on September 15, 1984 of Prince Henry of Wales, to give him his proper title, Prince Charles started to take more and more time off from his official duties—ostensibly to be with his children. With his public engagements cut to virtually zero, the prince suddenly underwent a heavy barrage of criticism from the press and Parliament. Vic Chapman explained to me that, far from "shirking," he was deliberately taking a breather to be with the boys: "He is very well prepared to take over as King if the need arises, but in the meantime he is building up the efficiency of the Duchy of Cornwall and devoting a few years to William and Harry while they are at such an impressionable age." There was a further reason: he was hunting regularly, and not just foxes.

All this unsettled the princess and she started to become very moody and to binge-eat—she once sat in the kitchen of Windsor Castle and ate a whole rice pudding, on another occasion a whole stack of pork pies. And she started to do things calculated to irritate others. The Queen, not a woman to cross, was furious with her daughter-in-law at the 1984 State Opening of Parliament, one of the most important dates in her calendar, when Diana turned up with a brand new hairstyle, which extravagantly bared her neck for the first time. The Queen, I was told, felt that "this bit of nonsense" detracted from the solemnity of the occasion. Perhaps more to the point, the princess got her photograph all over the front page of most papers, including *The Times*. Pictures of the Queen, when there were any, were postage-stamp size.

In December of that year, at the christening of Prince Harry at Windsor Castle, Princess Anne was the first royal to make a public gesture at what she saw as Diana's increasingly tiresome behavior. She and her then husband, Captain Mark Phillips, did not attend the ceremony, an unprecedented snub. The Phillipses chose instead to go pheasant-shooting on their Gloucestershire estate. Palace officials made an attempt to defuse the situation by suggesting that the shooting party had been previously arranged and that Anne and Mark had a responsibility to their guests, but it fooled no one. Diana herself couldn't have cared less whether Anne was at Windsor or not and roared with laughter when the story was put out that she would choose Anne as a godmother to any daugh-

ter she might one day have. This was the last
thing on her mind: "I just don't like her," said
Diana. "She may be wonderful doing all that charity work for Save the Children and others, but I
can do it as well." The Princess Royal's response
to this was to label Diana "the Dope."

Following this display of mutual disregard,
Diana was asked by Charles if she couldn't try
to get along better with Anne, if only for public
consumption. At the same time he spoke to his
sister in similar terms: harmony within the royals
was paramount, he argued. But a few weeks later,
when Diana was asked whether she felt that in
any sense there was a rivalry with Anne, she was
still not prepared to be conciliatory. Her less than
convincing reply was, "None at all. Princess
Anne's been working incredibly hard for Save the
Children and I'm her biggest fan because what
she crams into a day I could never achieve." She
added, almost tongue in cheek, "We've always hit
it off very well and I just think she's marvelous."

And the Princess Royal continued to be irritated by her sister-in-law. The publicity about her
clothes and the way she was so "charming" with
everybody touched a raw nerve: charm was never
Anne's strong suit, and she always looked best
when on horseback, never on her own feet. The
fact that the public could take to their hearts
someone who could offer so little intellectually
stung her, just as it annoyed her brother. I was
told, "Anne knows a lot of this isn't Diana's fault,

but it still bugs her." It was also significant that when Anne and Mark and their children entertained the Waleses and their children, the grownups were almost never present. Anne gave lots of barbecues, but hid behind her children.

By 1985 Diana was tired of Highgrove. The house had been bought by Charles before their romance began, she felt hemmed in by its smallness—though her father was a mere earl, his house by comparison with the prince's was truly a palace, and she felt that a move might benefit them both. She felt cut off when she was there, cut off from both her friends and her interests. Also, the house was far too close to the Parker Bowleses' home. A vague attempt to look at other possible houses ensued. Charles and Diana were spotted more than once looking at the empty Belton House in Lincolnshire, a much more substantial pile, owned by Lord Brownlow and conveniently situated in prime hunting country far away from the Parker Bowleses'.

But the idea came to nothing. The couple were tied to Highgrove for a number of reasons, principal among which was that far too many wedding presents had been given that were in some way connected to the house, and the donors would be upset if the Waleses were to move away. Vic Chapman explained, "It would be rude and bad-mannered if they gave the place up. For example, the wrought-iron front gates were a present from the villagers. The swimming pool came from thousands of small donations from members of the army."

It is also the case that, because of its size, security at Highgrove is manageable. There is a safe room in the house where the family can run in the event of an attack, with steel-lined walls and doors and shutters that seal. Inside are food provisions for several weeks, supplies of water and enough medical equipment to last for months. There is also an armory, radio transmitters and other communication devices. The place is designed to withstand any sort of attack and is said to be so strong it would survive intact even if it crashed to the ground floor if the building were demolished by a rocket attack. This kind of security in a family home left Diana feeling inhibited, but Charles was entirely comfortable with it. Diana was left feeling that it was his, rather than their, home.

And Charles was at his best with the little princes when he was at Highgrove. One of his neighbors who worked part time on the land said, "The three are always together when they are here, and Charles is really good with the boys: it's more like big brother than big father and you hear Charles educating and teaching them all the time. He is incredibly patient, explaining the ways of the country and everything that is going on around them. Charles also loves taking the boys on tractors."

Another employee who worked in the house

talked loyally to me at this period about how "matters have improved dramatically between the prince and princess." After admitting there had been problems she told me, "I won't accept that the problems were that bad. You should see them all together here, they're really close. Things are much better now." But she was deluding herself, in the most decent sort of way. Like everybody else, this lady loved the idea of the Waleses, and loved the reality of them, and was desperately "willing" with all her strength for the couple to make things work. But there was never a chance while Camilla was around. And she was around constantly.

Diana and Charles began to seriously drift apart during 1985, and for the first time the princess started to carry out engagements on her own, events at which husbands would normally be expected to accompany their wives. But for Charles the notion of attending, for example, anything as frivolous as an event organized by the fashion world, even if it *was* for charity, was anathema. Nevertheless, Diana went to a charity ball organized by the designer Bruce Oldfield. She was escorted into the ball wearing, of course, a Bruce Oldfield gown. She positively sparkled, and her evening was made when, after flirting with Jean-Michel Jarre, the composer asked her to dance. She did so with almost indecent pleasure. His wife Charlotte Rampling was not nearly so happy;

it was reported that she ended the evening in tears.

At about this time Diana's former flatmate Carolyn Pride took part in a program with me for Australian television about the lives of Charles and Diana. The interviewer, Michael Barratt, asked her what the royal couple had in common. There was a lengthy pause before she finally replied, not very convincingly, "The children." I wasn't surprised at her hesitancy. From my own observations of them it was clear the couple had almost nothing going together.

And then, that autumn, the prince stopped pretending. After their usual family gathering at Balmoral, Diana left complaining of the boredom of the place and the amount of rain that fell. Charles stayed on and on after she left, making no attempt to return to Kensington Palace. In November 1985 they went on tour to Australia for the 150th anniversary celebrations for the State of Victoria. Following the rules laid down after their previous trip, they took neither child, which made Diana extremely unhappy.

That unhappiness manifested itself in a number of ways, not least in her dissatisfaction with staff. At that time I recorded that nearly forty members of staff had left since her marriage. The most notable departure had been Charles's private secretary, Edward Adeane, who, it had been made clear on his appointment, was to remain with the prince until he became King. The height of the exodus occurred between 1983 and 1985. A member of staff drew up a list of those who had left, dividing the departers into three groups—those who had been asked to leave, those who were fed up and those who left because of retirement or a career move.

In the latter category came Adeane, Charles's assistant private secretary Oliver Everett (now the librarian at Windsor Castle), their butler Alan Fisher (who told me that he left the Waleses because they were "so boring, never giving proper dinner parties"), chauffeur David Garforth and two maids. Among others who left were royal bodyguards Paul Officer (the man who was assigned to Diana the day of the royal engagement) and Jim McMaster, footman Bishnu Pun, another chauffeur, Ron Pike, maid Julie Spinelli and valet Paul Chant. During this same period, described by apologists as "transitional," the princess built up a hard core of staff who were completely loyal to her. Rival camps, even at this stage of the marriage, were being formed.

With the appointment of typically Establishment figure Sir John Riddell (Eton, Oxford, Credit Suisse/First Boston Bank) as private secretary, the Wales household went through a period of consolidation, even though Riddell did describe the press as "the enemy." The problem now, nearly everyone agreed, was the prince himself. Certainly his father was worried about how Charles was performing and to whom he was listening. He regarded his eldest son as an "intellectual pillow"—bearing the impression of the last person to catch his attention. Illustrating the gulf between them, there is a photograph of the Duke of Edinburgh in Charles's rooms. Underneath, in Charles's own handwriting, are the words, "I was not born to follow in my father's footsteps."

The duke was particularly wary of two gurus who were greatly influencing Charles at the time—the octogenarian oil magnate Armand Hammer and the philosopher (and godfather to Prince William) Laurens van der Post. These men were in part substitute father-figures, for since the death of Earl Mountbatten Charles had from time to time felt rudderless and in need of guidance. The influence over Charles by these two mentors was eyed with suspicion by Philip, who was particularly concerned with what he defined as "the buy-up syndrome." This is when a member of the royal family is made to jump through hoops in order to raise cash for a pet charity.

He particularly frowned on the arrangements for a charity dinner in West Palm Beach in November 1985. For the evening the ticket prices varied according to how close the purchaser was placed to the Prince and Princess of Wales. It led to a string of cruel but accurate jokes at their expense in Palm Beach's jet-set community. And it did nothing but damage to the royals' non-commercial image; not only was Prince Philip concerned, but Diana too.

However, Charles was in thrall to Dr. Hammer, one of the richest men in the world—he admired his global view, and every bit as much he admired his riches. Not everyone felt quite so warmly toward him. I recall being told on this same Florida visit how the dictatorial Hammer had made a late and unexpected entrance at a lunch that was supposed to be just for the two participating polo teams, Charles and Diana. The princess, sensing a man on the make even with all his riches, turned to a lunch companion and said, "Oh, my God, not that man again—I can't stand it!" Charles could, and he went down in Diana's estimation even more. It is interesting, though, that Hammer, who contributed millions to many of Charles's pet schemes, never received an official honor from the Queen. Philip's deep suspicion of the man—seconded by many others—may have played a significant part in this decision.

Prince Philip was also worried, but much less so, about his son's admiration for Laurens van der Post, the explorer and writer who had been a close friend of the psychoanalyst Carl Jung. He was the man responsible for some of Charles's more obscure-sounding thoughts on issues such as alternative medicine and Buddhism.

During a visit to Japan in May 1986 the prince admitted to a Buddhist priest that he meditated for hours at Kensington Palace. He told the Zen high priest Tensan Yasuda that he hoped his children would follow the same beliefs and find the same calm as monks are able to by deep contemplation. While there is nothing intrinsically wrong with this, there is concern that as the future Supreme Governor of the Church of England Charles should not be seen to be too closely associated with beliefs not part of the religious mainstream.

Charles's relationship with his father was always fraught with difficulty, and it is fair to say that his awkwardness in personal relationships could well stem from the artificiality of his childhood regime. While Charles tended toward being a "softie," his iron-disciplined father could not bear to see where this was leading. Poetry, the arts, philosophy—all his interests were anathema to the older man. Prince Philip's biographer John Parker noted, "Whereas Charles once saw his father as a rather god-like, heavy-duty, all-action figure whom he wanted to imitate, his new vision (as he grew older) was of a demanding, strict and heavy-handed man."

Charles's training for kingship was rigorous and unbending: "No further weaklings could be permitted in this century; Philip was going to make damn sure that his son could face the pressures." But as has been pointed out, the prince had inherited, along with his mother, the same diffident streak that was so large a part of George VI's character. But he was not allowed to let that diffidence develop, and along with learning to provide himself with a tougher exterior, he absorbed some

other things too. With a father whose days as a
roué did not quite cease upon his marriage,
Charles learned an uneasy set of rules about man-
hood which were to pay him ill in later life.

It was on this same trip to Japan that I discovered
Diana was still not eating; she was surviving on a
salad a day. I recall how her two chefs, Mervyn
Wycherley and Graham Newbold, were in despair.
The staff at Kensington Palace used to joke that
the place should be renamed Ethiopia because
both Charles and Diana were so thin. Just prior
to Japan the royal couple had been in Canada for
Expo '86 in Vancouver, and it was while visiting
the Californian pavilion that the princess fainted.
There was consternation as she whispered to her
husband, "I'm going," and then slumped to the
floor. Her bodyguard caught her and she was half
carried, half dragged away by David Roycroft, the
Waleses' deputy private secretary, and the princess's lady-in-waiting, Anne Beckwith-Smith. It
was reported at the time that there was little sympathy from the prince. Vic Chapman got his message across forcibly: "She's not pregnant. For
Crissakes she just got too hot and people were
crowding in." But later, over a drink, Vic said, "I
can tell you, she's eating virtually nothing."

But her sometimes frail condition did not
weaken her steely resolve that her husband should
not grind her down. It was at this time that Diana
made her celebrated Covent Garden "début" as

THE HONEYMOON IS OVER

ex–Royal Ballet dancer Wayne Sleep's partner.
The prince's reaction at the time was one of disap-
proval. He felt that Diana had made a spectacle
of herself, which seemed unfathomable. In retrospect what one witnessed that night was a gesture
of defiance by Diana—"Look what I can do!"

And how she liked to dance! Her sister Sarah,
coming to Diana's rescue when Charles was away
on one of his interminable visits abroad, invited
Diana to a local Lincolnshire party. I reported the
next day how Diana was still "dragging young men
onto the floor" for "one more dance" late into
the night.

Diana's main comfort in 1985 and 1986 was
the arrival of Sarah Ferguson on the scene as the
girlfriend, then wife, of Prince Andrew. In those
days they were described as best friends, but the
relationship was not to last. Following the Yorks'
summer wedding in Westminster Abbey, the
prince and princess's tottering marriage reached a
watershed. They went on a bucket-and-spade holiday with the children to stay with King Juan Carlos at his Marivent Palace near Palma on the
Balearic island of Majorca.

One day the King—a charming man whom one
or two of us who bought him drinks at the Palma
Yacht Club nicknamed "Juan for the road Carlos"—took the Wales party to Cabrera, a tiny
group of islands sixty miles off Majorca. They
traveled there on the King's £3-million, 80-knot
yacht, the *Fortuna*. A few colleagues and I fol-

lowed at a respectful distance on a yacht similar in size, if not in luxury or speed.

When we pulled into one of the tiny, idyllic bays which make up Cabrera, the royal party had no idea we were nearby. I stayed below deck out of sight and watched what was occurring on the *Fortuna* for the next five hours. It was illuminating. Everything I had believed was happening in the marriage of the Prince and Princess of Wales was demonstrably true. Not once during this lengthy period did Charles or Diana sit anywhere near one another, let alone speak. When he came up from his air-conditioned quarters to go wind-surfing, she walked off in the opposite direction. When she went diving off the back of the boat, he deliberately looked the other way. They read, they sunbathed, they chatted to others, but never once did they address a single word to each other.

I watched through my field glasses, completely mesmerized. I had heard the stories, listened to the excuses, hoped that what I had been told was exaggerated or wrong. But clearly it wasn't. The five-year-old marriage, I was forced to conclude, was dead. With no official confirmation that it was over, however, I wrote a story which was headlined "Are Charles and Di still in tune?" in which I spelt out what I had seen that hot and sunny day. I don't know why I even bothered to make a question of it.

I have since been told that following this week in the Majorcan sun the prince and princess never slept together again.

SIX

Downfall of a Marriage

The Majorca holiday collapsed, with Prince Charles quitting two days ahead of schedule, all the sooner to be in his beloved Scotland with his beloved Camilla. The official reason was that he was going fishing. He was happy to leave Diana behind with the King to enjoy two more days of sea and sun with the two children, and she was happy for him to go. The pattern of their future lives together was set at that instant. Privately they were to have absolutely nothing more to do with one another, unless the children were involved. Professionally they were determined to soldier on with no thought in their minds that the marriage would end: their union was now merely an extension of the job. Indeed, in November 1986 the royal couple quite convincingly hid their indifference towards one another to fly off to the Gulf states of Oman, Qatar, Bahrain and Saudi Arabia. The following February they made a joint visit to Portugal.

It was here, for the first time on a tour such as this, that I learned that Charles had one bedroom and Diana had insisted on another—palace aides tried to dismiss this, but hotel staff confirmed it. With this added breathing space, we also saw for the first time in months Diana back in skittish mood: at a gala ballet evening in Lisbon she astonished a beribboned gathering of the country's luminaries by twanging the braces of the country's president, Mario Soares, in full public view. The president was pleased enough at this outrageous flirtation but Charles was less relaxed: he thought her behavior unacceptable on a state occasion— but Diana didn't give a damn.

Not that Charles was on top diplomatic form either. On one particularly dreary morning, with the scudding clouds bringing in rain from the Atlantic, the royal couple were listening to a dismal speech from the Mayor of Lisbon, delivered at snail's pace while everything was translated. The prince turned to a few reporters standing nearby and muttered, "Can anybody tell me what I am supposed to be doing here? In *Lisbon*? In *FEBRUARY*?" The answer to Charles's question was very simple: he was there because his prime minister wanted him there. Margaret Thatcher needed his presence to cement Anglo-Portuguese relations at a time when the country, sponsored by Britain, was applying for membership of the European Economic Community. For the same reason the prince and princess were in Spain a couple of months later, on a trip that was to spell the end of any remaining relationship between Charles and the popular media.

On each royal visit, for many years, the prince and princess had given a reception for the traveling press, the idea being that the two sides could have a frank exchange of views on neutral territory. It was understood that all conversations were off the record, but journalists, using their discretion, could utilize any information gleaned for background material. In theory the system worked well and had the added advantage—to the royals—that they could themselves score some points. Once Diana good-naturedly remonstrated with me for writing about her wearing thermal underwear—accusing me of looking up her skirt with my binoculars and for writing too much about her clothes. But on recent tours the system had started to break down and the Waleses had found themselves being quoted directly.

At the Spanish media reception we were given a final warning from Vic Chapman. "Look, you guys," he rasped, "for Crissakes remember the rules. You don't go out and write *anything,* otherwise that's it." We agreed, despite the fact that Diana was peculiarly hyped-up and talking incessantly. But an hour later a photographer came rushing in to say the Spanish national news agency was filing an extraordinary story, quoting Prince Charles talking about ETA, the IRA and terrorism. Talking to a group of Spanish journalists who had quizzed him about whether he was worried that Basque separatists might have a shot at him, Charles had apparently replied that he was a fatalist: "I feel that if your name's on the bullet there's nothing much you can do about it." It was a good story and the Spanish journalists, who rightly reasoned that they were unlikely to meet the prince again for several years, immediately broke the off-the-record rules and filed their stories, citing the prince by name.

The British contingent, after consulting Vic Chapman, followed suit—the story was already winging its way round the world anyway. What, we ventured the next morning, did HRH think of this? "Not a lot," growled Chapman. "In fact he's Goddam furious." How furious we were soon to discover—Charles said he would never hold a media reception again. The princess later resumed them on her own account in the autumn of 1991, by which time she had mentally ditched her husband and just about everything he felt or believed in.

But at the reception in Madrid in 1987, Diana was in full flow when she suddenly said, "When we first got married we were everybody's idea of the world's most perfect couple. Now they're saying we are leading separate lives. The next thing is I'll start reading that I've got a black lover." I asked the princess whether the rumor that she was expecting another child was true. She patted her tummy and said no, very firmly. Someone else asked her if it was true that she and her husband were drifting apart. I watched, fascinated, as she talked of "the truth about our so-called separate lives." She said, "It's very simple. My husband and I get around two thousand invitations every six months. We can't do them all but if we split them up, with him doing some and me others, we can fulfil twice as many." It's hard to know why Diana spoke so supportively of Charles at that reception: she knew that at the end of the week he was going off on yet another solo visit, this time to Bologna, Italy, to collect an award for his book *The Old Man of Lochnagar*. She also knew that following the ceremony he was going on a painting tour of Tuscany, staying in Florence and Padua. And she worried that the chances of Camilla Parker Bowles slipping out to be with him were high.

By then the princess was fully aware of Charles's affair—but at this stage she didn't care. She had reconciled herself to the idea of only rarely seeing her husband. In June I gauged that Charles had taken at least seven partnerless jaunts, including one celebrated trek into Africa's Kalahari desert with Sir Laurens van der Post. The *News of the World* kept a scoresheet of how often the couple met. It recorded that in a three-month period Charles and Diana had spent thirty-five days away from each other. Official duties were to blame for some of the absences, but the prince actually chose to be away from his wife for twenty-six nights. A new pattern had become established: in February, after eight days of skiing, Diana left early to return to London; in March Charles went skiing in Switzerland while Diana stayed at home; then in April Charles babysat William and Harry at Balmoral while Diana went to Kensington Palace. At the end of April he was back in Italy, ostensibly to gaze at the art, in fact to meet Camilla discreetly; then in May he flew alone to a remote Hebridean island where he spent three days helping farmers on the land.

Marriage-guidance counsellors murmured that the royal timetable was a cocktail for disaster, even though frequent separations were the norm for members of the House of Windsor. After the early, shaky realization that theirs could never be a marriage in the conventional sense, Diana was now ready to relax and enjoy the freedom this new arrangement gave her. On her skiing trip in February—the first time the Yorks and the Waleses had holidayed together as married couples—Fergie invited along Philip Dunne and David Waterhouse. At this same period the princess started to develop her hobbies. Two or three times a week she would play tennis at the Vanderbilt Racquet club in Shepherd's Bush, west London, and she stepped up her keep-fit exercise classes. But she allowed nothing to take precedence over her children: she adored them and took comfort from them. No matter what engagements she had, she would take them to school each morning, arranging her schedule so as to be home in time for their return. And with a full diary of official engagements to occupy her—it was at about this time that she first began her AIDS work—the princess was determined to fill whatever empty moments there were in a social way. She was a lady who lunched, a lady who shopped and a lady who met friends and gossiped. The only thing that was missing was any sort of relationship with her husband. If this period of her life seemed bleak it was to get worse. Her friendship with the Duchess of York seemed to attract adverse publicity: their larks led the public to believe she was leading a gilded life free from care while a recession was starting to bite. Although professing not to read about herself in the newspapers, she always seemed to know about the negative pieces. After a few such pieces appeared in print, she told me, "A couple of days later the postman arrives with a big bag of hate mail that somehow gets through. I read it and I do get upset."

By the fall the cracks in the Waleses' marriage were becoming plain for all to see. At the end of September I wrote that every senior member of the royal family, from the Queen downwards, had begun to realize that many of their fears about the Prince and Princess of Wales were coming horribly true. Diana, bored with her stuffy husband, was spending almost no time at all with him. She was going out at nights with anybody other than Charles.

Even when he was around she was avoiding dinner parties with her husband in their own home; dinners, she complained, "were with boring old men, clever and worthy though they might be." Instead of graciously hosting such evenings she would go to bed early. It was clear that 1987 was the year when Prince Charles stopped trying to persuade his wife to join him at these parties.

When I talked to a guest at one of these evenings I was told, "We would ask where the princess was and would be told, 'Oh, she's just feeling tired and sends her apologies.' Later, we would learn she'd been to the cinema or theater and had then crept up to bed on her return to the palace." Then, in the same patronizing tone Charles so often used about Diana, the prince's friend added, "Quite honestly, I think this was sensible of her because mentally she just couldn't cope with the conversation, which was philosophical and highbrow. That's the sort of talk the prince encourages at these evenings. If she'd been there he would have been embarrassed and annoyed with her, being forced to explain what was being discussed. Charles is no towering intellect, but he does read a lot and can hold his own in conversation."

Her absence from these soirées was no great loss to Diana who, notwithstanding her husband's patronizing attitude, was growing in confidence daily. She had begun to relish the knowledge that she was a highly desirable woman, that she was a world star and worshipped by the masses. Previously this sort of thing had terrified her, but, as she charted a course for herself without Charles, the knowledge of it buoyed her up. The moments of weakness in front of her husband, though increasingly rare, were still there however. A security man who worked at Kensington Palace told me of hearing the princess sobbing in her bedroom while he was doing his rounds. He reported that he heard her saying to Charles, "You had a difficult upbringing with your father; why can't you understand your problem? You should." Charles, reported the guard, failed to respond in any way.

The day the Klosters avalanche was triggered—March 10, 1988—was the day Diana finally hardened her heart against her husband. It was a perfect skiing day and the prince was on the piste early. We lunched at the same place, the Conterser Schwendi, but then, because the temperature had gone up and the afternoon skiing wasn't looking good, I went back to the village. The prince kept going. He is a good, extremely fit skier, but not as good as instructors encourage him to think.

What happened next has been analyzed many times since; how, after pushing his party to go down an off-piste run when there were clear signs warning them not to, Charles was forced to take responsibility for the tragedy that followed. An equerry, Major Hugh Lindsay, died, and a friend, Patty Palmer-Tomkinson, very nearly lost her life, taking many months to recover from her injuries.

But what upset Diana above and beyond Hugh Lindsay's death was her husband's—to her—inexplicable attitude to the affair. Diana told Hugh's widow Sarah, who was pregnant when he died, that she would never set foot in Klosters again, yet Prince Charles was back there the following year, skiing away as if nothing had happened. Such insensitivity chilled her blood.

There was an amusing (for my colleagues) by-product of that day. I spent four hours in the local jail after being arrested for apparently running away from a car crash. Having heard that the avalanche had taken place—first reports said that Prince Charles was dead and that both Princess Diana and the Duchess of York had been injured—I rushed from my hotel to the bottom of the Gotschna cable lift. On the way I skidded on a bend and grazed an oncoming car, whose Swiss occupants did not speak a word of English. I tried to communicate with them for three or four minutes but, failing to do so, I went to find out the full extent of the accident up the mountain. After discovering that neither Diana nor Fergie had been involved at all I was grabbed by a Klosters policeman for leaving the scene of an accident. Despite all protests I had to accompany my inquisitor to the police station where I was incarcerated—although I was kindly let out for twenty minutes to file a story to my newspaper. Months later, I was found guilty in my absence and fined the equivalent of £300.

Soon after this incident Diana's friend Carolyn Bartholomew (neé Pride) was horrified to discover that not simply were the princess's nerves jangled by Major Lindsay's death, but that the princess's bulimia had now become severe. A specialist explained to Carolyn that chronic deprivation of vital minerals could lead to depression and tiredness. Her duty, she felt, was clear. Carolyn telephoned Diana to say that either she should contact a doctor or she would go to the press. The princess was recommended to a Dr. Maurice Lipsedge, a specialist in eating disorders at Guy's Hospital in London. In this unstable state, it has been reported, Diana finally confronted Camilla Parker Bowles at a fortieth birthday party for Camilla's sister, Annabel Elliott. She is alleged to have said, "Why don't you leave my husband alone?" but I am told by friends of Camilla Parker Bowles the confrontation never happened.

But in any event Camilla and Charles were now accepted as an "item" in the circle in which they moved. Said one, "Everybody knew they were in love, and having an affair. They never made any secret of it among those with whom they stayed." In May 1988 Charles, and probably Camilla, was on another visit to Italy when he was informed on his way there from Paris that Harry had been taken into hospital for an emergency hernia operation. He immediately offered to fly home but Diana said no. It did not take long for the world to learn that she had refused to go home after the operation at Great Ormond Street Hospital, preferring instead to spend the night dozing in a chair at the foot of her son's bed. She learned from the following day's glowing headlines just how easy it was to score a hit off an absent husband. Charles was furious.

At about this time Diana's father Earl Spencer spoke up for his daughter, trying to defuse the stories of marital disharmony which were gathering momentum by the minute. He spoke to *Woman's Own* magazine about his daughter as a wife and a mother, and allowed a frank admission that Charles and Diana had had "the odd row." It was a touching interview, charming and supportive as one would expect, but it showed how completely out of touch with reality he was. Lord Spencer dismissed the rumors with a wave of his hand, saying, "They're trivial, just like mosquitoes. Of course Charles and Diana have their rows, what couple doesn't? But they are nothing out of the ordinary. What makes it so different for them is that they're on show the whole time. They might have had a disagreement, then they have to step out in front of the cameras and pretend that everything is going well—and that's not easy." He added, "She's still very much in love with Charles." And then he went on to discount stories saying that Diana and Fergie had fallen out: "Of course all that stuff is nonsense—the two of them are great friends. Her arrival has made things much easier for Diana. She was so thrilled when Sarah and Andrew got married. After all, Diana was the matchmaker."

But the earl was wrong. By mid-1988 Diana was beginning to distance herself from the duchess. I recall Vic Chapman telling me, "They're very different animals. One is the Duchess of York while the other is the Princess of Wales, a very superior person. They both know their positions and they don't forget them."

Things had changed. In 1982, on Diana's twenty-first birthday, Sarah was the only person to turn up for lunch at Buckingham Palace. The Merry Wives of Windsor became a laugh-a-minute double act, or so it seemed, and just weeks after her wedding the newest member of the House of Windsor was, in the words of *People* magazine, "a wildly popular co-star in the royal road show." This was particularly so in the United States. Diana was for many a little too cool, a little too reserved to be admired—not so the duchess. The Americans loved her relaxed, boisterous, up-front act—if *she* could make it to the top, they argued, anyone could.

And Fergie was so much better equipped to handle the Queen. They went riding together, they could converse easily and the duchess actually enjoyed having lunch with her, which most certainly was not the case with Diana. But Diana had developed a fine sense of smell for impending trouble and the duchess had started to upset people. In many ways she was too honest: when she felt something she showed it, when she wanted to say something she would do it without thinking of the consequences. For a time it was refreshing, but only for a time.

The year had begun well enough for Fergie and her family, but when it was announced in November 1987 that she was pregnant and she confided that the baby hadn't been planned—"I'm not that worried," she said, "but I wouldn't have had one now by choice"—the news was received in chilly silence by the public. A trip by the Yorks to California was seen by their American hosts as a success, but back home they suffered a particularly vicious attack in the *Sunday Times* under the headline "The Duke and Duchess of Yuk."

In Australia later that year she talked to me frankly about the adverse publicity she was suddenly attracting: "Of course I get hurt when attacked. I try not to show I'm upset but it does get to me." Personally, I found her candor refreshing, but palace officials disapproved—and the streetwise Diana thought she was crazy to give so much away. Fergie, she assessed, was an accident waiting to happen. She offered to help her sister-in-law on her return from Australia, but the help was rejected. And then her father was discovered to be a regular visitor to a seedy massage parlor in London's West End. No amount of assistance from the princess could help Major Ron.

And now the princess had problems of her own to contend with. Her marriage continued to deteriorate at an alarming rate, her husband was spending more and more time with Camilla—he used to confess to close friends, including Major Ferguson, "I just want to be with her all the time"—and though Diana was trying to have fun of her own with "available" men, she was forever frightened she would be caught up in controversy. It was a miserable existence. Which makes all the more remarkable her capacity to lose herself in the sorrows and joys of others. In May 1990 I watched with fascination as the princess, during the playing of the Hungarian national anthem, took the hand of the new president's wife; Zsuzsa Goncz, following that country's release from Communism, was overcome with emotion, and was crying. It was not done ostentatiously; in fact, none of the photographers spotted what had happened until they looked closely at their films after I had told them what I had seen.

People observed that Diana's most engaging trait was the ability to be thoroughly modern in her role. Relaxed, cheerful and energetic, she was regarded as largely disproving the Victorian constitutionalist Walter Bagehot's decree that to retain the royal mystique, "We must not let in daylight upon magic." People felt that however much daylight Diana was subjected to, she rarely revealed a blemish.

A member of her personal staff told me that, in an unsanctimonious way, she felt it was her duty to improve the lot of others and at the end of 1989 she resolved to start visiting the children of the Third World. Commenting on this at the time I said I was sad that she was undertaking this new stage of her career without her husband at her side. She said, "I will be going solo on these trips. My husband is too busy with his own organizations." But actually she had discovered a new role for herself, one which did not require her to be an adjunct to the Prince of Wales but allowed her to be someone in her own right. This development was prompted by television footage of starving children, coupled with a briefing from Bob Geldof.

Diana's aide told me that Diana's work priority for the nineties was "the family unit." He said, "This applies not only abroad, where economic circumstances often force families to split up to survive, but in this country too." Another commitment made by Diana was to give additional time to Relate, the organization formerly known as the Marriage Guidance Council. Her aide told me, "The princess wants to make everybody aware of the tremendous importance of marriages working." The organization's spokeswoman, Zelda West-Meads, spelt out the difference Diana's royal patronage would make. In 1988, before

Diana had become officially involved with the charity, it raised from various events a total of £9,402. In 1989, after Diana became patron, that figure soared to £238,976. Said Miss West-Meads, "Before the Princess of Wales started actively supporting us we hardly dared put on a gala film première because we couldn't sell the tickets. And if we had a charity ball we might have raised £8,000. Now with the princess's involvement we would be looking to raise £30,000 to £50,000." The charity was beguiled by her commitment: once during a visit Diana was reminded it was lunchtime. Because she was listening to what someone was telling her, her response was, "Oh, blow lunch." Another time she attended the Family of the Year award, which Relate had organized. I was at this small lunch that day in Park Lane, and her speech was full of hidden depths. She said, "I have seen the tears, the anguish, the raw emotions, hurt and pain caused by the split between couples."

Certainly the princess's own personal relationship with her husband was a disaster. Writing an article as their tenth wedding anniversary approached I highlighted three public events in which Diana—and I would think the prince too—suffered. My story was written just after Diana had commented that she had "never been happier." I listed three examples which showed just how far their relationship had gone downhill.

The first was November 8, 1988. The setting

was the River Seine in Paris and the occasion had been planned as an evening of relaxation for Prince Charles and Princess Diana during a hectic visit. The idea was to allow the couple to savor an evening of magic on one of the boats which glide down the river, while a gourmet dinner was served by candlelight. It was a disaster for virtually everybody: as the band played "I Love Paris" there was a sourness in the air coming from the prince and princess which could not help but communicate itself to their hosts. I had asked a member of the band to tell me later how the couple enjoyed their evening. He reported that they had not looked at each other once, nor had they addressed a single word to each other all evening.

The second episode was on August 2, 1990, the occasion, a special evening at Buckingham Palace arranged by Charles for the Queen Mother as part of her ninetieth birthday celebrations. The prince rushed about checking that everybody was comfortable before the concert, given by the London Symphony Orchestra, with music specially written for the evening, began. Diana went up to her husband to ask gently where one of her friends should be seated, but Charles couldn't even be bothered to turn round to look at her. He told her to "sort it out," then went back to fussing over an ancient European royal who had flown in for the occasion.

The third date was September 10, 1990, a traumatic day in the lives of the Wales family: Prince William was to begin at boarding school. Dozens of photographers were at Ludgrove Preparatory School, near Wokingham in Berkshire, to witness the event. A couple of them were to be allowed to the front door to record for posterity the moment the young prince stepped out of the family car to shake hands with the joint headmasters, Gerald Barber and Nicol Marston. It all looked very cozy—but it wasn't. Much of the occasion I witnessed was a sham. Although Charles, Diana and William appeared to arrive together in their Turbo Bentley as a family unit, the true story was less appealing: Charles, still suffering a badly broken arm, had driven the car from Highgrove. Diana and William on the other hand had driven in her Jaguar XJS from Kensington Palace, where they had spent the weekend. The two cars slipped into the school grounds through a back entrance a few minutes apart. Their actions concealed by laurel bushes, the princess and William then transferred from her car into the Bentley. Then, together, the family drove the hundred yards or so to the front door for the arrival. After saying farewell to their son—which made Diana cry—the departure took place in reverse: Charles and Diana got back into the Bentley, drove out of sight back to Diana's car, then parted company. She drove back to Kensington Palace, he went to Highgrove. Their meeting, which lasted for a total of thirty minutes, would mark the last time they would see each other for thirty-nine days.

At that time I thought it inconceivable that the

two might separate, let alone divorce, but there were no indications as to how little Charles was working to save the marriage. A significant factor in the worsening of the relationship was Charles's accident at the Cirencester polo ground in June 1990, when he fell from his pony after some particularly rough play. So severe was the fall that spectators a hundred yards away heard the crack of his arm breaking.

Initial surgery did nothing to heal the break, and Charles was finally moved to the University Hospital, Nottingham, where space was cleared for him and new furniture brought in. Ostensibly he was treated as a patient of the National Health Service, but few of his fellow patients were accustomed to the attention he received.

During the long summer that followed, the prince only allowed one person to nurse him: Camilla. Diana went to Highgrove from time to time but the joke among staff was that as she drove in one entrance, Camilla was driving out of another. Comments that Diana made about her rival were passed on to me by staff and polo friends. At first muted, they became angrier and angrier.

Camilla was now regarded by their friends as Charles's official hostess in Gloucestershire. She boasted about the roses she was growing in the Highgrove garden, she threw dinner parties for Charles and she sunbathed in the grounds in a bikini while Charles pottered in the garden nearby. Set against the standards of most civilized people, this behavior was outrageous. A neighbor told me, "It was as if neither cared who saw what was going on. They were, to all intents and purposes, living as man and wife." There was even a story from one of the estate policemen who guarded the property, that he had found the prince and Camilla in a downstairs room making love.

Charles and Diana endured another joint holiday with King Juan Carlos in Majorca for the sake of the children, but even then the prince went there early, and when Diana arrived with the boys he took his sketchbooks and disappeared. He couldn't wait to finish the holiday and get up to Scotland once more. In America *People* magazine warned that the marriage was "a fake" and a "pretense sustained only because of the messy constitutional problems that would arise from a formal separation or divorce."

It was in the early summer of 1991 that stories started to emanate from Gloucestershire that Diana had been warned she would have to accept that a certain amount of time was set aside for Camilla. This started to circulate as Charles and Camilla were discovered on holiday in Italy. She was on her own, she said, he was on *his* own—their trips just happened to overlap. Camilla protested there was nothing wrong in the arrangement, but her relationship with Charles, a secret for so long, was now in the public domain.

If there was initial public approval of this hitherto little known woman it was prompted by her curiosity value when matched against the flawless icon Diana. But meanwhile, backstage, Diana was taking a drubbing from Charles's powerful friends: she was seeing too many mystics, fortune tellers, aromatherapists, soothsayers and other strange "experts." People were beginning to say she was "loony" and that she had become dangerous and unpredictable. And even Diana's own self-denigrating phrases—with which in the early days of her marriage she had put people at their ease—were now being hauled out to be used against her.

Gritty and resourceful were not among the adjectives used by Charles's friends to describe her, yet in June 1991, when Prince William was hit on the head with a golf club by a fellow pupil at Ludgrove, these were the very qualities that bubbled instantly to the surface. As William was rushed to hospital while calls were put out to both parents—typically, Diana was having lunch in San Lorenzo and Charles was at home in Gloucestershire—it was arranged that the royal couple would meet at the Royal Berkshire Hospital in Reading. Both parents were shocked and upset but it was a steely Diana who controlled what happened next. As Charles dithered, suggesting that William should go to the hospital in Nottingham that had fixed his arm, Diana told him to shut up. Although the consultants were stunned at the ferocity of the princess's command they responded instantly when Diana asked where was the best place for her injured son. Without hesitation they nominated the Great Ormond Street Hospital in London. Addressing her husband in just the way he had come to address her, Diana uttered a curt order as she left the room. She didn't even look at her husband as she said, "You heard what was said. Fix it!"

The whole drama was to turn to Diana's benefit. Later that day Charles was due to host a party of European environmentalists and British ministers who were arriving at Covent Garden to see *Tosca* at the Royal Opera House. The engagement had been planned for months and had already been postponed once because of Charles's broken arm the year before. When William's accident occurred and an operation could not be scheduled until eight-forty that evening, Charles was ready to cancel. But the consultants said he should not; it was a straightforward operation and there was no need to worry. They urged Charles to keep to his plans—and so did Diana. "It's all right," she said, "just go." But the newspaper headlines the next morning trumpeted his lack of judgment: "What sort of a Dad are you?" bellowed one. Diana, the one who stayed at the hospital, again smiled to herself.

She allowed herself another small triumph in September 1991 when she undertook her first solo tour to Pakistan. It was rated a huge success. India the following February was less rewarding, as Diana was back as the distaff side of the Wales team, bickering about whether she and Charles would sleep in the same suite at the Viceroy's Palace in New Delhi. They didn't—she slept on a different floor.

Even in the early days of 1992, which the Queen was to call her *annus horribilis*, there were unpleasant rumblings on the royal scene. Anti-hunt saboteurs barracked the prince while he was out with the Meynell Hunt and, losing his cool, he barked back, "Shut up!" But the next day he was forced to adopt a more conciliatory tone when an onlooker, watching him take William and Harry to church, yelled, "Where's Di?" With a pained expression he fell back on the old chestnut: "She's not here today, so you can get your money back."

The increasing speculation on the state of the Waleses' marriage briefly took a back seat to allow the lesser royals center stage. The popular and pretty Lady Helen Windsor, daughter of the Duke of Kent, announced she was to marry her long-standing boyfriend Tim Taylor. A week later intimate photographs of the Duchess of York and Steve Wyatt surfaced. Wyatt tried to dismiss the incriminating pictures as a "joke," but the damage had been done. During the next five days, while Fergie was in Florida with her father to promote a charity polo match, she denied being intimate with the Texan—in itself a gross error of judgment. And it convinced no one.

The Princess of Wales's deliberate distancing of herself from Fergie proved justified as, on her return to London, the duchess suffered what some described as a "mini nervous breakdown" in her first-class seat. She had made phone calls at Miami airport to both Wyatt and her husband, and had concluded both in tears. On the flight, fortified by champagne, the duchess started throwing wet towels, peanuts and tissues. Then she put a sick-bag over her head and started making telephone noises into it. Her father, trying his best to calm her with the help of Sarah's bodyguard John Askew, admitted she was "deeply troubled." Unsurprisingly, in an opinion poll which followed hard on the heels of this demeaning display the duchess was nominated as the person who had done most harm to the royal family. At the other end of the scale Diana topped the poll as Britain's favorite royal, comfortably outstripping her mother-in-law and her husband.

But at the same time the princess made a rare tactical error. Against Buckingham Palace's habitual buy-British policy she took delivery of a leased Mercedes-Benz 500SL sports car, valued at £72,000. Some argued this was a statement saying, "I'm my own woman and I'll do what I want," but the car was not British, and motor manufacturing bosses labeled her irresponsible. Initially she refused to acknowledge her mistake, but within a few months the car was returned.

And so began the Indian tour, yet another foreign minefield for the Waleses to traverse. Diana posed alone for pictures in front of the Taj Mahal, built by the seventeenth-century Moghul emperor Shah Jehan—a romantic edifice at the best of times, but made all the more so by a dashing bachelor Prince of Wales who promised some years before: "One day I will come back and bring my wife with me." In the event his wife went by herself. The prince was in Delhi, unromantically addressing a group of business leaders, and once again miscalculating the balance between doing good locally and providing photo-opportunities for a voracious and impatient outside world. He shunned the anticipated photo-call outside the Taj Mahal because of its gruesome superficiality, yet a photograph of him and his wife at the world's greatest temple to love would have been the lasting image of the tour. Instead the image that is retained is of the Prince of Wales looking a complete idiot.

On the eve of St. Valentine's Day the couple were in Jaipur, the temperature was in the high eighties and Charles had just played a hectic game of polo. As usual bored by polo, the princess had sat on a balcony to watch the second half of the match, but now Charles was standing in line with his teammates to receive a trophy from his wife. For the whole of the previous week there had been some fairly intense speculation as to whether they might kiss, giving the serried ranks of photographers a picture for their front pages on the most romantic day of the year. Once, I recalled, it had been normal practice for the royal couple to kiss one another on the lips at the end of a game—they obviously enjoyed doing so. But that seemed like a long time ago. Now the air was heavy with expectation. Would they or wouldn't they? The answer was not slow in coming as I watched one of the cruelest, most public put-downs of any man by his wife, executed in front of a hundred professional cameramen and 5,000 laughing Indians. With triumph in her eyes, Diana waited until her husband's lips were almost on hers, then she turned her head away. Not so fast that Charles would be able to pull back—no, it was much more calculating than that. Instead, she moved her head to the left, slowly. Charles who knew the world would see what happened next—television was there too—politely and gallantly tried to follow Diana's turning head. He chased it all the way round until he could reach no further without falling over. He ended up kissing Diana half in mid-air, half on her gold earring.

Four days later Diana wept as she listened to nuns sing a hymn written by their leader, Mother Teresa of Calcutta. As if by way of atonement for her extraordinary public cruelty she then moved to the mission's hospice where she sat on the beds of dozens of incurables as they lay waiting to die. The patients were so ill they were unable to take either solids or liquids. Their one comfort came from something sweet that they could slowly suck, and Diana sat gently dropping boiled sweets into their open mouths. Such horrors seemed to boost her; she seemed to gain an inner strength from them.

Two or three days after returning to Britain the princess arranged to fly to Rome to see Mother Teresa, who had earlier been taken ill and had been unable to get back to India to greet Diana on her tour. They met, they prayed together and Mother Teresa prayed for Diana and her personal happiness. The meeting was deeply uplifting for Diana and, I was told, it strengthened her resolve to forget her own problems and to concentrate on others who were far worse off. She had given herself a new mission.

Back in London, toward the end of March 1992, it was announced that the Duke and Duchess of York were to separate. Fergie was no longer a member of the royal family: she could not represent them any more, she no longer warranted a bodyguard of her own (though her two daughters did). The following day a deeply sad Prince Andrew declared, "It is a very difficult time for me," while solicitors started to draw up settlement plans. Unlike the Waleses, the Yorks maintained a civilized relationship following the separation, and a couple of days later Andrew and Sarah enjoyed a candlelit dinner together at the family home before attending a showbiz party given by Elton John. Then, for the sake of the children, the Yorks gave a second birthday party for Eugenie the following week. If divorce is a battle, this was the phony war.

On April 13, an event I had forecast in 1989 finally came to pass: Princess Anne began divorce proceedings against Captain Mark Phillips and immediately attention turned to her romance with a former equerry to the Queen, Commander Timothy Laurence, a serving naval officer. Forces within Buckingham Palace put out negative stories about Tim, and I was told that the "old guard" did not like a former servant making eyes at a Princess Royal. Newspaper columnist Sir John Junor had warned Anne earlier: "Keep your hands off the hired help." Everyone studiously avoided making references to the fact that Laurence's family name had originally been Levy, but one could not avoid the idea that it was his Jewish ancestors who were in their thoughts nevertheless.

Charles and Diana were allowed a brief publicity respite as the spotlight turned once again to the Duchess of York. She quietly and suddenly disappeared just before Easter for a holiday with her two daughters, apparently slipping out of Southampton on a private plane and flying to Germany where she caught a scheduled flight to Thailand. Her cover was blown when three days later the *Daily Mail* published an out-of-focus photo of the duchess with a bald-headed man, quickly identified as John Bryan. It became clear that Bryan had masterminded the holiday, successfully keeping her moving ahead of the pursuing press pack. By the beginning of May Fergie and her children were in Indonesia, still ahead of photographers who were after them. On May 8 I flew to Jakarta to accompany the duchess and the children back to London: Fergie looked tanned but terrible. This could be accounted for by subsequent suggestions from close friends that she had suffered a miscarriage. One told me, "She lost a lot of blood, and a doctor had to fly out from England to give her more."

Shortly after, a television documentary showed Prince Charles digging potatoes and pulling lobster pots in the remote Scottish island of Berneray. Meanwhile, the subject of the documentary flew to Turkey for a holiday, while his wife undertook another solo tour, this time of Egypt. Such was the cynical view of the health of the Waleses' marriage that several newspapers dispatched reporters to Turkey to try and catch Charles with Camilla Parker Bowles. They were unlucky.

By the end of the Egyptian tour it was patently clear that Diana had the capacity to be an ambassador for Britain in her own right. Certainly she was happier being in charge of her own show; when, later that month, the Waleses traveled together to Seville in Spain for the Expo World Fair, she was noticeably unhappy.

On June 7 the book Diana apparently sanctioned was serialized in the *Sunday Times*. Yet within a week she was a member of the Queen's party at Royal Ascot, riding the storm and effectively telling the inquisitive, "It's not over yet." But though Charles and Diana left the racecourse together, a mile down the road they separated and she drove back to London rather than stay at Windsor, which she had done in previous years. One afternoon during race week I watched Prince Philip snub Diana in the royal box—as she walked in, fresh from the carriage drive down the course where she was applauded wildly by thousands, he studiously ignored her. I noted she didn't seem particularly to care.

A week later it was reported Diana and Charles had had a crisis meeting with the Queen during which Diana said firmly, "I know my duty." The implication was that Diana would not walk out of her marriage, and indeed the couple were together at the end of the month when the Queen cele-brated forty years on the throne with a dinner party whose guests included five British prime ministers, past and present.

At the beginning of August the Wales family made one last effort by jetting off together to Greece to join a holiday cruise provided by the shipping billionaire John Latsis. The trip, though luxurious, was a disaster: the princess insisted on her own cabin and quarters and on eating with the children. There were also reports toward the end of the voyage that the princess caught Charles, more than once, taking telephone calls from Camilla. Did Diana really care any more? I think not. By this stage of her married life I think she just wanted out.

According to people who worked for the Wales family, the prince had begun in the early summer a campaign of verbal abuse against his wife. One Kensington Palace employee told me how the prince would spit at Diana, "You stupid woman," or, "You silly young girl," over and over again. He said, "It was awful. I felt so sorry for Diana. But it was obvious the two hated each other and I knew that the couple were bound to separate. I could tell by the way they talked to one another." Another employee heard arguments between the prince and princess, during which Diana would tell her husband to "shut up" and he would reply, "I can't stand living with you." He said, "Diana cried really hard. Then he told her that he didn't like the way the children were being brought up; that she was far too casual with them and didn't respect their positions in life. And he told her that he thought her encouragement of the boys to go Go-Karting all the time was stupid. That actually stopped Diana crying. She just said to him, 'Oh, shut up.' "

On another occasion, at Marble Arch, a witness who saw the royal couple passing by in their official car watched in fascination as Diana tried to force open her door and get out while the car was moving, after a particularly vicious exchange of words. The witness, a road-sweeper, later told me that the princess was hysterical and crying. He said, "She was clearly saying something like, 'I've had enough of this,' and then I watched as a man in the front, who I presumed was a detective, held her back."

Other Kensington Palace employees told how Sir Robert Fellowes and Charles Anson would openly discuss the Waleses' collapsing marriage. This was between June and August 1992, four months before the official announcement. In the end the marriage might have staggered on into 1993, as Sir Robert predicted it would. Diana's early announcement spoiled the Princess Royal's wedding to Tim Laurence. Anne had earlier been quoted as saying in a rather pompous way, "I'm not getting married just to bail those two silly girls [Diana and Fergie] out."

With August came the publication in the *Sun* of the Squidgy tapes. At first Buckingham Palace denounced them as fakes, but pretty soon they said they weren't sure. The end was now very near: the remaining differences revolved around the children, about whom both Charles and the princess were enormously concerned. Indeed, putting their personal problems to one side, they managed to link up for a rare joint outing to take Harry to Ludgrove prep school for the first time in early September. That was a day of misery for Diana—for the first time she had to return to Kensington Palace all alone, without anyone to greet her except the staff. The next day the prince and princess made an official visit to Nottingham, but the crowds noticed that the couple did not exchange a single word with one another. Soon after that it emerged that the Queen's lawyers, Farrer's, were asking historical and constitutional experts whether the prince and princess could part and still leave the monarchy in one piece.

By early October Diana was under attack from within the royal family and was suffering. Her brother Earl Spencer decided that somebody should speak out on her behalf: "Diana has warmth, love and femininity, all very rare qualities. She is probably unique." A week later Diana attended a Relate conference and heard a sociologist describe how it was always the children who came out worst in a marriage breakup. A counsellor told me that day, "Of course Princess Diana knows this, that is why she hasn't walked away yet. But I think it's getting close."

At the beginning of November came the infamous tour of Korea. It was clear to me from the way Charles and Diana behaved toward one another that everything was now lost. On November 20 Windsor Castle caught fire, and on November 24 the Queen, standing in the ancient Guildhall in the City of London, talked of her *annus horribilis,* a Latin phrase rendered slightly less surprising when it was discovered to have been borrowed from a letter of sympathy sent by one of her more erudite ex-employees. Despite all the auguries, when the end came on December 9 1992, it was still shocking. The prime minister rose to address a packed House of Commons with these words:

> It is announced from Buckingham Palace that, with regret, the Prince and Princess of Wales have decided to separate.
>
> Their Royal Highnesses have no plans to divorce and their constitutional positions are unaffected. This decision has been reached amicably, and they will both continue to participate fully in the upbringing of their children. Their Royal Highnesses will continue to carry out full and separate programs of public engagements and will, from time to time, attend family occasions and national events together.
>
> The Queen and the Duke of Edinburgh, though saddened, understand and sympathize with the difficulties that have led to this decision. Her Majesty and His Royal Highness particularly hope that the intrusions into the privacy of the Prince and Princess may now cease. They believe that a degree of privacy and understanding is essential if Their Royal Highnesses are to provide a happy and secure upbringing for their children while continuing to give a wholehearted commitment to their public duties.

Those who questioned the wisdom of handing the prime minister the job of reading out the Buckingham Palace statement were confirmed in their beliefs when Mr. Major, in reply to the barrage of questions shouted at him, stated that there was nothing to stop Diana eventually becoming Queen. Even in the heat of the moment such an idea seemed absurd, and once the implications of this unprecedented statement had time to sink in, it became even more so.

That same day I wrote about the "End of a Fairy-tale." It was rather more personal for me than for any other royal commentator. I was the only one who had been in at the very beginning, and now I was reading the last rites.

SEVEN

Spencers at War

It could be argued that, because of the events it triggered, the death of the 8th Earl Spencer had more historical significance than his life. Though the Spencer line was long and distinguished, Johnnie's life had been remarkable for its lack of achievement.

Apart from a particularly ugly divorce in the late 1960s, and a brief spell as equerry to King George VI and then the Queen in the early 1950s, there was little of note to draw him to the attention of the newspaper-reading public. The private battle he waged to preserve the roof of his country house is one familiar to many Englishmen in his position. It might have daunted a lesser man, but Spencer accepted it as the burden of privilege. His career was typical of his class: Eton, the cavalry, member of the county council, High Sheriff. By virtue of his birthright he was able to interview and appoint vicars of the twelve parishes around

Althorp, Northamptonshire. But though he was a member of the Turf Club and Brooks's, his name did not figure in the membership book at White's. Whatever he may have appeared at first sight, Johnnie Spencer was no grandee.

His early life on the Sandringham estate, which brought him so close to the royal family, is well recorded. Less well documented is Spencer's darker side, which manifested itself in a number of ways. Though his appearance to the outside world was avuncular and jolly, the treatment of his first wife spoke of a less sunny nature, and though Spencer spoke warmly and often of the relationship with his youngest daughter, it was not always reciprocated, as we shall see.

To understand Diana's relationship with her father and mother, it is necessary to go back to the late 1960s. Spencer, then Viscount Althorp, was living and farming in Norfolk. He and his father hated each other and kept apart for much of Johnnie's adult life. Though they had little in common, one thing they did share was a ferocious temper. This took his bride, the Hon. Frances Roche, daughter of the 4th Lord Fermoy, by surprise. Nevertheless she bore him five children: Sarah, Jane, a boy who died the day he was born, Diana and his heir Charles.

But after thirteen years of marriage Lady Althorp had had enough. The word in society was that she was a "bolter," who ran off with the man she subsequently married, Peter Shand Kydd.

Certainly when it came to a separation she lost custody of the children. And when divorce followed, it was again Lady Althorp who lost. But in order to understand the deeper tides running in the Princess of Wales, it is important to re-examine what actually happened. Here is what Lady Althorp, now Mrs. Frances Shand Kydd, says about the matter:

In the summer of 1967 Johnnie and I agreed to a trial separation. It was decided that I should take Diana and Charles with me to London, where they would both go to school in September—Sarah and Jane were already at boarding school.

A furnished house was rented in London and Diana, then aged six, and Charles, who was four, were enrolled at a girls' day school and a kindergarten respectively, both of which had been seen and approved by Johnnie.

In early September I left Park House (at Sandringham) and drove to London. The following day Diana, Charles and a nanny were put on a train by Johnnie and came to live with me. During the school term the two children returned to Park House most weekends to see their father, who in turn came to stay with us on his trips to London. In October I joined him and all four of our children, including Sarah and Jane, at Park House for the half-term holiday.

The whole family were reunited again at Christmas at Park House. It was my last Christmas there, for by now it had become apparent that the marriage had completely broken down. Johnnie now insisted that Diana and Charles should be sent to school in King's

Lynn, not far from Park House, and that they should thenceforth stay at the house with him.

He refused to let them return in the New Year to London. I strongly objected to this, and in a court action in June 1968 sought that the children be allowed to live with and be cared for by their mother. I lost the case and the custody of the children.

But this is only part of the story. Mrs. Shand Kydd's upbringing would never allow her to say that her husband was a wife-beater, but there was little doubt in the minds of Norfolk society—and in the wider world—that it was so. Years later Erin Pizzey, who set up the first battered women's refuge in Chiswick at around that time, turned to novel writing and used her knowledge of the Spencer marriage, gleaned from friends, to write *In the Shadow of the Castle,* which gives a terrifying account of wife-beating in high society.

Though Frances lost her custody case—hardly surprising when even her own mother Ruth, Lady Fermoy, turned against her, as well as a host of Johnnie's high-powered aristocratic friends—it was she who instituted divorce proceedings. In December 1968 she sued Johnnie for divorce on the grounds of his cruelty.

Shattered by the fact that she had left him, and fearful that the details of his cruelty to her would become public, Johnnie launched a massive counterattack designed to squash his wife at all costs. His lawyers cross-petitioned on the grounds of her adultery with Peter Shand Kydd. In the climate of the late sixties, she didn't stand a chance. She had lost the custody battle and she had found herself another man. Bruises disappear, but adultery does not.

When the divorce was heard on April 15, 1969 Spencer won. He was given a decree nisi and his wife offered no evidence on the cruelty charges. She had been told by her lawyers she had no chance, and that it would be far better for her if she went without a fuss. The humiliation was complete: she was not allowed to air her justified grievances, she had lost her children *and* she was ordered to pay £3,000 toward her husband's costs. And Johnnie's barbarous behavior was compounded by her mother giving evidence against her. Penny Junor understands it this way: "She really could not believe that her daughter would leave a belted earl for a man in trade."

Some have suggested that it was the motherless years that brought a shadow over the Spencer children. But those who know the family ascribe both Diana's bulimia and Sarah's anorexia to the violent scenes which went on before Frances Shand Kydd finally quit. To be left in the custody of a man they knew had been unkind to their mother was a burden they had to endure throughout their childhood. Significantly, just before Johnnie's death all the children were in touch with their mother; they were barely speaking to their father.

All this was of no significance the weekend Earl Spencer quite unexpectedly died. His death brought about the ultimate public breach between Charles and Diana. After that, no one had any faith the marriage could ever be restored.

Admitted to hospital suffering from pneumonia on March 22, 1992, Earl Spencer gave no indication that his condition was in any way life-threatening. Though there had been a certain coolness between them, Diana was naturally concerned as she made final preparations to take William and Harry off on their annual skiing holiday. But after a couple of reassuring telephone calls from the consultant surgeons looking after Lord Spencer, she saw no reason to alter her arrangements. The plan was to return to Lech, the Austrian resort Diana had adopted after the accident in Klosters.

Told that her father was expected to return home on the following Tuesday, Diana set off with the boys. She was following the dismal pattern of the previous year, when Charles had taken his skiing holiday separately from the rest of the family. That decision, in 1991, had cost him dear in terms of personal popularity, and he was heavily criticized for not accompanying Diana and the boys. Buckingham Palace officials and members of his household had predicted in private conversations with me that such a public split with his family at holiday-time would create problems, but there was little they could do to counteract it and Charles was in no mood to listen. The only excuse they could feed to the press, and a lame one at that, was that Charles had to go up to Scotland that particular weekend because he had some important speeches to write. The truth, which I subsequently uncovered, was slightly different. Camilla Parker Bowles was also in Scotland that weekend on the Balmoral estate, the place, ironically, where Charles and Diana first went on returning from their honeymoon cruise on the royal yacht.

In private conversations with officials I repeatedly queried the wisdom of Charles going to Scotland: Diana's appearance on the Austrian slopes without him would give rise to further speculation about the state of the marriage. The speeches were a feeble excuse, because surely he could ski all day and work in the evenings. But the truth was that Charles had no official engagements at that time, and all he was doing was spending time with Camilla while the focus of attention was on Diana and the boys on the ski slopes. Charles's behavior seemed unduly cynical.

Nonetheless the criticism must have stung the prince, because this time it was announced at the very last moment that he would join his family for a few days at Lech. Diana had taken a wing at the end of the Arlberg Hotel, and it was agreed he would join her there. This was a major disaster for Diana the gilded media manipulator, who by now had perfected her act as mother-protector of the boys and wanted no assistance from her husband. I began to suspect a flanking maneuver by Charles's supporters, and I was not disappointed.

The prince flew in from Milan on the Friday evening. The press had been alerted to the time he would be arriving at the hotel, and between forty and fifty photographers gathered in anticipation. Three or four minutes before Charles was due I noticed William and Harry in the hotel foyer, hiding behind the front doors, waiting for their father to arrive. Suddenly it became apparent that this was to be a very public greeting: the little princes were being wheeled out to perform a cynically constructed PR exercise for their father's benefit.

The presence of Scotsman Philip Mackie started to make sense. A part-time member of the Buckingham Palace press office (jocularly known to those he dealt with as the Silly Ghillie), Mackie had been in Lech for a couple of days. It was obvious that his job was to make sure this "informal" encounter between father and sons went off smoothly; his role as liaison between the Princess of Wales and the press was merely a convenient blind. The previous year, on an identical holiday in identical circumstances, no one had felt the need of his undoubted talents.

Attracted by the jostling banks of photographers, a crowd had now gathered outside, and although William and Harry were in view there was no sign of Diana: I later learned she had been banned from the photo-call for her husband; this was an attempt to establish that Diana was not the only parent in the children's lives.

With radio contact between Charles's car and the hotel established, William and Harry appeared on the steps with thirty seconds to go. As the car pulled up they both raced up to their father excitedly and kissed him.

Normally photographs of such an encounter are difficult to achieve as the opportunity is rapidly past, but on this occasion there was at least a minute for the photographers to get what they wanted, and the pictures duly appeared the next day.

This maneuver was an indication to me that the tide had turned. While it is difficult to accept that Charles would have personally ordered such a blatant photo-opportunity, it could not have happened without his consent. All indications were that the impetus came from Commander Richard Aylard. But this new initiative ran counter to my other conversations with the commander, when he had told me there would be no attempt by the prince's side to engage in media manipulation.

But by this stage things were collapsing badly: few were left in any doubt that the marriage was in real trouble. Diana's intuitive use of her public engagements to foster sympathy for her cause, and the extraordinary ability she had to be photographed with the princes, had led to a one-sided view in the public's mind: Diana the caring mother, Charles the remote father. Something had to be done.

Next morning there was more. Having arrived at Lech Charles was now expected to deliver to the media happy-family shots of the Waleses disporting themselves on the Austrian ski slopes. There was a brief foray onto the slopes, with the family surrounded by aides, friends, detectives and photographers. Diana seemed remarkably tense and distracted. When the entourage, which had struggled up on the T-bars and chairlifts, hit the top of the mountain I found myself next to her and we had a brief and rather bizarre conversation. Pointing at my skis, Diana asked, "Are you going down on those?" I replied, "Well, yes, that's what skis are for, Ma'am." Then she said, "Wouldn't you rather I gave you a piggyback down the mountain?" It was most peculiar. Her nerves were clearly very jangled by Charles's presence, and she was trying to reassert herself in a situation where her husband seemed to have stolen the initiative. For once she was coming out second-best in the publicity war, and she didn't like it. He'd won the opening round the previous night and she was trying to get back—and as she went down the mountain with the boys she was giggling a lot and was clearly very wound up.

The whole circus was repellent to Charles. On the one hand he was pleased to be with the boys and to see that they were skiing reasonably well, on the other he could not bear to be near his wife. He didn't like the gang of press people, and he hated the way she was behaving with them. It was a very uncomfortable experience for him, but it was obvious that he felt the need to go through with it.

The family did a simple run down to Oberlech, but as they went back up to start another, Charles veered off to the other side of the piste so there was a vast gap between him and Diana and the boys. And of course the photographers went after Diana. By then he'd had enough and in the afternoon he went off with a guide and his bodyguard to ski by himself over much more difficult terrain. A further attempt at a "togetherness" photo-call the next day failed just as miserably, and though Charles tried to spend time skiing with his family he eventually went off again by himself. At the end of the day Charles took the boys out for an impromptu snowball fight. It could not have escaped his notice that the spot he chose was in direct line of vision of the Schneiderhof Hotel, where many press photographers were staying. The pictures that appeared the following morning showed Charles as he would like to be seen—as a father who enjoys ragging around with his sons. At first sight it appeared that he'd achieved the public-relations coup he was looking for. But the headlines which accompanied the pictures told a different story.

For the previous day, while Charles and Diana were straining to make their marriage seem a going concern, Lord Spencer had suddenly and unexpectedly died.

He had entered the Humana Wellington Hospital in St. John's Wood, north London, apparently suffering from mild pneumonia. Though severely weakened by a stroke in 1979 which had all but killed him, Lord Spencer had remained tolerably well in the intervening years. The decision to spend a few days in hospital seemed no more than a wise precaution, but unknown at the time was the fact that a team of six heart specialists was drafted in by Countess Spencer to attend her husband. Ferocious in her will to preserve her husband's life, Raine was still exhibiting the steely determination that had seen him through a massive stroke thirteen years before. Consultants agreed that Spencer was in poor shape and that his condition had deteriorated over the past six months, but he was expected to survive even though he was incoherent at times. The condition manifested itself in a number of different ways, but he was prone to spasms of bad temper and by the end was almost impossible to understand.

Staff, pleased to have such a famous patient, paid particular attention to Earl Spencer's needs. As they bustled in and out of his room they came to the conclusion that urgent business still needed to be done at Althorp: Spencer went through at least one, possibly two, check books that week, signing check after check for Raine to take away. Clearly both wanted everything to be in apple-pie order.

On the day Diana had flown out to Austria, Lord Spencer had been inspected by the cardiac team, who had predicted he would be able to go home in the next few days. His son was quoted in *Hello!* magazine, saying, "He is very well. I haven't seen him so well in years." It was on that basis alone that Diana had continued with her holiday, having twice telephoned a consultant to check her father's progress.

When Lord Spencer died, Raine was on her way to Althorp for Sunday lunch. She had visited her husband that morning, repeating the daily routine she had established on the first day he was admitted to hospital. She arrived just after ten-thirty and went to sit with her husband. But after about half an hour staff reported hearing what they later described as "a hell of a row." It had become difficult to understand what Spencer was saying, but he was clearly very upset about something. He was finally heard to explode, "Get out! Go away! Leave me—go!"

Unfortunately these were the last words Spencer would speak to the wife who had so devotedly looked after him. Just over an hour later as she arrived home she was told that there had been a setback in Spencer's condition and that she should return to London immediately. She turned around and drove back, but by the time she arrived at the Wellington her husband was dead,

after an heroic ninety-minute battle. Four surgeons, led by cardiologist Dr. Rodney Foale, had
tried everything they could to revive him from a
massive heart attack, but his heart had been so
severely damaged by the 1979 stroke that there
was nothing that could be done.

Raine's manner on arrival startled some of the
hospital staff. She walked in "very grandly and
very composed," according to one member of
staff, and said, "Would you like to tell me about
it." The details were given to her and then she
was asked if she would like to see her husband.
She replied, "I am hungry and I would like to
eat." Startled staff found a nurse with a menu
who asked what she would like. She was shown
into the sitting room which had been hired for the
duration of Johnnie's stay and she commanded, "I
do not wish to be disturbed." Half an hour later,
after a lunch of smoked salmon, she emerged,
composed, and went to see her husband.

The specialist team was waiting for her with
further assurances that Spencer's death had been
inevitable. They suggested that an autopsy should
be undertaken, but on this she was resolute. "Absolutely not. I don't want one," she said forcefully,
adding that the very idea of autopsies had always
distressed her. Not wishing to upset her further
the team agreed.

By arrangement, the new Earl Spencer waited
until his mother had left the hospital before making his appearance. The two no longer spoke to

one another, and Charles Spencer blamed his stepmother for the deterioration in relations between himself and his father. Indeed, the acrimonious quarrel between father and son remained unresolved at Johnnie's death.

That may have explained the heightened sense of distress displayed by Charles as he entered the hospital. Staff felt that his agitation was close to hysteria as he kept saying, "What should I do? How can I cope with this?" One of the consultants took him to one side; a nurse heard him say, "You've been on bad terms with your father—why don't you go in and make peace with him? Go in, sit there and talk to him. Say how sorry you are you didn't manage to make it up before he died and how sorry you are there was this conflict in the first place."

Charles, who was crying and in a confused state, looked down at his jeans and said, "I'm not even dressed to go in." It was gently explained to him that it didn't matter how he was dressed. He was told a nurse would be put on the door and no one would disturb him. Eventually he went in and spent forty-five minutes alone with his father, talking to him. Later he admitted that the advice had been right, that he had been able to unburden himself and as a result felt much happier.

Nevertheless, as he left the hospital the new earl made a heavily pointed remark. "It is a matter of great regret that no one was with him when he died," he said, bitterly. At the time his comment appeared to be one of self-blame; in the light of subsequent events it would seem to have been more directly pointed at his stepmother.

Meanwhile, Diana was making desperate attempts to get home. Though she insisted that she must pack and leave immediately it was explained there were no scheduled flights that night and it would be far too difficult to get to Zurich: it was two hours' drive and a specially ordered Queen's Flight plane would need at least eight hours notice before it could receive clearance to land.

A temporary truce came into force between the warring prince and princess, and Charles agreed to take the boys out to supper to give Diana time on her own. An interim plan to fly the whole family out next morning was drawn up, but then it was decided that to spare their feelings it would be better for the young princes to finish their skiing holiday and miss the funeral.

At RAF Northolt, after the Bae 146 of the Queen's Flight taxied to a halt, Charles descended with Richard Aylard and for a minute or two they stood talking on the tarmac. Suddenly, framed in the doorway, was the sight of a stony-faced Diana struggling with a heavy bag. As she came down the steps, photographers froze the image—unfeeling Charles deep in conversation, tragic wife carrying her own luggage.

Of course it made headlines the next day. But I was told by one of Charles's aides, "It wasn't like that and it was so unfair that it should come

out that way. Diana insisted she didn't want anybody touching her case. Charles had offered, but
she'd said she could carry it herself."

So was it Diana, who knows in an instant how
to create a powerful photographic image, up to
her old tricks? Or was Prince Charles's disinformation machine at work? Either way it was not a
fitting image for a future Queen, and it compared
unfavorably with a similar one from another age—
when the new Queen Elizabeth II flew in from
Nairobi to face her father's death forty years
before.

Johnnie Spencer's funeral marked the final public breach between Charles and Diana. The prince
made a fleeting appearance at the thirteenth-cen-
tury church of St. Mary the Virgin at Great
Brington, Northamptonshire, then flew back to
London in a royal helicopter before the funeral
reception was half over. He did not wait for the
cremation service. Buckingham Palace stated that
Charles had an "important" meeting with the
Crown Prince of Bahrain, but such meetings can
be easily moved to accommodate special circumstances. Similarly, Charles had delayed his arrival
in Northamptonshire till the very last moment,
leaving Diana to drive up from Kensington Palace
by herself. The "prior engagement" that kept him
from his wife's side on this occasion was a meeting with some anonymous businessmen.

Diana had instructed that a wreath from her
should be just that—Charles would have to send

a floral tribute of his own. Later palace officials tried to suggest to me that there was a mix-up which had resulted in separate wreaths, but they were not convincing. Charles's behavior since her father's death had angered Diana so much she wanted to make a bold statement of her new independence. The card that accompanied her wreath said poignantly: "I miss you dreadfully Darling Daddy, but will love you forever. Diana." Charles's more reserved inscription read: "In most affectionate memory," but in truth the two men hardly knew each other.

Naturally the public noticed. The funeral was a public-relations disaster for Charles, but a coup for Diana. Red-eyed with grief but looking stunning in a broad-brimmed black hat, she managed to convey the idea that there was a *rapprochement* with her stepmother after sixteen years of acrimonious family warfare. *The Times* misjudged the mood completely and headlined their funeral report: "Earl Spencer goes to rest at peace with his family." But things were not quite what they seemed.

In his oration Lord St. John of Fawsley, ever-conscious of the headlines, reminded the congregation unnecessarily of the recent bickering in the family. "Birds twitter and peck in their nests," he observed, "even when they are gilded ones. But love is not so easily disarmed. Johnnie loved all his family, but had a special affinity with the Princess of Wales." Well, up to a point, murmured some members of the congregation to themselves.

Diana and Raine, who had sat on opposite sides of the church, walked out together behind the oak coffin with its simple spray of daffodils. But Lady Spencer's personal assistant, Sue Ingram, remained unconvinced by the sudden and apparently spontaneous show of affection by Diana. "Perhaps I sound cynical but the sight of Diana reaching for her ladyship's arm at the funeral service made me feel quite sick," she said. "Her ladyship was bemused, but not surprised. The graveside note about missing her 'Darling Daddy' just did not make sense. She hardly ever saw him. She hadn't been to Althorp since her brother's wedding in 1989 and she made very little effort to see him in London."

This is borne out by others, who paint a picture of a mournful Spencer arriving at Kensington Palace to see his daughter reportedly only to be told she was too busy. On one occasion he was turned away, on another he was allowed in to see his grandsons but did not get to see his daughter.

Early on the earl had had to face up to the fact that he would never be seeing a great deal of William and Harry. With energy and enthusiasm he had bought two houses at Bognor Regis, then a third, thinking that this was where the boys could escape the pressure of court life and have simple bucket-and-spade holidays. He'd enjoyed similar holidays on the same beaches in the 1920s in his pre-Eton days, and fondly recalled the excitements of the English seaside.

But seven years after the birth of Prince William neither he nor Harry had paid a single visit to the two main houses, Trade Winds and La Hacienda, and it became clear they would never see the treehouse their grandfather had had built for them. Instead, bucket-and-spade holidays were to be had in the company of King Juan Carlos of Spain at his Majorcan retreat. Even when the Waleses didn't go abroad for a summer holiday they still spurned Johnnie's open invitation, and in 1989 he put the houses up for rent, another dream evaporated.

The sticking point in all this, of course, was "Acid" Raine. Though she had been married to Johnnie Spencer longer than her predecessor Frances Shand Kydd—and by every account it was clear he was happier with his second wife—it made no difference. She was reviled by the Spencer children to a quite extraordinary degree.

By far the most startling manifestation of this ill feeling came from Diana herself. On the eve of her brother Charles's wedding to Victoria Lockwood in 1989, when the princess was staying at Althorp, Raine arranged a family tea party at which Mrs. Shand Kydd was a guest. The countess poured tea and ensured that her husband's grandchildren were being properly catered for.

She left the nursery for a moment and was followed by Diana, whose face was flushed with rage.

At the end of the passageway that connected the nursery with the grand staircase, and just as Raine was about to descend the flight of stairs onto the landing, Diana shot forward, seemingly catching her stepmother from behind and sending Raine flying forward onto her knees. Frightened and shocked, the countess, then fifty-eight, found herself crashing down the steps, ending up in a heap on the landing. Before she could struggle to her feet Diana had sidestepped her and strode off back to the party.

The scene was witnessed by Sue Ingram, who later recalled, "I wanted to run upstairs and ask her ladyship if she was all right, but I was too embarrassed, not only for myself but for her. The servants and I pretended that nothing had happened—we just looked away."

But later, in the privacy of her bedroom Raine asked her, "What has happened to Diana? Why such an occurrence? I just don't understand that girl." The answer, as she probably knew, lay in the nursery, where the two wives of the 8th earl had circled each other warily, barely speaking to each other. Diana, witness to this uncomfortable stand-off, had sensed a snub and taken her mother's side.

Such behavior was merely a continuation of what Raine had endured from her husband's children for many years. To Sarah, Jane, Diana and Charles she exemplified the fast, glossy, metropolitan approach to life that jarred with their more rural, aristocratic upbringing. While Diana was still dressing herself in Laura Ashley, Raine went to Paris and clad herself in Balmain.

Possessed of a quick mind, and multi-lingual, Raine had arrived at Althorp with a half-page of her achievements already listed in *Who's Who*. The dozing stately home had never seen anything so exotic; Sarah once sourly asked Sue: "Tell me, what does my stepmother look like with wet hair?" Word among the aristocratic house parties in the mid-1970s was that Raine held Johnnie in sexual thrall. That did *not* go down well with the children, who felt their father's affection was being seriously diverted.

During her seventeen years of service with the Spencers, Sue Ingram witnessed a variety of tactics employed by the children against their stepmother. They would laugh at Raine behind her back and walk out of rooms when she entered, while Raine herself recalls how Jane refused to speak to her for the first two years of the marriage, and how as a boy Charles Althorp threatened her.

What may have been childish pranks gradually hardened into an uncompromising hatred. Jokes were nothing short of cruel—salt was poured into Raine's drinking water; poison-pen letters were sent; any attempts by their stepmother to win the children's friendship were met with sullen silence or a rebuff. Sarah and Jane would change her orders to the staff. All three sisters were rude to her in public. Christmas cards were sent to "Darling

Daddy and Raine" and thoughtful and expensive Christmas presents from the countess would be rewarded with packets of soap or drawer-liners. In fact the endless reappearance of these became a standing joke between Lady Spencer and her assistant.

But in the face of such unremitting hostility, Raine would occasionally crack. "Lord Spencer would ring me at home some evenings and ask me to go round because her ladyship was in floods of tears and he was unable to cope," recalled Sue Ingram. The countess's tears would evaporate as she tried to dismiss the problem. Nothing was ever going to change their feelings, she told her secretary. She had tried everything, to no avail. Why go on bothering to try to understand their behavior?

By now, Charles was living with his new wife at the Falconry, one of the larger houses on the 13,000-acre estate, and only dropped in to the big house to collect his mail. One September night, Charles asked to see his father and stepmother in the library at Althorp.

The meeting between father and son was to prove painful and destructive, escalating at one point to near-hysteria with Charles screaming at his father. Johnnie's response was despairing: "If that is what you think of me . . . fine," and from then on the slightest misunderstanding would ignite Charles's temper. He had taken on the role of managing the estate and when he found out that his father had questioned one of the employees about a brace of pheasants, he waited until he knew that the earl and countess would be leaving the house. He drove to a halt in front of his father's car, causing it to come to an abrupt stop, walked over to his father and once again began to shout at him to mind his own business and never again to question *his* workers.

The earl was speechless, but it was only history repeating itself. His own father, the 7th earl, was a difficult man with a short temper and the two did not get on—which is why Johnnie had chosen to go and live on the Sandringham estate all those years before. Althorp wasn't big enough for both of them. Now with this confrontation mirroring his relationship with his own father, Johnnie could only shake his head in bewilderment and hurt.

That Raine endured this unremitting hostility with such equanimity was remarkable, but it was born of years of practice. What did infuriate her, however, was when the snubs extended to take in other members of her family.

Earl Mountbatten of Burma's former private secretary John Barratt recalls Diana's humiliation of Raine's mother, Dame Barbara Cartland, at the time of the royal wedding.

> I assumed, as everyone did, that Barbara would be going to the wedding, and soon after I received my invitation I asked if she had received hers. She told me she was not getting one, and asked me if there was anything I could do about it.

I went to see if Michael Colbourne, who worked in the Prince of Wales's office, could intercede. I heard that her name had been taken off the list of guests on the express instructions of Lady Diana, who said she did not want Barbara Cartland upstaging her on her wedding day.

I really resented this. I knew that Diana and her siblings did not get on well with their stepmother. But she had not been the cause of the breakup of their parents' marriage, and when their father was desperately ill she nursed him devotedly.

I told Michael that the one way of making sure that Barbara would upstage the bride was by not inviting her: it fed a great story of family disunity to the hungry press, who were devouring every titbit about the marriage.

Barbara was distraught—really deeply hurt. I would like to think that if Diana had known how much she hurt an old lady she would have reconsidered her actions, but she was very young and naïve then, and for some crazy reason the palace advisers let her have her way. Barbara asked me if she should go abroad for the wedding day, but I told her it would make her look as though she had been banished.

Then I had a brainwave. Barbara had always been very active in the St. John's Ambulance Brigade, so I suggested she give a party for the St. John's volunteers in her district. I told her it was imperative she did not dress up in her usual over-the-top finery, but that she should wear St. John's uniform. Which she did, with the net result that she got great credit for it—masses of coverage in all the newspapers—and was thrilled to bits. Had she been one of the hundreds of famous guests trooping into St. Paul's Cathedral she would hardly have been noticed. Although it would be going too far to say she upstaged the Prince and Princess of Wales, she came as near as anyone could.

The ritual humiliation never let up. Johnnie Spencer had made a provision in his will to ensure that after his death there would be a smooth transition to the new regime at Althorp: he ordered that Raine should be given six months grace in order to organize her affairs before moving out to make way for the new earl. Instead an unseemly row broke just days after the funeral. Neither the countess nor her personal assistant were in the least surprised. The new earl had told staff often enough, "The moment my father dies there will be three taxis at the back door. One for Raine, one for Sue and one for the estate manager, Richard Stanley." His decision was endorsed by Diana and the other sisters.

Why? "They always hated their stepmother. They felt she was a gold digger after their father's money and status," says Sue. Indeed, such was the ill feeling of the Spencer children that when Sue arrived at Althorp immediately after the earl's death she was told she was not allowed to touch anything in the house. In the week between Johnnie's death and funeral, more humiliations were to come. When she called to collect Raine's papers she faced a similar reception, and a few days later she was made redundant.

And when the countess herself tried to enter the house with a roll of red stickers to identify which property was hers, she was told she would have to supply proof of purchase to the executors of the will before the items could be removed. And still it went on: when her maid Pauline arrived to collect Raine's clothes, Diana and her brother Charles positioned themselves outside one of the side doors of the house.

"What have you got in there?" demanded Diana as the maid emerged carrying two Louis Vuitton cases embellished with the Spencer "S." "Those are my father's cases. They don't belong to you." The maid replied nervously that they were her ladyship's clothes and the suitcases had been bought for a trip to Japan. There were four cases, the other two with the initials "RS."

Both Charles and Diana stooped down to examine the contents, and ordered everything to be transferred to plastic dustbin liners; the cases would remain with them. Another dress bag was brought down and Diana laid it on the ground, unzipping it and feeling inside between the layers of clothing before kicking it to one side.

"The Spencer children did not come near their stepmother after their father's death," says Sue Ingram. "She had to telephone the new earl for details of the memorial service, and he told his solicitor to send her a fax." She was not invited to the ceremony when her husband's ashes were placed in the Spencer vault.

All she had wanted was to be their friend, so they could gather together occasionally, as a family, in an atmosphere of love and respect. But her steely determination to cure Althorp of its financial ailments was as repugnant to them as it was vital to her. Who, they asked themselves, was Raine to tell them how to turn their family business into a going concern?

Her problem, of course, was that she was cleverer than the Spencers—too clever, probably. She saw Althorp as a wasting asset, a dilapidated house that needed brightening up and reviving; a family business that needed some pep put into it.

Silver and paintings were sold to get the renovations under way, a move which caused the final showdown between the Spencer children and their stepmother, whom they blamed wholly and completely. "A lot of mischievous gossips talked about vans leaving Althorp packed with paintings and furniture—absolutely true," says Sue Ingram. "The vans were packed with goods but they were being taken to restorers and cleaners, not the sale rooms."

The Princess of Wales also jumped to the wrong conclusion on at least one occasion. On spying an empty space on one of the walls she demanded to know where the picture was. When Raine tried to calm her, explaining the picture had been sent away to be cleaned, Diana refused to believe her. The painting had to be brought back in order to satisfy her. Charles Althorp shared her fears. When the earl and countess were in London, usually from Tuesday to Thursday, he could be seen walking round the house with a briefcase full of papers, checking to see if anything had disappeared.

Admittedly not all Raine's ideas were successes. The immense dining room at Althorp was redecorated at breathtaking cost in a bizarre shade of blue, and the souvenir shop where she and Johnnie would meet the tourists face to face sold rather tacky items. Diana was infuriated at the idea of rubbernecking members of the public being able to buy themselves a place at dinner with the earl and countess, and loathed the idea of a £75-a-couple Wine-and-Dine Lovers' Evening where Johnnie poured the wine and a pianist tinkled romantic melodies in the corner. She felt no better about the hordes of Japanese who increasingly were filling the house with their chatter and their cameras.

The snide comments about Raine's determination to refurbish the entire house angered Spencer. Sensing that the breach with his children was more or less permanent, he said that Diana had been on the telephone to him. "I think it's Raine's new décor she doesn't like. But she has done a magnificent job, nobody could have done it better. She's a natural interior decorator—all the pictures have been cleaned and relined and the furniture has been re-covered. I love it."

He was also loving every moment of his new-found entrepreneurial activities. But the pressure between the earl and his children continued to grow and, towards the end, he abandoned all hopes of a *rapprochement* with any of them. In September 1991 he indulged himself in a rare public outburst, railing at the children—and particularly Diana—who had turned against him. "I have given Diana a hell of a lot of money—between £500,000 and £1 million to invest for Harry," he said. "Diana doesn't understand about money. She has no experience. She is too young." And, he added bitterly, "Why she has to make such a fuss I don't know, because she seldom visits—only at Easter and Christmas."

Raine joined in. Referring to the young Spencers' complaints about selling off the family heritage, she said, "I don't make the decisions to sell paintings or cottages." Pointing at her husband she added, "I take my orders from him. He tells me what to do and I do it. This idea that I have some great influence is not right. These possessions are his to do what he likes with." Warming to her theme, the countess went on, "Do you think that for one minute if I didn't love Lord Spencer that I would put up with all this hassle and bad blood? I don't need it."

Referring to her nickname Acid Raine, the countess added, "All these names go over my head. I'm only interested in John and what he is trying to do for posterity. He loves Althorp and everything we have done with it."

The earl and countess were beginning to feel under increasing pressure, not only from the younger generation, but from a burgeoning press interest in their private affairs. Newspapers itemized the family heirlooms which had gone missing—including eleven Van Dycks—and estimated that over two hundred significant items had been taken from the house and sold. More than one publication sent a reporter with a fine-art expert to check the official photographs of Althorp's treasures against what remained.

The schism in the Spencer family over the sale of works of art and heirlooms could no longer remain private. Jokes about the patches on the wall at Althorp did the rounds, and indeed there did seem to be some point to them.

Johnnie Spencer hit back at his critics, claiming the sales were vital to fund a £2-million restoration of his house, and he accused his children of "financial immaturity," saying they were "ungrateful" and did not understand the responsibility of owning Althorp.

The implication was that his children were stupid, and Diana, as we have seen, came in for special mention by her father. But she got her revenge. Come Christmas and Johnnie's regular party for the grandchildren at Althorp, rumors began to circulate that neither Diana nor the two princes would be going—that the four-month rift between her and her father was as wide as ever. In the end the boys went, though "public engagements" kept the princess herself away.

This made up Johnnie's mind and he shamelessly began to exploit the family heritage. His wife's entreaties to make money in the Orient were at last to bear fruit. He even boasted to me that Raine had learned Japanese so she could further her commercial ambitions. In late 1991 it emerged that Spencer had effectively flogged the family name, title, crest and arms to the Japanese. More, he had sold his daughter's wedding dress, or so it appeared at first. In fact, it turned out to be merely replicas of the Emanuel gown—but Spencer was forced to acknowledge that he was debasing the family coinage by such commercial activity. He told his son he was going to do "this rather awful thing." A highly placed source at Althorp was quoted at the time, saying, "He was almost apologetic. He agreed it was somewhat tacky."

It triggered another row between the earl and the viscount. The argument intensified when it emerged that a second merchandising scheme, even cheekier than the first, was also on the cards. This involved Spencer lending his name to something which proposed to call itself the Royal Spencer Golf Club. Based at Kushiro on Japan's northern island of Hokkaido, it would offer membership to social aspirants at between £26,000 and £80,000 a time. In return the Spencers would receive a licensing fee.

As the news emerged, the Spencers rather guiltily left Britain for the South of France on a short holiday. But the storm clouds grew, for even discounting the matter of taste in lending the family name to an industry that, in Japan, was linked to scandal, corruption and organized crime, there was also the matter of the word "royal."

Critics lost no time in pointing out that Spencer himself was not royal, nor had the family ever been. His daughter was royal by virtue of her marriage, but that was all. I learned that Buckingham Palace officials were beside themselves with rage because of Johnnie's blatant breach of protocol—he'd been an equerry, after all. He knew the ropes, and should have known better. Not the least of his critics was his son-in-law, Sir Robert Fellowes. It became known that Spencer had not been sanctioned to use the word "royal," nor had he applied through the proper channels in order to gain such sanction—and that as far as the Queen was concerned, Spencer was now *persona non grata*.

Whether by the combined efforts of his four children, the special influence of his youngest daughter or the power of his son-in-law, Earl Spencer and his wife were sidelined by the Queen, becoming as Mark Phillips before them and Ronald Ferguson after them not so much royal in-laws as out-laws. If Spencer, with his long history of family service and duty to the Crown, recognized this dynastic ruthlessness and accepted it, Raine never did.

The fuss rumbled slowly away into the distance, and the Spencers' commercial plans continued unabated—as indeed they needed to. Flying back to Britain after another meeting with their Japanese paymasters, they discovered just how much they were going to have to rely on the land of the rising sun. A homespun, money-spinning venture to turn Althorp into one of Britain's major equestrian centers had run aground. The plan was that Althorp would be the backdrop for the final Olympic Trials to pick the British team for the Barcelona games, but sponsors dropped out and an estimated £50,000 income evaporated.

All the grandiose plans, in the end, came to nothing. Before the first ball had been played down an oriental fairway, before the first Japanese bride was able to try on her Lady Di lookalike gown, the 8th Earl Spencer's earthly remains were transformed to dust on April 1, 1992. The same day his wife was forbidden her home for ever.

At Johnnie Spencer's memorial service in that traditional shrine for the great and the good, St. Margaret's, Westminster, Raine gently acknowledged the tributes given to her late husband. Prince Charles, who had sent her a five-page handwritten letter after Johnnie's death, had the decency to turn up. The Queen sent a former private secretary. Some other royals attended, though not many.

Raine, Countess Spencer walked out into the weak May sunlight and accepted the public kisses of the stepdaughter who once pushed her down the stairs.

EIGHT

The Way Forward

The virtually unbroken line of Britain's monarchy, stretching back over a thousand years, is one of the most remarkable acts of continuity in history. But the question is—can it go on? No one can doubt that events in 1992 and 1993 horribly wounded the royals: the Queen herself admitted as much. But the key to survival lies in the ability to adapt and change; and if the smugness of the House of Windsor's supporters can be set aside, then there is hope.

In a recent book the Countess of Longford, the wife of an hereditary peer and Knight of the Garter, published a book about the royal family. As an insider's view, it gives a striking picture of the royals as they themselves would like to be seen. Prince Charles is painted as a visionary, a Renais-

sance man whose private dalliances are nobody's
business but his. The scandal over Fergie's toe-
sucking incident was the fault of the press rather
than her own uncertain morals. Prince Philip,
though gruff, is warm-hearted and lovely. The
Queen Mother is a living saint, and those who
write of her withdrawal to her Castle of Mey,
home in Scotland, while Princess Margaret in
London found her life in tatters following the crisis over her broken romance with Group-Captain
Townsend in the 1950s, are no better than they
should be. And so on.

This is where the House of Windsor, and especially its supporters, part from reality—and in
doing so endanger the future of the royal line.
Nobody likes criticism, and in this the royals are
no different to the rest of us. But in order to have
our respect, most people feel, the royal family
must earn it; there is precious little point in ignor-
ing an angry and unsettled nation in the hope that
the problem will go away.

The difficulty the House of Windsor faces is
that it really doesn't know how much trouble it is
in. A perfect illustration of the point occurred in
April 1993 when the Prince of Wales, misjudging
the mood of the nation, flew to the funeral mass
of Don Juan de Borbon y Battenberg, the father
of the King of Spain. At the same moment all
attention was focused not on Madrid but at home
on the town of Warrington, where a memorial service for Jonathan Ball and Tim Parry, two young

boys who had been killed in an IRA bomb attack, was taking place.

Strictly speaking, Charles had no business being in Spain. Notwithstanding his attempts to forge an alliance with King Juan Carlos, the person who should have been there was the Duke of Edinburgh. Don Juan was Philip's mother's first cousin and so there was some vestigial reason for the duke to go. But how many people go to the funeral of their first cousin twice removed? And, most particularly, go when duty calls at home?

It was difficult to disagree with a Member of Parliament, Ian McCartney, when he declared, "As the King-to-be, he should have known that his place was with his future subjects at such a traumatic time." Even Charles's staunchest supporters were rendered speechless by his extraordinary absence—but that was only the start of it. The Princess of Wales had made clear her desire to go to the Warrington service, to be attended by the prime minister, the opposition leader and the Irish president, but was told she could not. What followed was, in the growing war between the two Wales camps, an ugly, depressing and unnecessary skirmish. This was not the sort of thing that should be happening.

Diana telephoned twelve-year-old Tim's mother the day before the memorial to offer words of consolation. The princess believes that she has healing powers, and indeed that is hard to dispute, since a compassionate word from her has changed

the lives of thousands of people. The call to Mrs.
Parry was one of many Diana makes each year
which are never made public. On this occasion,
however, a television crew was waiting to interview Mrs. Parry, and she told them that Diana
had said she was sorry she could not attend the
service. This was interpreted as a further attempt
at marginalizing the princess from mainstream
royal public engagements. Angry reactions from
all quarters were printed in the newspapers, turning what should have been a moving and healing
occasion into a national controversy centering on
the House of Wales. Denied the presence of both
Charles and Diana—though the Duke of Edinburgh did a splendid job, saying to Jonathan's father, "Don't stand on ceremony. Call me Phil, I'm
just a bit older than you"—Warringtonians voiced
their deep disappointment. Another own-goal by
the Buckingham Palace mandarins.

I have laid stress on this particular event because, though the royal family undertakes thousands of successful public engagements each year,
they are quite often guilty of getting it wrong on
the big occasion. In moments of glory and, more
particularly, tragedy, the country requires the
royal family to be the public face of their joy or
anguish. Though the world is changing and with
it people's need for a royal presence, some things
are immutable—and by now they should get it
right every time.

Buckingham Palace explained this particular

episode away like this: the Queen never attends memorial services, and it was always the royals' intention to send the duke as her representative. But Prince Charles had gone to Warrington to visit the bomb victims, and the townsfolk expected him to return for the memorial service.

Raised once again is the question of how remote the sovereign should be, a question Charles must address as he prepares for kinghood. Compare, for example, the actions of Queen Beatrix of the Netherlands with those of our own royal family over two comparable tragedies.

On October 5, 1992 an El Al cargo plane hit a block of flats on the outskirts of Amsterdam, killing forty-three people. Queen Beatrix, accompanied by her prime minister Ruud Lubbers, immediately attended the scene, then went on to meet the survivors and bereaved at the Bijlmermeer sports stadium. She broke down in tears when confronted with a nine-year-old boy who had just been orphaned.

In December 1988 at Clapham, south London, a British Rail train ploughed into the back of another, causing the deaths of thirty-five people. No member of the royal family attended the scene, and when the time came for a memorial service the Queen sent neither her husband nor her son: she dispatched Fergie as her representative.

For a man studying to be King, such gross errors of judgment should be absorbed and learned from. It would have been wiser—if the Queen herself could not stomach looking tragedy in the face—for Charles to have gone to Lockerbie after the Pan Am air disaster. Instead Prince Andrew was dispatched, and delivered a public performance of embarrassing ineptitude.

These public-relations disasters are habitually swept aside by the palace. I truly believe from my own observations that the royals, and more particularly those who advise them, discount all public criticism as worthless. Only when the Queen's popularity ratings went down dramatically after the Windsor Castle fire, when it was announced by the Heritage minister that the country would be *proud* to pay for its restoration, was there a flurry of unaccustomed activity which ended up with two concessions—that Her Majesty would contribute part of the cost of repairs rather than leaving it to her subjects to pay, and that she would finally consent to pay income tax. The mood of the nation, dangerously rebellious, was only partly mollified.*

When Prince Charles made a visit to the East End after the Camillagate tapes were published, he was shaken to the core when a man shouted angrily at him, "You should be ashamed of your-

---

*In the end, the Queen read the public mood correctly. After first retreating from her pledge to help toward the cost of the fire, she then, in an unprecedented move, agreed to open Buckingham Palace to tourists for two months every summer for the next five years. The money from the admission fees will, it is hoped, pay for a large part of the repairs.

self!" Later, the *Sunday Telegraph* was briefed by friends that he intended to be King and was prepared to "accept a celibate way of life to win back the public confidence he believes is vital to guarantee succession to the throne." Laudable sentiments perhaps, but the way they were expressed made him a laughingstock. Again, the courtiers were misjudging the public mood.

One thing they *must* get right is the future of the Princess of Wales. No matter how hard the forces within Buckingham Palace try to minimize her—and they are trying very hard, as we shall see—she is, after twelve years of marriage, the object of global admiration. In every opinion poll published she emerges as the most popular member of the family she married into. Instead of trying to counter this irresistible force, and failing, Buckingham Palace should be turning it to its own advantage. Diana's great value is that she is good news for the financial, as well as the spiritual, health of the country.

Take, for example, the tour she made of the United States in November 1985. During it she stopped off in the charming town of Springfield, Virginia, and headed for its shopping mall. Inside one of the stores, the lower-middle-market J. C. Penney's, she chatted with company executives and sales staff and then paused—with cameras recording her every nod—to admire racks of British-made sweaters, skirts, dresses, coats, shoes and scarves. Penney's was delighted. "Her fresh young image—to be associated with that is invaluable to us. When the Queen came to this country she went to Bloomingdale's, but Diana is coming to Penney's. There could not be a better person for us," said an excited company executive. All in a day's work for Diana: for Penney's had recently purchased $50 million worth of British goods, and her presence meant that the stuff was shifted off the racks in record time. Perfect for Penney's— and brilliant for Britain, though not so good for me: Springfield police weren't exactly used to visiting royalty, and a trigger-happy "Fed" threatened to blow my head off as I quickly left the store in pursuit of the royal party. I'm happy to say I was able to change his mind.

Prince Charles himself acknowledged Diana's assets as an export ambassador and stressed what the Waleses could do in "creating a positive atmosphere toward Britain. I would like to hope that through trying to engender that sort of awareness and interest, other things would follow, like increased trade and export opportunities," he said. "This is an area which hasn't really been concentrated on enough. It's very difficult for us to say how much can be achieved, but it's amazing what can be achieved through good will."

Despite the official separation, nothing has changed: Diana still has the capacity to fly the flag for Britain and, in an article that was only half joking, one American magazine reckoned that in 1985 Diana-related business generated $650 million in commercial transactions. Though it's difficult to see how they arrived at that figure, the magazine cited some concrete examples—in 1981 she wore a sweater decorated with little sheep: the manufacturer sold more than $1,000,000 worth. In 1982 she made flat shoes a fashion fad: one company, Clark's, credited her with helping them sell 2.8 million pairs—about $63 million worth.

From the American point of view, Diana and her image were the best British import since the Beatles. *The Book of Money* assesses her tourism value to Britain at a "conservative" $10 million— "somewhat higher than Blackpool Tower, Trafalgar Square and the Houses of Parliament put together." The well-known fashion PR Lynne Franks enthused, "Diana has done incredible things for British fashion and its exports," and a spokesman for the Branded Stocking Group, a trade association, added, "We can safely say that Princess Diana has had a hell of an impact on the hosiery industry, particularly on pattern styles. Since Di began wearing them, they've really taken off." Hats? "Diana has been a great influence," said a milliners' association spokeswoman. "The past four years have seen a great upsurge in the sale of hats."

People magazine approached an advertising agency to ask them if they were to create a campaign designed to bring Great Britain as much positive publicity as Diana has brought, how much would it cost? "About $500 million," said Malcolm Miles, then managing director of McCann Erickson Advertising, a leading British firm.

The middle years of marriage taught Diana a great deal and helped forge her public persona. Ever conscious of which way the wind was blowing, she took account of public opinion after Sarah Ferguson joined the royal family. Sarah's belief that this royal caper was a laugh, that she could wing it, soon transmitted itself to the outside world. The double-act the two women had worked up was in danger of capsizing Diana's canoe as well.

In July 1987 one American magazine summed up the House of Windsor as seen from the western side of the Atlantic:

See Fergie, the Duchess of York, leaping into sister-in-law Diana's lap at the royal box at Ascot and refusing to dislodge herself until Princess Anne drops by for a chat. See Diana give Fergie the giggles by standing up to straighten her clingy yellow dress, then shaking the royal bum with the finesse of a stripper. See Fergie and Di at the races, jabbing well-dressed gentry in the behinds with their umbrellas. Listen to Di taunting snooty Princess Michael of Kent: "Isn't that *Princess Michael?*" she asks Fergie with mock awe, within earshot of the starchy royal in-law . . . See Fergie gushing over David Bowie like an awestruck schoolgirl. See Diana turning to her sister-in-law and suggesting jokingly: "Let's get drunk."

This series of unrelated high jinks, when put together like that, could do nothing but damage to the royal family's necessarily sober image, and in the twinkling of an eye Diana understood. Sarah never did. In March 1993, with her royal reputation in tatters, she lashed out at Diana and Charles in a fit of jealous rage: "It's always me who gets the blame," she exploded. "I'm tired of carrying the can for them. I have been the scapegoat for the Waleses for the past four years. It's always my fault and I've had enough of it." Such wooden-headed incomprehension of what was required of her, by the palace and by the people, is the hallmark of Sarah's brief period within the royal family. She complained that she had been stopped from taking part in official royal engagements while Diana suffered no such restriction, signally failing to understand that all that had ever been required of her was a little self-restraint.

That is the quality Diana has—in public, at least. She must have shaken her head when, a week later, Fergie popped up in the *Sun* wailing: "I've messed up my life." She gave the world the benefit of her experience. "Life is about growing up," she said. "We all have to grow up. We all make serious mistakes and we learn by them. And that's it—to say 'I'm sorry' and get on. I think that's what it's all about. It's been a difficult time, but onwards and upwards—best foot forward now." Reading this was like listening to a schoolgirl who promised not to be naughty again. It was an ostrich-like performance from a woman who had blown away all royal credibility but was desperately clinging to the hope that all would be well. Having trod red carpets all over the world, she suddenly realized that people were rolling them up and putting them away—and that loss of status was much more frightening to her than the loss of her marriage.

Compare this battered and bruised image with that of Diana, who around the same time found herself in receipt of plaudits from the most unlikely source. Camille Paglia is the world's most controversial feminist, with a well-deserved reputation for iconoclasm in her native America. From her pen came the following assessment, delivered after Diana's tour of Nepal in early 1993, when she met and embraced inmates of a leper colony: "The truth is that today Diana's power is now greater than her husband's. Through her rapport with millions of people in the world who are poor and uneducated, she has now attained a near-mythic status."

But despite the deliberate attempts to downgrade Diana's status while in Nepal—on her arrival in Kathmandu she was not accorded the national anthem—and despite the fact that she was momentarily thrown by what was transparently a piece of palace chicanery, never once did she display any displeasure or show even the slightest sign of irritation. All through the arduous tour in a country of few resources, in stifling heat and often at literally breathtaking altitude, she remained totally in control. It was a triumph, a tour where Diana came of age—but back at St. James's Palace they were hoping for a disaster.

It is on occasions like this that one questions the recruitment policy in the royal household. To a man—and I mean to a *man*—"upstairs" royal courtiers are recruited from the officer classes, the aristocracy and the public schools. Only very occasionally does an outsider like the Queen's former private secretary Sir William Heseltine get in. There are few women in positions of any responsibility—Prince Charles's adviser Belinda Harley is a rare exception. One of the most effective courtiers I can recall in my time was Anne Hawkins, who later married and was honored, becoming Dame Anne Wall. She served long and brilliantly in the Buckingham Palace press office but was never allowed to rise to use her considerable skills to the full. Ludicrously, she was forced to leave full-time palace service because she chose to marry a divorced man.

Similarly, no people of either sex of African, Asian or Eurasian ancestry are employed in positions of responsibility. The courtier class is one-dimensional, and its narrow attitudes are doing the House of Windsor quite considerable damage.

Diana faces the added difficulty that it is her brother-in-law, Sir Robert Fellowes, who is at the center of the plot to sideline her, but in the end she cannot completely lose. She is the mother of the future King.

After being briefed by Buckingham Palace courtiers, the Countess of Longford wrote that Diana is convinced that Charles will not succeed to the throne. She suggests that this is a worry, insofar as Diana will bring up her son in this belief, damaging relations with his father.

This is nonsense, of course. Charles has equal access to his son and is perfectly able to counterbalance any disinformation the boy may be fed. But it is an indication of the fear and loathing with which Diana is regarded in court circles that such words should find their way into a palace-supported book. And if Diana didn't know already, it was now clear where the weak spot is when confronting her husband's supporters. William.

So what of the future for Diana? Divorce is inevitable; it is simply a question of when, not if—and on this there are two prevailing schools of thought. One is that the prince and princess now so heartily dislike each other that they want to end their marriage as soon as possible. That would mean a divorce in the first half of 1995, after a two-year separation. To move sooner would require a petition citing adultery or unreasonable behavior, a course of action neither is keen to pursue. The other option is that the Waleses will wait for the children to grow up, and complete the marriage breakup when William is eighteen. I am told by someone who knows Charles and Diana: "I believe this is the option they will go for. Obviously, they do both care for their children and I believe they will put their differences aside sufficiently to think first of them, not themselves. The benefit of waiting so long before divorcing is that, with a delay, the children will get used to the idea so the shock isn't so great when it happens." Is divorce at all avoidable? Not really. Though Charles wanted neither separation nor divorce, Diana did. Her husband was content to let the marriage ride as long as he could maintain his relationship with Camilla Parker Bowles, but this was totally unacceptable to Diana.

It is my belief that no hard-and-fast plans have been made for the future. Though waiting until William is of age before divorcing seems an acceptable formula, there are flaws: the plan does not take into account the possibility that one or the other party might wish to marry again—and that cannot be ruled out—nor does it address the problem of what is to happen if the Queen should die. If that were to occur tomorrow, Diana would automatically become Queen. Divorce then would become virtually impossible, and the couple would find themselves, and such liaisons as they were able to forge, under perpetual public scrutiny: a hopeless situation for them both. King George IV was caught in that trap, with the consequence that his situation degenerated to such a point that Queen Caroline was locked out of Westminster Abbey as he went to his Coronation.

Instead, a possible scenario could go like this. Charles and Diana divorce within the next five

years, and she is made a duchess in her own right.
Unlike the Duchess of York, who merely takes her
title from her husband, Diana's title would be her
own, and would be of considerable benefit if she
chose to marry again. Children of this second
marriage would carry courtesy titles, according
them the dignities befitting their half-brother or
half-sister relationship with the future King. Diana's future husband would have no title, unless
he already possessed one. Picking some random
name, Diana would become, say, the Duchess of
Connaught. Prince William would add to his titles
that of Marquess of Egerton. Any further children
Diana produced would bear courtesy titles, so that
if she married James Gilbey their children would
be known as Lord Arthur and Lady Emma (for
example) Gilbey. When Diana died, William
would succeed to the dukedom, becoming Duke
of Connaught, though he would not be known by
this title. (Prince Charles similarly carries a number of rarely used subsidiary titles, including Duke
of Rothesay, Earl of Chester and Earl of Carrick,
and Baron Renfrew.)

The only drawback to this solution might be the
prevailing political climate, which does not encourage the bestowal of hereditary peerages. However, against that is the fact that the Queen can,
in her personal gift, nominate peers who are
attached to her family. She did it in the case of
the Earl of Snowdon when he married Princess
Margaret, and was prepared to do it with Mark

Phillips when he married Princess Anne (though she is not with Anne's second husband, Tim Laurence).

There are no precedents for taking this suggested course, but then the situation in which Charles and Diana find themselves is itself without precedent. In different circumstances King Charles II created dukedoms for his bastard children, and these peerages still exist today in the persons of the Dukes of Grafton, St. Albans, and Richmond and Gordon. The present Earl of Munster descends from the bastard son of King William IV. The royal family has always shown great flexibility when creating its own peerages, and there seems no good reason why they should not display such ingenuity again. Certainly some title may have to be found for Diana, for should Prince Charles choose to marry again, there would be no proper room on the world stage for two Princesses of Wales.

And Diana has no intention of stepping down from this platform. Strangely, if she had never married Prince Charles she might well now have been an upper-class housewife living in the country amidst children and horses, with no job, no direction and no inkling of the quite extraordinary powers she possesses. Instead, her early status as the world's most photographed woman gave her entry to a more powerful world, and latterly a self-imposed sense of direction has sent her off in pursuit of helping others. Her selfless espousal of the plight of AIDS sufferers and her continuing work with lepers is just a hint of what is to come.

Translating good intentions into concrete actions is another thing, however. But since the official separation Diana has made a strong start: her trip to Nepal was in the company of Britain's Overseas Development Minister, Baroness Chalker—a "dream ticket," according to charity circles. As one observer had it: "Visits from a glamorous figure of world renown and the globetrotting minister—these are the two faces of British benevolence with headlines and bottom lines in one go." Diana's work for the International Red Cross goes on, and as Mike Whitlam, the director-general of the British end of the charity told me, "The princess will figure largely in our future worldwide plans. She will do what we ask her to do, but obviously we won't put her into any dangerous situations—and in each case the Foreign Office will have to approve our suggestions. We anticipate the princess will undertake many other trips on our behalf. She has made a commitment to us and we reciprocate that commitment." Moving forces within UNICEF have suggested that Diana take on the role left vacant by the death of Audrey Hepburn, and a source there told me, "We would welcome her as a roving ambassador for UNICEF. At present there is a slight problem in that the Duchess of Kent is the UK patron of our charity, but we are hopeful she can do something for us."

She will also continue to tour Britain and the rest of the world, even though her "royalness" is somewhat diminished now she and Charles are no longer together. A difficulty here is that she is a bigger crowd-puller than her husband—as an analysis by the *Daily Mail* in April 1993 proved. The newspaper followed both Charles and Diana on their separate engagements over a similar period. Though Charles appeared to be working twice as hard as Diana, judged solely by the number of engagements undertaken, it was to less effect. In the period measured, Diana drew crowds of more than 9,000 in sixteen public engagements, an average of 567 spectators per engagement. Charles's score was an average of 134 spectators per engagement. "Her royal visits are dramatically more productive in PR terms," the newspaper commented.

But the *Mail* added, "There is still an underlying perception that his work is somehow more 'worthy' than Diana's, despite her increasingly dedicated efforts for charity. Like the tortoise racing against the hare, there is a chance that his more reserved approach could pay popularity dividends later." Here lies the problem, however: the Waleses are now in competition with each other, each vying for a sort of Nobel Prize for Good Works. But the reason newspapers and the public believe this to be the case is because the Waleses' own courtiers are convinced it is so. Early in 1993, when charity organizers and others were making their applications to have a Wales present at their functions, they were getting back the response, "Diana isn't available. But the Prince of Wales is . . ."

But the charm offensive mounted by the prince in 1993 has done wonders for his image and, after a torpid interlude, for his own self-esteem. Triggered by the angry shout of "You should be ashamed of yourself!"—Charles had no idea his popularity had sunk so low—some of the charm offensive comes over as more offensive than charm, but then that is often the way with sensitive people who are determinedly out to please.

In April it was noted that after church at Sandringham he posed together with his sons for photographers. "It really was the most remarkable scene," a member of the congregation said later. "The prince led the boys up toward the photographers and got them to smile for the cameras. It's as if he was trying to say, 'We're all just one happy family. Make sure you get a picture of us.' It's just the sort of posing we'd expect from Diana. But never from Charles."

This was followed up by more twists in Charles's drive to be all things to all men. First he launched a book on the gardens at his beloved Highgrove; then he agreed to take part in a video animation of his children's book *The Old Man of Lochnagar*. But one public-relations executive who has worked with the royals on charity events was left with a lurking feeling that the charm offensive could backfire. "I believe he is being badly advised and has overstepped the mark," he said. "The biggest error in my opinion is the involvement in the TV project. Writing a children's book was fine, an admirable gesture from a man who apparently loves children, and it raised a lot of money for charity. But what benefit is there in agreeing to shrink to a twelve-inch-high cartoon character? It's demeaning—I haven't heard such nonsense since Fergie and Prince Edward starred in that awful television game show, *It's a Royal Knockout*. He's being filmed with children and trying to look like everyone's favorite uncle. Unfortunately, we all know a little too much about him to feel comfortable with that image. It comes across as cynical."

That sort of criticism falls into the heads-Diana-wins, tails-Charles-loses category, and is as sad as it may appear unfair. To an extent, the prince has recognized that he is off course and has tried to rectify matters. He is not surrounded by public-relations geniuses, media gurus and spin-doctors. Instead he has chaps who speak with a convincing accent and who struggle like their master to keep up with a rapidly changing world. It's not surprising he doesn't get it right all the time.

Diana has a remarkable and instinctive flair when it comes to the media—except for her public speaking, which despite patient coaching by Sir Richard Attenborough and the actor Terence Stamp, is still wooden. Charles makes good speeches, but hates the press and sees no reason to court it. He has resolutely turned his face against the media. His view is that they are there to ridicule him and, in an atmosphere of mutual mistrust and contempt, that is often what happens. But his new campaign to re-win the hearts and minds of the population, however enlightened, cannot be disseminated to the world except through the media. He must learn to live with them in a way that his predecessors did not have to do.

But to assess Charles's worth purely in media terms is to do him a disservice. Too much of the good works achieved by Charles in recent years have been subsumed by the publicity surrounding his private life. In fact he has much to be proud of, and has prepared himself for kingship with laudable dedication. Though dilatory about reading State papers—an accusation angrily but unconvincingly denied by his private secretary on a visit to one tabloid newspaper—he works in other directions in exemplary fashion. His book *A Vision of Britain* illustrated his utopian desire for a society in harmony with itself, pursuing philosophical as well as material goals. Some have argued that these hopes are fanciful or just plain naïve, but Charles has a practical side too.

He has put his money where his mouth is. Within the far-flung lands of the Duchy of Cornwall lies Dorchester, the Dorset town which Thomas Hardy immortalized in *The Mayor of*

Casterbridge. Here, with the architect Leon Kriel, he is developing a mini-town called Poundbury which he hopes will reflect the architectural virtues he extols.

It is too early to gauge what success he will have, but within Dorchester already lie the fruits of his labors in two major buildings and a number of smaller projects. The town is no convenient and uncomplaining vehicle for Charles's thrusting architectural ambitions—it has voiced its fair share of complaints—but as part-owner, Charles has been able to win round the population by demonstrating what a responsible and benevolent landlord he can be. He has given, or leased, large chunks of land so the townsfolk can enjoy leisure pursuits. He has renovated Victorian terraces and injected cash into the redevelopment of the arts center. A hospice for the chronically ill will rise, due to an advantageous land deal arranged by Duchy officials. A five-and-a-half-acre site now houses the town's sports center, thanks to him. Land sold to a private contractor has resulted in some handsome new upmarket houses being developed, and at the other end of the scale, warden-controlled homes have been built by the local council on Duchy land. On the Maiden Castle estate a play area of two and a half acres has been leased at a peppercorn rent, and at the Sawmills site five acres have been given over to provide a home for Scouts, Guides, Boys' Brigade, and a YMCA.

Two monuments to his architectural zeal stand comfortably and inconspicuously in the Georgian town—a football stadium and a supermarket. They were achieved by selling off Duchy land, formerly the site of Dorchester Rugby Club, during the property boom years. The deal secured the club, with a pair of new pitches on an improved site, a magnificent clubhouse thrown in, the new football stadium—and the most remarkable supermarket in the country.

The Tesco store which helped pay for all this is quite breathtaking. Much of its exterior is Charles's responsibility—he labored with the company's architects to try to bring a sense of graciousness to the tiresome chore of weekly shopping. Customers driving onto the site are greeted by cascading water fountains and a huge vaulted façade; they park their cars among rows of lime trees, make their way down avenues past mini-follies (used to house trolleys) and enter the store. The elegantly tiled roof is adorned by a huge cupola, redolent of Kensington Palace, and every detail, down to the litter bins, bears the royal touch.

Dorchester Town Football Club used to be housed in what was little more than a corrugated iron hut. Now, though the team itself is in the lowly Beazer League, it boasts a magnificent stadium: its façade is dominated by three pedimented porches supported on light blue circular steel columns, with a central pediment emerging from a pitched roof. It is faced in local Swanage brick, banded by Portland stone, and has lots of wrought iron.

Low-key in his approach to the redevelopment of Dorchester, Charles nevertheless opened an office in the High Street so local people could come and air their views. "The Duchy had run the place pretty disastrously for most of this century," said a former mayor, Mrs. Betty Boothman. "When Charles came out of the Royal Navy in 1977 and assumed his responsibilities as landlord, he saw things needed to change. There were practical, not idealistic, decisions which had to be taken. Up till then I don't think he'd set foot in the place, but when he started to take an interest he took the view that people came first and buildings second. Certainly there was no talk of building new things a decade ago. I think he's felt his way very carefully, learned a great deal, and only now is he putting his ideas into practice."

Charles's work in Dorchester is significant in more than one respect. Most importantly, he has set about practicing what he preaches without fanfare—to the present day, no proper analysis of the scale and depth of what he has achieved in the town has appeared in print. But he has also shown himself to be a caring and thoughtful landlord—and it could be said that his stewardship of the Duchy of Cornwall is a useful pointer to the way he will take on his greater responsibilities in the years ahead.

Other lights are also well and truly hidden under a bushel. With few accurate yardsticks to go by, it is nevertheless a fair certainty that the Prince of Wales has become the biggest individual charity fundraiser in the world. In the past fifteen years or so, Charles has done more than any other single individual to help the poor, needy and dispossessed. A figure of £100 million raised is probably on the conservative side, but since he refuses to discuss this aspect of his life, it is hard to know the extent of his success. In all, Charles lends his name to nearly two hundred charitable institutions as patron, president or chairman.

In many cases the principal fundraising is done by the charity's workers and the only contribution the prince can make is to turn out for events staged by the charity, or make speeches. However, Charles also goes gunning for the big money himself. He took the late oil billionaire Armand Hammer for a walk along a windswept beach, and came back with the full price—$14.5 million—of a new United World College.

Those kind of donations don't happen every day, and Charles is happy to settle for smaller sums. The sale of prints from his watercolors will raise around £2.7 million, and that money goes directly to charity. And if *he* can't reach people with money or influence, he knows those who can. Eric Clapton, Mark Knopfler and Phil Collins have all played free at Prince's Trust concerts, along with a multitude of other equally eminent rock stars, and have raised millions in the process.

The Prince's Trust and its companion organization, the Prince's Youth Business Trust, are the cornerstone of Charles's charitable crusade. Funded by Charles's own Royal Navy allowance until it was formally incorporated, the Prince's Trust was set up in 1976 to provide small grants to help disadvantaged young people, including the handicapped. The gifts from the Trust have no strings attached and come in the form of cash. To the recipients, mostly from deprived backgrounds, these may often be the first indicator that someone trusts and believes in them.

To date, though they are unforthcoming on their accounts, the Prince's Trust reckons to have handed over about £10 million. But this pales into insignificance when compared with the Prince's Youth Business Trust, started a decade after the Prince's Trust. This raised £40 million, which was then matched, in a pre-arranged deal, by a government grant. The original figure staggered the prince, who laughed and shrugged his shoulders when it was first suggested trying to raise that amount to coincide with his fortieth birthday. "The figure was plucked out of the air," I was told by someone who attended that meeting. "There was very little belief it could be done." But it was, and a new and vibrant charity was born, more questioning and more practically helpful toward its beneficiaries than its senior partner. The PYBT set out to provide bursaries and loans, professional advice and marketing opportunities for people between the ages of eighteen and twenty-five who want to start up in business. Over 9,000 such businesses have been started in this way in the past few years.

One of Charles's former private secretaries told me, "He's an extraordinary catalyst for raising money, there's no doubt about that. But virtue has to be its own reward, because there is no other. The prince is not a fount of honors. The accusation is put that people contribute to the Prince's causes because they want a knighthood. But you don't get a knighthood that way, not from him. Some people who've been associated with his charities have got decorations, but they've been the workers. The reward has to be the royal handshake or, more importantly, that you've done something worthwhile with your money."

Because it might be seen that favoring some charities as against others was a form of discrimination, the Buckingham Palace line has always been that the royal family do not make direct appeals for funds. "But," says the former courtier, "that's a line that's rather wavy. It is totally true in the case of the Queen, and certainly true as far as some other members of the family are concerned. But it's not absolutely true in the case of the Prince of Wales—he puts a great deal of effort in, by going to lunches with lots of business people and making speeches which indicate he thinks the charity is a good thing. Then he leaves. He doesn't actually say, kindly give money to this charity, nor does he need to, because the penny drops soon enough. So he honors the letter, if not the spirit, of the Buckingham Palace ruling."

Charles has had to work hard to achieve this position for himself, since charities are often ruthless in their determination to raise money. It is not unknown for members of the royal family to fall victim to the overweening ambition—social as well as fiscal—of some charity organizers. "Sometimes it's difficult to dissociate it (fundraising) from a certain amount of ghastliness and vulgarity." Indeed, some diehards in Buckingham Palace argue that it would be far safer for the royals to stay away from charity fundraising altogether, but Charles vehemently disagrees, even though sometimes it seems he acts against his better judgment. In 1986 a film was made called *The Prince and Princess of Wales in Public and Private*. It did what it set out to do—raise £400,000 for the then ailing Operation Raleigh youth charity—but it left Charles fuming. Having set out with the best of intentions, he felt the film made him look a fool, and though he never complained publicly, he is unlikely to undertake such a venture again for charity.

There are other ventures, however, where he does feel safe. Also in 1986 he attended a gala organized by his polo friend Galen Weston, head of the company that controls Fortnum and Mason. Held in Palm Beach, it attracted no adverse criticism and, within the space of a single day, raised over \$1 million for his charities.

These indicators as to the development of the future King are of far more relevance, I would argue, than the state of his private life. By the time he ascends the throne the divorce from his wife and the scandal of Camilla Parker Bowles will have receded into the distance. The reconstruction of his image is already under way, and by and large the British still want him as their next sovereign—though they are in no hurry to get rid of their present one.

An amusing sidelight to the question of succession was written about by James Blair Lovell. Over twenty years ago, when interviewing the woman who claimed to be Anastasia, the "surviving" daughter of the murdered Tsar Nicholas II of Russia, he mentioned that he would shortly be in London. At this she said he should see the Queen while he could, as she would be the last but one sovereign in Britain, according to a prophecy Rasputin had made. He said that when a Battenburg came to the throne, the dynasty would end. The Battenburgs changed their name to Mountbatten during the First World War, and Charles, as the son of the Duke of Edinburgh, previously Lieutenant Philip Mountbatten, would be the fulfilment of "Father Gregory's" prophecy.

That aside, one major hurdle Charles must face is resolving his future role as Defender of the Faith. In 1993 on the BBC television program *The*

Heart of the Matter the Archbishop of York, Dr. John Habgood, fired a warning shot at the prince, effectively saying he must resolve his personal problems before becoming King. Having taken his marriage vows in the church he cannot divorce and still become Defender of the Faith. Yet divorce, for all the reasons given above, is inevitable. But to abandon the traditional tie with the church, which goes back to King Henry VIII, will inevitably weaken the monarchy, not only in Charles's reign but in subsequent generations, and history will rightly point an accusing finger at him. He may additionally find it difficult to find bishops willing to attend his Coronation and crown him King.

It might be argued that Charles has plenty of time to consider his options and that he should do nothing hasty. But there are elements within the church who want the issue settled. In April 1993 the Bishop of Oxford, the Right Reverend Richard Harries, gave a hint of this in an interview: "While one of the Queen's titles is Defender of the Faith, I don't think people take that literally now," he said. "It's been very good when monarchs have presented themselves as ideal role models, but it is not expected of them these days." For Charles, this must have been the most ominous and depressing statement. What it was saying was that the church was no longer looking to the royal family to provide either a religious or moral lead to the country. A major reason for the royal family's existence had just been torn up.

All this—just because Charles maintained throughout his marriage a sexual liaison with Camilla Parker Bowles? After all, he has the right to argue that his good works have far outweighed his misdeeds, that he has trained himself for kingship and created a role for himself where there was none, and that kings and princes throughout history have enjoyed extramarital relations without damage to their reigns. Why should things be more difficult for him?

The answer lies in the actions of his predecessor, who selfishly allowed his obsession with a woman to rock the throne. In the days and months following the Abdication, Britain came close to joining some of its European cousins who had lost faith in their monarchies—and the country resented the fact that one man could jeopardize an institution it ordinarily cherished. As Kaiser Wilhelm once pointed out, "Monarchy is like virginity—once lost, you can't get it back." So Charles suffers from an inheritance factor that cannot take into account all his good works or his future potential. However, if it was Diana's intention, when she apparently sanctioned her friends' help on Andrew Morton's book, to derail the prince, she has failed. The likelihood is he will become King. Only one thing would almost certainly stop him. Should Brigadier Andrew Parker Bowles choose to name the prince in a divorce action, and should Charles, subsequent to that action, decide to marry Camilla, the prince may well be forced to implement a course of action he has outlined to his closest friends: wash his hands of the whole thing and live in exile in his beloved Italy. After all, he has a son who can do the job.

Prince Charles has to sort out this literally King-sized problem. Echoing eerily across history, the words of Sir Alan Lascelles to King Edward VIII in just such another crisis may well be called to mind: "Sir, you can have the Throne, or you can have the woman. You cannot have both."

UPDATE TO THE
SIGNET EDITION

A year after the shattering announcement that the Prince and Princess of Wales were to officially separate—made by Prime Minister John Major on December 9, 1992—the heir to the throne of Great Britain is on the point of making an historic decision. It concerns not only his own future but that of the Royal Family itself.

That decision was not reached alone. As the months have ticked by since the dreadful news was given to a packed House of Commons, Prince Charles spent hours, days and weeks weighing the pros and cons of this dilemma.

On the one hand is his continued love for Mrs. Camilla Parker Bowles. On the other is his innate sense of duty—a flawed characteristic, which many members of his immediate family believe has been found consistently wanting in the years he has spent waiting to succeed to the throne.

In the words of his fated predecessor, something had to be done. A public relations initiative was instituted, wise heads nodded, and fingers were crossed.

One person stands head and shoulders above all others in influencing Prince Charles as to what should be his correct course of action now.

That person is Queen Elizabeth, the Queen Mother. A senior Buckingham Palace official who has been guiding me for some considerable time now firmly believes that the Queen Mother's influence will be the deciding factor as to whether Charles steps down as heir-presumptive or continues to be the Crown Prince in waiting.

The choice is simple: Camilla—or the Crown.

Having talked to the senior aide, and one other, I am convinced that the stage is now set for Prince Charles to relinquish any thoughts of marriage to a woman he has loved for virtually all his adult life. The thoughts were there all right, but now he acknowledges that he must concentrate on resuscitating the sense of duty which has been missing for too long.

My Buckingham Palace source, who has known and worked with Prince Charles for the best part of ten years, says that it is no secret to the most senior courtiers that the Queen Mother has read the riot act not only to Charles about his "appalling" lack of sense of duty but to Andrew Parker Bowles as well. I am told: "Of course, she could hardly be furious with Andrew Parker Bowles, as he has been the injured party, so to speak—but even he has not escaped her wrath. The Queen Mother has deliberately kept up a strong relationship with Bowles, particularly in the past year or so, to help sort the whole wretched business out.

"Incredibly, at the height of the controversy following the release in full of the Camillagate tape, the Queen Mother had Andrew Parker Bowles to stay with her at Royal Lodge (her home in the Windsor Park) to discuss what should happen now. The conversation revolved around the necessity for the Parker Bowleses to sort themselves out. I know that Her Majesty is a great believer in families sticking together through thick and thin, particularly in this case where any split-up would involve the Prince of Wales."

The informant is positive that the Queen Mother has lobbied hard to sort the current mess out; he also believes that she will not be unsuccessful. He asks, "How do you think Prince Charles will react to his grandmother—a woman he admires almost more than the Queen herself—telling him to think of his duty, not his heart?"

Nobody in the world knows more about this side of things than the Queen Mother. In 1936 she watched with horror what the abdication of Edward VIII did to Bertie, the man she loved and married. She has always believed that this single act led directly to the death of her husband in 1952, when he was just 56 years old. She believes the strain that kingship placed on George VI was intolerable, and that no such act of selfishness should ever happen again.

She also believes that but for the guts and fortitude subsequently displayed by Bertie as he battled during his short reign with the ravages of war and with personal ill-health, the House of Windsor could easily have folded like a pack of cards at the time. She considered David Windsor's marriage to Wallis was "a terrible scandal," and she views what Prince Charles was seriously contemplating with Camilla as the same.

My source believes that the Queen Mother's dying words will be to urge Prince Charles to "do your duty," and that there is little chance he will ignore this plea. "Stand by to witness a distancing between Charles and Camilla," I am advised.

Another Palace source, agreeing with these general sentiments, feels that the level of pressure put on the Prince in the months since the Camillagate revelations—not only by the Queen Mother but other members of his family too—will swing the pendulum away from temptation. Despite the shattering of the Waleses' marriage through Charles's obsession with Camilla, I am told succinctly: "No divorce between Brigadier Parker Bowles and his wife"—and therefore no marriage between Charles and Camilla.

But, despite all this behind-the-scenes activity by the House of Windsor and its members, there is derision amongst the inner circle at reports that the Prince and Mrs. Parker Bowles have not seen each other since before Christmas 1992. They have not only met—at Charles's Gloucestershire home, Highgrove, and at the "safe" homes of friends in the way they have always done (as was revealed on the Camillagate tape)—but they have been in regular contact, amazingly, by mobile telephone.

Despite the acknowledged bugging of royal phone lines, particularly mobiles, by members of Britain's secret services—mainly either army or naval intelligence units, often operating as mavericks outside the jurisdiction of either MI5 or MI6—Prince Charles has not seen fit to modify his communications with Camilla.

He has always (or ever since I've known and reported on him) been adamant that he will carry on as normal, without bowing to outside pressure. Some believe that this is typical, a mark of Teutonic obduracy that often comes out in the House of Windsor. But Charles simply doesn't care. The only difference between the mobile he uses today and the mobile he used when Camillagate was recorded and then transmitted by the secret services in 1989 is that on his current telephone he has a scrambler fitted.

Such rudimentary protection is a joke, say his detractors. Modern technicians believe that such machines can soon be cracked—and that if Charles continues to talk to Camilla on such a machine he will eventually be caught up in another scandal.

There have been signs that in the months since Charles and Camilla's love for each other became so exposed, that the Parker Bowleses are trying to weather the storm, and are fighting to stay together. This would not only be for the sake of the country but also for the sake of their children.

Although it was hardly triumphant, there was a gathering of sorts at the family's Wiltshire home on the eve of their twentieth wedding anniversary on July 4, 1993, which was attended by their friend and neighbor, the former government minister for Northern Ireland, Tom King.

The beleaguered couple continued to live together on an irregular basis as they fought to sort things out. Their friends pointed out that the two always had an open marriage, with Camilla regularly seeing Prince Charles (a fact most definitely known by her husband) and Andrew Parker Bowles himself having a number of "girlfriends" throughout the seventies, eighties, and now the nineties.

Andrew always sought the companionship of other women during the marriage. Following the publication of *Diana vs. Charles: Royal Blood Feud* in May 1993, it was discovered by *The People* newspaper, a sister to the *Daily Mirror*, that Andrew Parker Bowles was regularly visiting, often late at night, the Battersea home of one of Camilla's best friends.

Naturally, it was denied all round that there was anything untoward going on. But those who knew were not impressed. A friend told me at the time: "I don't think Andrew really cared that people found out what was going on. He was totally humiliated at the release of the contents of that telephone conversation between Charles and Camilla, and thought, 'Why should I care any more?' In fact, in a way, it helped him get some sort of standing back among his friends—the fact that he could pull one of the best friends of his unfaithful wife. It's a childish way of looking at things, but it helped."

The belief among many of their friends and family is that this is just part of the pattern of things to come: Andrew enjoying relationships outside his marriage and Camilla being able to do nothing about them. With Prince Charles being directed more and more towards his "duty" and Andrew Parker Bowles absenting himself more frequently, the one who will be left at home alone will be Camilla.

The heavy burden of the past twelve months since the exposure of her relationship with Charles has left its mark. Never a conventionally beautiful woman, her looks have been hit hard by the pressure of constant media attention. That, paradoxically, will have the effect of bringing out the prince's latent sympathy, and of one thing we can be certain: this complex and catastrophic relationship is far from over, even if the passion has been watered down.

Although there was much fury and disbelief at stories chronicling the clandestine routine bug-

ging of Royal telephone lines and conversations—
and even a denial from the Foreign Office that
such covert operations even happened—there was
enough concern for an investigation, ironically by
MI5 itself, to be instituted.

Naturally, there was little public discussion
about the inquiries—such matters are never discussed in Parliament or admitted openly—but in
June 1993 there was a fascinating and significant
announcement in the Court Circular page of *The
Times*. It read: "June 24. The Queen today visited
the headquarters of the security service and was
received by Mrs. Stella Rimington (Director
General)."

At the same time, another story appeared in *The
Times*, stating, without equivocation, that MI5 "is
investigating the source of transcripts of alleged
conversations involving members of the Royal
Family as part of a review of Buckingham Palace
security." The report went on to state that the
Royal Family's security is reviewed regularly,
mainly because of the IRA threat (particularly following the assassination of Earl Mountbatten in
1979).

But there was a further bombshell in this un-
derstated announcement. It was said—and there
was no denial—that the new investigation would
pay special attention to telecommunications, including mobile phones, at all royal residences.
These included Highgrove and, of course, Kensington Palace.

It is intriguing that MI5 should be carrying out the investigation. Many believe that they—or people who work loosely under their umbrella—were and are responsible for Royal "bugging" in the first place. Since the stories of the eavesdropping of conversations between Charles and Diana at Highgrove and of Diana and a girlfriend, again at Highgrove, there has been a wealth of disinformation put out by the Government (who often don't know what's going on) and the security services (who don't want people to know). Stories of these goings-on first surfaced in some detail in *The People* newspaper in January 1993. There was, at that time, no denial and no uproar.

Why? I believe that the authorities hoped the story would just go away. It didn't. I wrote about, and expanded on, the detail of those revelations in this book.

It seems appropriate that I should clarify some points. I still believe, without reservation, that conversations, both in their private homes and on their telephone lines, are recorded—without the use of out-of-date bugs. It happens on a regular basis. I still believe that people in authority know that such activities have been happening for years—which is why an investigation by MI5 is now under way: the truth is beginning to leak out.

There is no way Royal-watchers like myself or the public at large will ever learn the whole truth of these inquiries. But there is, at least, the comfort that the British government feels the matter has become one of public concern. This book played a part in wreaking that concession from a smug and secretive establishment, which sought to cover its mistakes and flaws with blanket denials and vicious criticism of what I had written.

My security sources tell me (and always have done) that independent cells are responsible for the bugging of private conversations. I am told: "The only authority they have is their own. They are naval and military units recording as *they* see fit. They do so in the belief they are acting 'in defence of the realm,' and they report only when they feel it is necessary. Even the Prime Minister has little idea of what is happening. They are, to all intents and purposes, out of control."

In a recent book the renowned spy writer John LeCarré spotlighted the groups of underutilised operatives hanging about Whitehall who have been left on the shelf following the cessation of the Cold War. Frustrated by the lack of "enemy" to spy upon, they have turned their spying skills inward and are searching out (or so they believe) the cancer within.

However shadowy, these people most certainly *do* exist, and some in authority will admit to this. A senior Member of Parliament who came to me following the publication of the hardback version of this book revealed to me that after taking up a certain position in the House of Commons, he was warned never to make a telephone call from the House if it was of a compromising nature.

He was asked: "Do you have a mistress? If so, don't ever call her from Westminster. Your conversations are listened to—constantly. Don't think you might just be unlucky on one day, you will always be caught out. Ask any Member if this is true. Unless they're totally naive they will confess that this is the way that things work 'in defence of the realm.' "

Listening in to other people's conversations, either on the telephone or into their very homes, has become remarkably easy these days, even for amateurs. Devices that can lock into conversations within a radius of several miles are readily available in electronics shops for as little as $400. The advice which has been given to the Royal Family is to be wary, especially when talking on mobile phones.

The younger Royals have had special warnings not to be lax, and generally they've heeded them as best they (and their Royal Protection Squad officers) can. It has been admitted that both Charles and Diana have had Highgrove and Kensington Palace swept for bugs—but surveillance experts just laughed at the futility of this exercise. They point out that bugs are a thing of the past, and modern techniques are ultrasophisticated.

The point of the current review, apparently not personally ordered by the Queen but probably requested by her private secretary, Sir Robert Fellowes, is to identify and isolate the source of these damaging tapes and conversations. It was fairly amazing that following the rows about whether the tapes were genuine—*of course* they are!—the Queen should actually make an unprecedented official visit to Stella Rimington, the boss of MI5, at the secret service's new headquarters on the banks of the River Thames near Parliament.

There was little doubt that royal security was at the top of their agenda. Although John Major none too convincingly denied that MI5 and the British government's listening service (the GCHQ building at Cheltenham) were involved in any bugging, his assurances did not preclude an investigation into who was responsible. Here was the tacit admission that somebody was.

At the time of writing the investigations have been going on for some months, with no indication as to how much longer they will take to complete. When they are complete, it seems unlikely that any proper explanation will be made public, despite the fact that it is universally acknowledged that the Royal Family have suffered more long-term damage by the publication of their private thoughts than by anything before or since.

What of the future for Charles, Diana, and the rest of the Royals now that these revelations have been made?

A major public relations campaign to win the hearts and minds of their British subjects is under way, with the little Princes William and Harry stuck uncomfortably in the middle. Both mother and father in turn wheel the boys out for photo opportunities as if the very confirmation that they are caring parents will reassure the nation.

Last summer, the public push-me-pull-you went on, with Charles taking the boys aboard the ocean-going yacht of Greek shipping billionaire Ionnis Latsis. Diana retaliated with her own photo calls when it was her turn with the boys, knowing that inevitably she would get more space in the newspapers and magazines.

Under an agreement reached earlier in the year, the two Princes spent a large part of their summer holidays this year with their father, as they had been with their mother at Nevis in the Caribbean for New Year's. Charles has taken the boys to the Greek Islands. When these arrangements were made at the time of the official separation in December 1992, it was easy for Diana to go along with them. After all, she was going to get them first. But by the time August 1993 came round and the two young Princes were heading for Greece with Charles, it was much harder for Diana to bear.

Admittedly, she had them for the first two and a half weeks after the boys had left their boarding school, Ludgrove, but it was a long, hot summer for her while they were away, again aboard the luxury yacht owned by Latsis.

To make matters worse—although she knew it was going to happen—the two Princes spent one brief day with their mother on their return from

Greece before linking up with Prince Charles again and heading north for Scotland and a few days holiday with the Queen at Balmoral Castle.

A Buckingham Palace aide had explained to me earlier in the year that such arrangements were never made at the last minute. He said, "It is known weeks ahead who the Princes will be with and when. These things are never decided at the last minute. They have to be organized because a lot of important people are involved."

But finally, before school began again for William and Harry on September 7, they were reunited with Diana for a holiday in the sun. Fun time came when she took Wills and Harry to Disney World in Florida before flying on to Nassau in the Bahamas for a long weekend at Lyford Cay, a millionaire's playground on New Providence Island. There she stayed with newsagent heiress, Kate Menzies, who had shown solid support and deep friendship to Diana in the months following the formal separation.

But even as Princess Diana rested in the low-rise beach house that looks over the aquamarine Atlantic Ocean, there was little peace of mind for her. Paparazzi cameramen hired expensive boats to get photos of her, but she couldn't cooperate with them even if she had wanted to. She had received instructions from the Queen not to be seen "flaunting herself" or the children. Her "performance" with William and Harry at Novis, in the Caribbean, earlier in the year, where she had been photographed in that orange swimsuit, had not gone down well at Buckingham Palace. She was told, "We want no repeat of that." So she stayed out of sight for the whole weekend, using the houses of friends.

At the same time, she had to fight off suggestions being made in the tabloids that she was in competition with her husband over who could give the boys the best holidays. This just wasn't true. Any visits, like the ones to Florida and Nassau, are made only with the permission of the Queen and Prince Charles—but the damage was being done to her as the Palace machinery supported her husband more and more. In this conflict there was only going to be one winner, and it wasn't going to be Diana. That was the reality of the situation as the Princes went back to their boarding schools on September 7. Some said that the two were the most spoiled children in the world. But both Princes would have swapped all their holidays and adventures for Mummy and Papa to have remained together. A friend commented: "It's agony and ecstasy for the Princess when it comes to her children and being with them. But she should have known it would be like this. It's one of the penalties."

When I set out to write this book, it was with a heavy heart. I have covered the British Royal Family's comings and goings for a quarter of a century, and I believe it to be worthwhile as an institution and a positive force. In the dying days of the twentieth century, however, it seems to have temporarily lost its way—due in no small part to those who advise it.

I look forward, as do millions of people, to the day when its position of esteem is restored in the eyes of the world.

INDEX

Abdication Crisis (1936),
    xvii–xviii, 52, 107
Adeane, Edward, 193–194
Airlie, Earl of, xiii, 120
Alexander, Brian, 24
Alexander of Tunis, Earl,
    24
Alexandra, Princess, 66
Allen, Gertrude, 139
Allsopp, Charles, 39
Allsopp, Fiona, 39
Althorp,
    Northamptonshire,
    79, 133, 238, 248,
    255, 256, 258, 259,
    260, 262, 264–268,
    270
ambulance strike (1989),
    46, 51–52
Amsterdam air disaster
    (1992), 275
"Anastasia", 300
Andrew, HRH Prince,
    Duke of York,
    134–135

and Bryan/Fergie photo-
    graphs, 116
and leak of separation,
    117–118, 121
MI5 monitoring of con-
    versations, 95, 97
separation from Sarah,
    118, 228
wedding, 199
Anne, HRH The Princess
    Royal, 170
    attends the Parker
    Bowles wedding, 23
    divorces Captain Phillips,
    229
    irritated by D, 188–190
    marries Captain Phillips,
    162, 287
    Parker Bowles's friend-
    ship with, 24, 55–56
Anson, Charles, 118, 120,
    121, 125, 233
Arundel, Earl of, 79
Ashcombe, Lord, 34, 39
Askew, Barry, 172–173

Attenborough, Sir Richard, 291
Aylard, Commander Richard, 127–130, 245, 252

Bagehot, Walter, 215
Bahrain, Crown Prince of, 253
Ball, Johnathan, 272, 274
Barratt, John, 260–262
Barry, Stephen, 22, 28, 153, 157
Bartholomew, Carolyn, 83, 116, 125, 211
Beatrice, Princess, 113
Beatrix, Queen of the Netherlands, 275
Beaufort, Duke of, 67
Beaufort Hunt, 54
Beaverbrook, Max, 1st Baron, 39
Beckwith-Smith, Anne, 83, 198
Bell, Ron, 63
Bell, Sir Tim, 119
Benson, Carolyn "Chubby", 39
Berni, Lorenzo, 82
Berni, Mara, 82–85, 116
Bingham, Sir Thomas, 96
Blandford, Marquess of, 70
Blues and Royals regiment, Household Cavalry, 20, 24
Bolehyde Manor, 32, 55, 152
Bolton, Ann, 134
Boothman, Mrs. Betty, 295
Borbon v Battenberg, Don Juan de, 272
Braemar Gathering, 168

Bryan, John, 111–113, 117
Butner, Paul, 105

Cabrera, 199
Cadogan, Earls of, 24
Calcutt, Sir David, 125
Camillagate tapes, xiv, 40–52, 95, 108–110, 276
Carey, Dr. George, Archbishop of Canterbury, xvi
Carington, Virginia, 39
Cartland, Dame Barbara, 63, 143, 260–262
Cavendish, Lady Elizabeth, 123, 126
Chalker, Baroness, 288
Chant, Paul, 194
Chantal (friend of Prince Charles), 146, 147
Chapman, Vic, 175–176, 187, 190–191, 198, 203, 204, 213
Charles, HRH Prince of Wales
  and ambulance strike, 46, 51
  Antipodean tour (1983), 64, 179–181
  attitude to his marriage, 166–168
  Australian tour (1985), 193
  and Camillagate see Camillagate
  Camilla Parker Bowles, attraction for, 53–55
  Canadian tours, 179, 180, 181, 198
  character, 49–51, 145
  charity work, 295–300

compared with Duke of
  Windsor, 52
Daily Mail crowd-pulling
  statistics, 289
as Defender of the Faith,
  301
divorce possibilities,
  284–285
drifts apart from D, 192
and Earl Spencer's fu-
  neral, 252–254
early meetings with D,
  147–153
early relationship with
  Camilla Parker
  Bowles, 24–25
engagement, 160,
  162–163, 178
fails to understand D's
  problems, 178, 182
"gurus" of, 195–196
and Hewitt, 75–76
Indian tours, 33, 155,
  223–224, 225–228
jealousy of D, xii–xiii,
  62–66, 170, 179
lack of things in common
  with D, 182–184
Lady Longford on, 271
and Lady Sarah Spencer,
  145–147
learns survival tech-
  niques, 186
at Lech, 243–247
letter to Raine, 270
living with Camilla, 310
Majorcan holidays,
  199–200, 201, 221
media offensive against
  D, 123–124
meets D, 133–134

meets Camilla Parker
  Bowles, 24, 34
monitoring of conversa-
  tions, 95, 96–102,
  103–104
polo accident, 220
Portuguese tour, 202
Poundbury project,
  293–295
question of remarriage,
  xvi–xvii
reaction to D's apparent
  relationship with
  Dunne, 68
relationship with father,
  196–197
resumes seeing Camilla,
  187
in Royal Navy, 25, 26
royal train scandal,
  28–33
separation announced,
  60, 94, 235, 305
South Korean trip,
  128–131, 234
Spanish tour, 203–204
training for kingship, 197
visit to Japan (1986), 198
and Warrington bomb at-
  tack, 272–273
wedding of, 19–23
Church of England, 197
Churchill, Jane, 39
Churchill, Sir Winston, 26
Cirencester polo ground,
  220
Clapham rail disaster
  (1988), 275
Clapton, Eric, 81, 296
Clifford, Brigadier Robert,
  57
Colbourne, Michael, 261

Collins, Phil, 296
Colloms, Martin, 109
Combermere Barracks,
    near Windsor, 70
Coronation (1953), xviii,
    20, 24
Cowdray Park, Sussex, 149
Crawley, Marita, 43n
Crawley, Sarah, 43n
Cubitt family, 34

Daily Express, 129
Daily Mail, 27, 108,
    117–119, 129–130,
    229, 289
Daily Mirror, 113–115,
    128, 310
Daily Record, 114
Daily Telegraph, 28, 76
Delhi, 226
Dempster, Nigel, 27, 124
Derby, Earls of, 24
Diana, HRH The Princess
    of Wales
  and age gap between her
    and C, 133–135
  and America, 277, 279
  as an icon, xi, 50, 62,
    65–66
  appearance, xi, 150, 188,
    254
  attitude of Buckingham
    Palace to, xv–xvi
  attitude to foreign tours,
    180–181
  attitude to Raine, Count-
    ess Spencer,
    144–145, 256–258,
    262–264, 270
  in Australia and New
    Zealand, 63–64,

    161–162, 179–181,
    193
  bulimia, 78, 124, 142,
    176–178, 187, 198,
    211, 241
  Caribbean holiday, 105
  character, xi–xii, 29, 137
  childhood of, 133–138
  choice as C's bride, xii
  compared with Camilla
    Parker Bowles, 53
  concern for others, 86,
    139, 207, 215–217,
    227–228, 273–274,
    282, 287–288, 289
  Daily Mail crowd-pulling
    statistics, 289
  dissatisfaction with staff,
    193–194
  divorce possibilities,
    284–285
  drifts apart from C, 192
  and Dunne, 66–68
  early meetings with C,
    147–153
  education, 139–141, 239
  effect of parents' divorce,
    129–140, 241
  end of friendship with
    Gilbey, 93–94
  engagement, 160, 162
  faints at Expo '86, 198
  father's death and fu-
    neral, 251–254
  and FG bracelet, 165
  first memory of C, 135
  first public appearance as
    Princess of Wales,
    168–169
  first solo tour, 223
  and Hewitt, 71–77

and the House of Windsor, 87
Indian tour, 223–224, 225–227
involvement in Morton biography, 126–127, 302
jealous of C's long-standing love affair, xiii, 127
Junor article on, 126–128
lack of things in common with C, 183–184
learns survival techniques, 186
Majorcan holidays, 199–200, 201, 221
meets C, 133–134
meets Gilbey, 79
miscarriage, 182
monitoring of conversations, 98–105
Nepal visit, 282, 288
popularity of, xi, xii, xvi, xvii, 105, 116, 171, 209, 225, 277–278
Portuguese tour, 202
and Prince William, xiv–xv
question of remarriage, xvii
and radio ham, 108
royal train scandal, 29–33
on "separate lives" rumor, 205
separation announced, 60, 94, 235, 305
friendship with Fergie, 199, 207, 213

South Korea trip, 128–131, 234
Spanish tour, 203–204
Squidgy tapes, see Squidgy tapes
and stepmother, 144–145
"suicide attempts" of, 78, 93, 126, 173
title of, 285–287
tour of Australia, 193
tour of Canada, 179, 181
visits Gilbey's flat, 80, 84
and Warrington bomb attack, 272–273
and Waterhouse, 68–70
as Wayne Sleep's dancing partner, 198–199
wedding of, 19–23
works at kindergarten, 151, 157, 162
Dire Straits, 63
Dodd-Noble, Julia, 83
Dorchester, Dorset, 292–293
Dumbrells, Ditchling, 35
Dunne, Millie, 83
Dunne, Philip, 66–69, 206
EastEnders (television series), 89
Edward, HRH Prince, 135
Edward VII, King, 34
Edward VIII, King (later Duke of Windsor), 52, 59, 106–107, 303, 307
Edwards, Bob, 29–30, 32, 33
Elizabeth II, Queen, 160, 182, 285
and abdication question, xvii–xviii

anger with D, 168–169, 174–175, 188
annus horribilis, xiii, 224, 234
and Bryan/Fergie photographs, 118
celebrates forty years on the throne, 231
family life, 135
friendship with Parker Bowles's mother, 24
as godmother to D's brother, 136
and homeopathy, 159
and intruder (Fagan), 185
jealousy of D, xiii
meeting with the Press, 172–173
nomination of peers attached to her family, 286
and payment of taxes, xiii, 276
Elizabeth, Queen, the Queen Mother, 148, 272
and D, 164, 175
birthday concert (1990), 218
as godmother to D's sister, 136
influence on C, 306
Parker Bowles's relationship to, 24
Elliott, Annabel, 211
Emanuel, David and Elizabeth, 22
English, Sir David, 119
Eugenie, Princess, 113, 228
Evening Standard, 177

Everett, Oliver, 194
Expo World Fair, Seville, 230

Falconry, the, Althorp, 259
Farrer, Sir Matthew, 111
Farrer's, 111, 234
Fellowes, Lady Jane, *see* Spencer, Lady Jane
Fellowes, Laura, 147
Fellowes, Sir Robert, xvii, 119–125, 147, 233, 269, 283
Fergie, *see* Sarah, Duchess of York
Ferguson, Brigadier-General Algernon, 121
Ferguson, Jane, 121
Ferguson, Major Ronald, 62, 76, 77, 116, 121, 122–123, 214–215
Fermoy, Lord, 136, 154
Fermoy, Maurice Roche, Lord, 238
Fermoy, Ruth, Lady, 240
Fisher, Alan, 194
Fitzgerald, Penelope, 35
Foale, Dr. Rodney, 250
4th Armoured Brigade, 75
Four Corners (television program), 109
Franks, Lynne, 279
Fraser, Jason, 69–70
Frost, Lady Carina, 79
Frost, Sir David, 79

Gainsborough, Earl of, 79
Garforth, David, 194
Gaselee, Nick, 161
GCHQ listening center, Cheltenham, 97, 110
Geldof, Bob, 216

George VI, King, 197, 237, 307
Gere, Richard, 103
Gilbey, Monsignor Alfred, 78
Gilbey, James, 92, 287
  background and education, 77–79
  and D's visit to his flat, 80, 84
  end of friendship with D, 94
  meets D, 79
  and Morton book about D, 79, 93
  at San Lorenzo restaurant, 81–83
  Squidgy tapes, *see* Squidgy tapes
Goldsmith, Harvey, 282
Goncz, Zsuzsa, 215
Gordon, Duke of, 287
Gore, Georgina, 79
Grafton, Duke of, 287
Great Ormond Street Hospital, London, 212, 223
Grenfell, Katya, 67
Guards Polo Club, 39, 58, 59, 146
Guinness, Sabrina, 69
Gulf War, 75

Haldon Investments, 79
Hambro, Rick, 56
Hambro, Rupert, 23
Hammer, Armand, 195–196, 296
Habgood, Dr. John, Archbishop of York, 301
Harries, Rt. Rev. Richard,

Bishop of Oxford, 301
Harry, Prince (Prince Henry of Wales), xii, 167, 186, 187, 188, 206, 211, 224, 233, 242, 244, 245, 255, 256, 266, 316, 317, 318
Hawkins, Anne (later Dame Anne Wall), 283
Heart of the Matter, The (television program), 301
Heath, Edward, 162
Hello! magazine, 249
Henry VIII, King, 301
Hepburn, Audrey, 288
Heseltine, Sir William, 283
Hewitt, Major James, 71–77, 81, 88, 92
  D gives presents to, 74–75
  and D's riding lessons, 71–73, 139
  Gilbey supercedes, 77
  girlfriend approaches *News of the World* about, 74
  in the Gulf War, 75
  plays against C at polo, 75–76
Highgrove, near Tetbury, Gloucestershire, 43*n*, 71, 74, 98, 102, 105, 153, 190–191, 219, 220, 290
Holbein Motor Company plc, 78
Household Cavalry, 20
Humana Wellington Hospital, 248, 249

Ian Johnson Associates, 105

In the Shadow of the Castle (Pizzey), 240

Ingram, Sue, 255, 257–259, 262, 263–264

Institut Alpin Videmanette, Château d'Oex, 141

International Red Cross, 288

IRA, 273

It's a Royal Knockout (television program), 291

Jaipur, 226

Jarre, Jean-Michel, 192

"Jennifer's Diary" (*Queen* magazine), 38–39

John, Elton, 228

Juan Carlos, King, 199, 221, 256, 273

Jung, Carl, 196

Junor, Penny, 126–127, 241

Junor, Sir John, 229

Kay, Richard, 108–109

Kent, Duchess of, 297

Kent, Duke of, 136, 224

Kenward, Betty, 38

Keppel, Alice, 34

King, Lord, 106

Klosters, 44*n*, 66, 69, 145, 160, 209–210, 242

Knatchbull, Amanda, 133

Knatchbull family, 26

Knight, Andrew, 125

Knopfler, Mark, 296

Kriel, Leon, 292

Lascelles, Sir Alan, 304

Latsis, John, 231

Laurence, Commander Timothy, 55, 56, 229, 233, 286

Lawrence, Murray, 43*n*

Learmond, Lieutenant General Sir John, 57

LeCarre, John, 314

Lech, 242, 244, 246

Leete, Lance-Corporal Malcolm, 72–74

Leigh, Colonel Gerard, 39

Life Guards, 71, 72

Lindsay, Major Hugh, 44*n*, 210, 211

Lindsay, Sarah, 210

Lipsedge, Dr. Maurice, 211

Lisbon, 202

Lloyd, Sir Nicholas, 129

Lockerbie air disaster, 276

Lockwood, Victoria, 256

London Symphony Orchestra, 218

Longford, Elizabeth, Countess of, 271, 284

Lovell, James Blair, 300

Lubbers, Ruud, 275

Ludgrove Preparatory School, near Wokingham, Berkshire, 219, 222, 233

Ludlow race meeting, 151

MacArthur, Brian, 114

McCartney, Ian, 273

Macclesfield, Earls of, 24

McCorquodale, Lady Sarah, *see* Spencer, Lady Sarah

McDonough, David and Kiki, 119

McGregor of Durris, Lord, 123, 124–126
Mackay of Clashfern, Lord, 125
Mackenzie, Kelvin, 111, 115
Mackie, Philip, 244
McLean, John, 145, 153
McMaster, Jim, 194
Macmillan, Sir Harold, 1st Earl of Stockton, 27
Macmillan, Maurice, 27
Mail on Sunday, 92
Major, John, 96, 126, 235, 305
Mannakee, Sergeant, 184–185
Margaret, HRH Princess, 31, 170, 182, 272, 286
Marivent Palace, Majorca, 199
Marlborough, Duke of, 24, 39
Marriage Guidance Council (now Relate), 216
Maugham, W. Somerset, 58, 117
Melbourne, 63
Menkes, Suzy, 54
Menwith Hill, Yorkshire, 110
Menzies, Kate, 69, 83
Mexborough, Earl of, 91
Meynell Hunt, 224
MI5 95, 96, 97, 99, 102, 106, 116, 185
Miles, Malcolm, 280
Millfield, 71
Minerva, HMS, 26
Morton, Andrew, 78, 93, 124, 128, 203

Morwenstow, Cornwall, 110
Mountbatten, Louis, 1st Earl Mountbatten of Burma, 26, 107, 133, 166, 195, 260
Munster, Earl of, 287

National Security Agency (NSA), 110
Newman, Jim, 30, 32
News of the World, 74, 92, 172, 205
Nice Matin, 112
Nicholas II, Tsar, 300
Noel, Thomas, 79
Norgrove, Jane, 108, 109
Nottingham General Hospital, 220, 222

Officer, Paul, 153, 194
Old Man of Lochnagar, The (Charles, Prince of Wales), 205, 290
Oldfield, Bruce, 192
Operation Raleigh youth charity, 299

Paglia, Camille, 282
Palm Beach, 195, 299
Palma Yacht Club, 199
Palmer-Tomkinson, Charles, 44, 46
Palmer-Tomkinson, Patty, 44, 210
Paravicini, Nicolas, 58
Parker Bowles, Dame Ann, 24
Parker Bowles, Laura, 55
Parker Bowles, Brigadier Andrew, 149, 159

INDEX

and ambulance strike,
46, 51–52
attitude to women, 26
background and educa-
tion, 24, 77
and Camillagate tapes,
45–46, 50
character, 26
and Charlotte Soames,
56
criticized within the
army, 57
and C's accession to
Throne, 302
denies C/Camilla rela-
tionship, 60
enjoying relationship
outside marriage,
310, 311
as leader of Sovereign's
Escort, 21
made Silver Stick in
Waiting to the
Queen, 57
marries, 23
at Queen's dinner party,
21
friendship with Princess
Anne, 24, 55–56
relationship with Queen
Mother, 306
relationship with wife,
55–56
in Rhodesia, 26, 27, 28
Parker Bowles, Mary Ann,
58
Parker Bowles, Camilla
(nee Shand), 90,
132, 157, 159, 163,
179, 182, 206, 215,
243, 285, 300, 301,
302–303

and Anna Wallace, 148
appearance, 23, 24, 25,
35–39, 53, 311
background, 34
birth, 33
C resumes seeing, 187
and Camillagate tapes,
see Camillagate tapes
as chaperone, 152–153
character, 23, 27, 35, 36,
37
compared with Diana,
53–54
and C's wedding, 165
as a debutante, 36,
38–39
early relationship with C,
24–25
education, 35–37
at Highgrove, 220
as horsewoman, 54
marries, 23–24
meets C, 24, 34
objects to the public
gaze, 58
at Queen's dinner party,
21
and question of C's
marrying, xvii
relationship with hus-
band, 55
and royal train scandal,
31–32, 33, 155
source of attraction to C,
53–55
takes secretarial job, 39
visits C in hospital, 220
Parker Bowles, Thomas,
26, 47, 50, 165
Parker, John, 197
Parry, Tim, 272, 273
Peel, Earl, 56

330

INDEX

People magazine, 213, 221, 279, 310, 313

Peters, Alan, 175

Philip, Prince, Duke of Edinburgh, 194–198, 231, 272, 273, 274, 300

Phillips, Captain Mark, 162, 188, 229, 269, 284

Pike, Ron, 284

Pitman, Virginia, 31

Pizzey, Erin, 240

Player, Lesley, 122, 123

Plusquick, 78

Poundbury, Dorset, 293–296

Pounds, Emma, 93

Pounds, Harry, 93

Press Complaints Commission, 123, 124, 126

Press Council, 32

Pride, Carolyn, 193

Prince and Princess of Wales in Public and Private, The (film), 299

Prince's Trust, 297

Prince's Youth Business Trust, 297

Private Eye magazine, 27

Pun, Bishnu, 194

Queen magazine, 38–39

Queen's Gate School, South Kensington, 35, 37

radio ham tape, 108–110

Rampling, Charlotte, 192–193

Rasputin, Gregory, 300

Redgrave, Lynn, 37

Redhead, Brian, 177

Reenan, Cyril, 107–109

Rees-Mogg, Lord, 109, 162

Relate (previously Marriage Guidance Council), 216–217, 234

Reynolds, Paul, 118, 120

Rhodesia, 26–27

Richmond, Duke of, 287

Riddell, Sir John, 194

Roche, Maurice, *see* Fermoy, Lord

Romsey, Lord and Lady, 173

Rothermere, Viscount, 119

Royal Army Veterinary Corps, 57

Royal Berkshire Hospital, Reading, 222

Royal Berkshire Polo Club, 75

Royal Horse Artillery, 20

Royal Opera House, Covent Garden, 81, 223

Royal Spencer Golf Club, Kushiro, 268

Roycroft, David, 198

Rusbridger, James, 97

St. Albans, Duke of, 287

St. John of Fawsley, Lord, 254–255

St. Mary the Virgin church, Great Brington, Northamptonshire, 253

St. Paul's Cathedral, 22, 261

Samuel, Julia, 69, 79

San Lorenzo restaurant, Beauchamp Place, 81–84, 222

Sarah, Duchess of York,
272, 286
 attacks the Waleses, 281
 bracketed with D, xvi,
 280
 Bryan claims to repre-
 sent, 111
 and Clapham rail disas-
 ter, 275
 conversations monitored,
 95
 in-flight episode, 225
 and leak of separation,
 117–119, 120, 121
 leaves Balmoral, 114
 Palace attack on,
 117–119
 photographed with
 Bryan, 112–114, 229
 photographed with
 Wyatt, 117, 224
 relationship with the
 Queen, 213
 separation from Andrew,
 117–119, 228
 friendship with D, 199,
 207, 213
 and Sir Robert Fellowes,
 120
 wedding, 199
SAS, 29, 32, 186
Save the Children Fund,
 189
Savile, Lady Alethea, 85,
 92
7th Armoured Brigade, 75
Shand, Major Bruce (Ca-
 milla Parker Bowles's
 father), 34, 58, 60–61,
 78
Shand Kydd, Mrs. Frances
 (D's mother), 21,

139, 153–154,
 156–157, 161,
 238–241, 256
Shand Kydd, Peter, 21,
 160, 238, 241
Sharp, Sergeant Dave ("Ra-
 zors"), 80
Shea, Michael, 29, 30, 32,
 172
Shelburne, Earl of, 44n
Shepherd, Richard, 96
Sillitoe, Anthony, 106
Sillitoe, Sir Percy, 106
Simpson, Wallis (later
 Duchess of Windsor),
 conversations moni-
 tored, 106
Smallwood, Kirsty, 39
Smith, Inspector Graham,
 185
Snowdon, Anthony Arm-
 strong-Jones, Earl of,
 286
Soames, Charlotte, 56
Soames, Lord Christopher,
 26, 27, 56
Soames, The Hon. Nicho-
 las, MP, 149
Soares, Mario, 202
Spencer, 7th Earl, 79, 260
Spencer, Charles, 9th Earl
 (D's brother), 136,
 138, 234, 239,
 250–252, 256, 257,
 258–260, 262, 263,
 264–265
Spencer, Edward John, 8th
 Earl (D's father), 21,
 133, 139, 143, 144,
 212, 213, 237
 career, 237

332

cerebral haemorrhage,
143–145
and commercial plans for
Althorp, 265–270
confrontation with son,
259–260
death, 237, 241–242,
248–251
divorce, 139, 237,
238–241
funeral of, 252–255, 270
at Queen's dinner party,
21
Woman's Own interview,
212–213
Spencer, Lady Jane (later
Fellowes; D's sister),
136, 147, 149, 238,
239, 257–258
Spencer, Raine, Countess
(second wife of 8th
Earl Spencer), 21,
143, 144–145,
248–251, 255–270
Spencer, Lady Sarah (later
McCorquodale; D's
sister), 136, 140,
171–172, 238, 239
anorexia nervosa of,
141–143, 177, 241
effect of parents' divorce,
139, 142–143, 241
as girlfriend of C,
145–147
meets C, 141–142
and stepmother,
143–144, 257, 258
Spinelli, Julie, 194
Springfield, Virginia, 277
Squidgy tapes, 80, 83–91,
94
D on Hewitt in, 74–75

D on the House of Wind-
sor in, 85
Mara Berni mentioned
in, 83–85
nature of, xiv, 85–87
publication of, 40, 85,
91, 94, 95, 96, 111,
115, 233
Stamp, Terence, 291
Stanley, Richard, 262
Stewardson, Emma, 74, 77,
92
Stuart-Smith, Lord Justice,
96
Sun, the
Fergie's comments in,
281
and radio ham tape, 109
Squidgy tapes published
in, 40, 85, 87, 111,
116, 233
Sunday Mirror,
royal train scandal, 28,
29
Sunday Telegraph, 119,
120, 277
Sunday Times, 114,
128–129
attacks the Yorks, 214
serializes Morton's book,
230

Taj Mahal, 225–226
Taylor, Tim, 224
Telephone bugging, 309,
312–316
Teresa of Calcutta, Mother,
227, 228
Thatcher, Margaret, 202
Thompson, Janet, 135,
136–137, 139
Times, The, 109, 156, 157,

158, 162, 188, 254, 282–283, 312
Today, 126, 177
Townsend, Group-Captain, 272
Tryon, Lady, 68, 163, 165
12th Lancers, 34
Twinkle, 36

UNICEF, 288
United World College, 296

van Cutsem, Hugh, 44*n*
van der Post, Sir Laurens, 195, 196, 205
Vanderbilt Racquet club, 206
Vestey, Lady, 148
Vestey, Lord, 148
Victoria, Queen, xviii
Vision of Britain, A (Charles, Prince of Wales), 292

Wakeham, Lord, 125–126
Wallace, Anna, 67, 133, 147–148, 150
Ward, Freda Dudley, 52
Ward, Jane, 146
Ward, Rachel, 67
Warrington, 273–274
Waterhouse, Major David, 68–69, 70, 206
Watkins, Laura Jo, 146
Wellesley, Lady Jane, 26, 133
West-Meads, Zelda, 216–217
Westmacott, Peter, 130
Westminster Abbey, 149, 199
Westminster, Anne, Duchess of ("Nancy"), 40, 42–43
Westminster, Duke of, 34
Weston, Galen, 299
Wharfe, Ken, 84, 185
White, Marco Pierre, 93
Whitlam, Mike, 288
Wildenstein, Guy, 146
Wilhelm II, Kaiser, 302
William IV, King, 287
William, Prince of Wales, xv, 71, 104, 138, 167, 174, 176, 179, 180, 181, 184, 187, 206, 218–219, 222–224, 242–245, 255–256, 266, 283–286, 316, 317, 318
Willoughby de Broke, David, Lord, 43, 46
Wilson, Christopher, 129
Windsor, 59, 141, 148, 188, 194, 231, 234, 276
Windsor, Duke of, *see* Edward VIII, King
Windsor, Lady Helen, 224
Woman's Own magazine, 212
Woomargama, 180
Worcester, Marquess and Marchioness of, 67
World at One (radio program), 118
Wyatt, Steve, 117, 224

Yass, New South Wales, 160–161
Young England Kindergarten, Pimlico, 151

Ziegler, Philip, 52, 107

By the year 2000, 2 out of 3 Americans could be illiterate.

It's true.

Today, 75 million adults...about one American in three, can't read adequately. And by the year 2000, U.S. News & World Report envisions an America with a literacy rate of only 30%.

Before that America comes to be, you can stop it...by joining the fight against illiteracy today.

Call the Coalition for Literacy at toll-free **1-800-228-8813** and volunteer.

Volunteer Against Illiteracy. The only degree you need is a degree of caring.